# MY HEART I GIVE TO CHILDREN

# MY HEART I GIVE TO CHILDREN

Vasily Sukhomlinsky

Translated by Alan Cockerill

EJR Language Service Pty Ltd

**National Library of Australia Cataloguing-in-Publication entry:**

Creator:
Sukhomlinskii, V. A. (Vasilii Aleksandrovich) author.
Title: My heart I give to children / Vasily Sukhomlinsky;
translated by Alan Cockerill.

ISBN: 978-0-9805885-7-6 (paperback)

Subjects:
Sukhomlinskii, V. A. (Vasilii Aleksandrovich)
Holistic education—Ukraine.
Education—Study and teaching (Primary)—Ukraine.
Education—Ukraine.
Other Creators/Contributors:
Cockerill, Alan, 1952– translator.
Dewey Number: 370.11

First published in 2016 by EJR Language Service Pty Ltd
[Trading online as Holistic Education Books]
181 Oxley Road, Graceville, QLD 4075 Australia
www.ejr.com.au
http://holistic-education-books.com/

Copyright © 2016 EJR Language Service Pty. Ltd. All rights reserved.
No part of this publication shall be reproduced, stored in or introduced into a retrieval system, or transmitted in any form or by any means (electronic, mechanical, photocopying, recording, scanning or otherwise), without the prior permission of the copyright owner and publisher of this book.

Cover background photograph taken by Alan Cockerill in the grounds of Sukhomlinsky's school in Pavlysh, 2009

Archival photographs reproduced by permission of Olga Sukhomlyns'ka

Copy-editing by Lisa Hill

Internal design by Paul Howson

Cover design by Julia Peddie

This book is dedicated to
Professor Olga Sukhomlyns'ka

# Contents

| | |
|---|---|
| Acknowledgements | ix |
| Translator's introduction | x |
| Preface | xix |

## THE SCHOOL OF JOY — 1

| | |
|---|---|
| My educational convictions | 2 |
| The first year — studying the children | 15 |
| My students' parents | 16 |
| A school under the open sky | 31 |
| Our Nook of Dreams | 47 |
| Nature—the source of health | 54 |
| Each child is an artist | 60 |
| Caring for the living and the beautiful | 63 |
| We listen to the music of nature | 71 |
| Our winter joys and concerns | 84 |
| Our first Day of the Lark | 88 |
| How we learnt to read and write | 89 |
| You live amongst other people | 100 |
| Our class is a friendly family | 108 |
| We live in the garden of health | 109 |
| Thoughts on the eve of the first school year | 110 |

## THE YEARS OF CHILDHOOD

| | |
|---|---|
| What is primary school? | 116 |
| Health, health and once again health | 121 |
| Study is a part of our spiritual life | 132 |
| Three hundred pages of the 'book of nature' | 152 |
| What comes from where? | 173 |
| A thousand problems from the maths book of life | 176 |
| Our journeys around the globe | 188 |
| Give children the joy of success in study | 195 |
| The story room | 212 |
| The story continues—our Island of Wonders | 222 |
| Song reveals to children the beauty of the world | 226 |
| Books in the spiritual life of a child | 233 |
| Love for our native language | 243 |
| Our Nook of Beauty | 266 |
| On the threshold of an ideal in life | 270 |
| Not a day without concern for others | 278 |
| Work inspired by noble feelings | 289 |
| You are future custodians of our homeland | 311 |
| The children join the Pioneer Organisation | 326 |
| To fight and overcome, like Lenin | 328 |
| The Brave and Fearless Patrol | 333 |
| We say farewell to summer | 341 |
| | |
| Other Publications | 345 |

# *Acknowledgements*

I WOULD LIKE TO ACKNOWLEDGE the continuing support I have received from Sukhomlinsky's daughter, Professor Olga Sukhomlyns'ka, who prepared the 2012 edition of *Serdtse otdayu detyam* [My heart I give to children] upon which this translation is based, and has given me permission to translate her father's works. Without her painstaking work to identify the 1966 manuscript of the work as the version that corresponds most closely to Sukhomlinsky's original purpose, and her preparation of the 2012 edition, this translation would simply not exist.

Next, I would like to thank my friend Paul Howson for his support throughout this project. Paul worked on the typesetting for *Each One Must Shine*, my book about Sukhomlinksy published in New York by Peter Lang in 1999. Since then he has shown a sustained interest in the work of Sukhomlinsky. He is responsible for the internal design of this book, and his advice throughout the project has been invaluable.

I am indebted to Lisa Hill for her thorough copy-editing of the text. Her enthusiasm for the project has been appreciated.

I would like to thank Julia Peddie for her attractive cover design, and for her patience in working with me.

Finally I would like to thank my wife Hiroko, and my son Christopher, for their patience while I have been working on this book. It has of necessity taken a lot of my spare time and attention, and I could not have completed the project without their support.

Alan Cockerill, translator

# Translator's introduction

VASILY SUKHOMLINSKY WAS A UKRAINIAN school teacher and principal who, through writing about his personal experience, became the most influential Soviet educator of the 1950s and 1960s. His school in the small rural town of Pavlysh was visited by thousands of school teachers, principals and academics, and his books have been read by millions. His books and articles were written in both Ukrainian and Russian, and up to the present time all translations of his work into English have been made from Russian. My own doctoral study of his work was based on Russian language sources. When transliterating his name from Russian, Progress Publishers spelt his name as Vasily Aleksandrovich Sukhomlinsky, and I have used this English version since I commenced studying his work in 1987. His name appears differently when transliterated from Ukrainian, with one possible transliteration being Vasyl Oleksandrovich Sukhomlynsky. I considered using this latter transliteration in recognition of the fact that Sukhomlinsky was Ukrainian and not Russian, but after consultation with Sukhomlinsky's daughter, Professor Olga Sukhomlyns'ka, I have opted to retain the spelling that has been used in most of my previous publications.

Sukhomlinsky's *My heart I give to children* is an educational classic. First published in a German translation in 1968 and published in Russian (the language in which it was written) in 1969, by 1998 it had been published at least fifty-five times in thirty languages, in print runs that numbered millions.[1] Since then, other editions

---

1 Sukhomlyns'ka, Olga, 'V poiskakh nastoyashchego' [In search of the genuine], an editorial preface to Sukhomlinsky, Vasily, *Serdtse otdayu detyam* [My heart I give to children], Kyiv: Akta, 2012, p. 22.

have appeared, including an abridged English language translation by Robert Weiss published in the United States, and a new Russian language edition prepared by Sukhomlinsky's daughter, published in Ukraine in 2012. It is this remarkable new Russian language edition that prompted me to undertake a fresh translation.

The work was written in a Ukrainian country school during the 1960s at the height of the Cold War. It bears many marks of the time and place in which it was written, but at the same time transcends them. More than anything this book is a narrative, a story of a teacher's work with a specific group of children over a period of five years. In 1951 Sukhomlinsky took the highly unusual step for a school principal, of asking parents in his district to send their children to school a year early so he could personally work with them. This gave him the freedom to work extremely creatively, unfettered by the prescriptions of the official curriculum. He continued to work with this group of children until they graduated from year eleven in 1963, and subsequently wrote about his experience. This book is the first in a planned trilogy. It describes Sukhomlinsky's work during the experimental preschool year, and the following four years (in the Soviet system) of primary schooling. It is a fascinating narrative set against the backdrop of the Second World War, whose shadow still lay over the lives of everyone in that rural community. Sukhomlinsky first describes each of the families his students came from and the impact of the war, and then goes on to describe a uniquely creative and therapeutic pedagogy he developed to meet the needs of the children in his care.

The new Russian language edition of the work, prepared by Sukhomlinsky's daughter, is based on a 1966 manuscript, which differs in significant respects from previous editions of the work. In Professor Sukhomlyns'ka's introduction to this new 2012 edition she writes:

> The content of the book, the methodology it puts forward, the manner of its exposition, while they may not align Sukhomlinsky

with the ideas of free education, most definitely distance him from Marxist-Leninist, Soviet educational thought. And although in his preface he refers to NK Krupskaya and AS Makarenko as the highest authorities, it seems to me that his book owes very little to the educational views of those authors. It is not to them that Vasily Aleksandrovich refers constantly in the text of the book, but to Leo Tolstoy, the founder of the idea of free education, who held that a school's main task was to stimulate interest in study, that study should respond to the questions posed by life (and above all by children themselves), rather than to those posed by the teacher.

In support of his argument Sukhomlinsky cites, on more than one occasion, the words of Konstantin Ushinsky about the characteristics of children's thought, about the necessity of developing a child's investigative thinking, and also about the fact that study involves work and will power, and is not just an amusement or a pleasant way of spending time.

*My heart I give to children* shows that Janusz Korczak exerted a major influence on Sukhomlinsky's personality and on his educational philosophy, and Sukhomlinsky refers to Korczak often in the book. He was inspired by the genuine humanism of the Polish educator, and he aligns himself with Korczak's ideas about the value and uniqueness of childhood, and the need to 'ascend' and not 'descend' to a child's level of understanding ... Respect for children and unconditional support for childhood is an absolute educational truth for Vasily Aleksandrovich, as it is for Korczak. Sukhomlinsky's special attentiveness to unfortunate children, who have difficult lives, and to those with various peculiarities in their development, can also be traced to Korczak.

If we look more widely at the educational context of this book, not limiting ourselves to references and quotations, we can see it has a lot in common with tendencies and directions existing at that time beyond the field of Soviet educational discourse. For example, one of the educators with whose ideas the book is in harmony is Rudolph Steiner, who promoted a phenomenological approach to the instruction and education of children, more specifically: living experience, observation, description, reflection, work of an investigative nature, the use of stories as a vital and graphic way of coming to know the world, and the view of a teacher as a spiritual mentor.

We could add to the list the name of Célestin Freinet, who created the 'modern school movement' (activity, initiative, cooperation, creativity) for poor and deprived children.[2]

Much of Sukhomlinsky's educational writing (he wrote around thirty books and 500 articles) can be seen as a heroic attempt to redirect the course of Soviet education towards a greater focus on the individual, as opposed to the 'collective'.

This new English language translation is made on the basis of the 2012 edition. The main difference between it and previous editions is that it contains less material of an ideological nature (which was included in the first edition in response to editorial pressure), more information about the real children that Sukhomlinsky was working with, and more of his personal views, which were to some extent censored in the first edition in order to secure publication of the work in the Soviet Union. In the 2012 edition, Professor Sukhomlyns'ka also presents the material that was incorporated into the first Russian language edition in 1969 due to editorial pressure, but she places these revisions in footnotes. I have included a small part of this additional material in my translation where I thought it would be of interest to

---

2 Sukhomlyns'ka, Olga, 'V poiskakh nastoyashchego' [In search of the genuine], an editorial preface to Sukhomlinsky, Vasily, *Serdtse otdayu detyam* [My heart I give to children], Kyiv: Akta, 2012, pp. 8–10.

English speaking educators. I have also cut out a small amount of text from the 1966 manuscript that I thought too overtly ideological for readers in western democracies. This amounts to no more than a page or two of text and does not in any way change the general thrust of the book.[3] Some ideological material does remain in the book. This is partly due to the fact that in order to be published at all, some deference had to be paid to communist ideology. It also reflects the fact that communism was the faith in which Sukhomlinsky had been raised, and which, almost at the cost of his life, he defended against Nazism.

Every translator has to make choices when trying to translate words that have no exact equivalent in the target language and when translating words whose precise meaning depends on knowledge of social and cultural context. Specialists in Soviet education (and even some non-specialists) may be interested in knowing about some of the choices I have made.

Two words that crop up again and again in Sukhomlinsky's writing are *vospitanie* (воспитание) and *dukhovnyi* (духовный). The first of these words (*vospitanie*) may refer to education that takes place in the family and in early childhood learning centres, to the broad education of character and to education considered from a more holistic perspective. In spite of the fact that many have previously translated this word as 'upbringing', I have nearly everywhere translated it simply as 'education'. This is partly due to my own belief that education should be viewed as a holistic process, and also because Sukhomlinsky often combines the word with a qualifier to produce expressions such as 'work education', 'aesthetic education' and 'intellectual education', and the use of 'upbringing' in such expressions seems awkward.

---

3  Where I have cut a short passage of text, I have indicated the hiatus with three asterisks: * * *.

The second of these words (*dukhovnyi*) I have nearly always translated as 'spiritual', despite being fully aware that usage of the Russian word does not correspond fully to usage of this word in English. In an earlier work, *The spiritual world of a school student*, Sukhomlinsky writes:

> People's spiritual life encompasses the development, shaping, and satisfying of their moral, intellectual and aesthetic needs in the process of activity.[4]

There were many occasions when I thought it might be more appropriate to translate this word as 'inner' to more closely correspond with English usage. When Sukhomlinsky writes about 'the spiritual world of a child', I might have written 'the inner world of a child'. However, there were occasions when 'inner' did not seem adequate or appropriate. Sukhomlinsky also writes about the 'spiritual life of a collective', and neither 'inner' nor 'psychological' seemed to convey his meaning as well as the world 'spiritual'. As the reader progresses through this book, it becomes evident that Sukhomlinsky is deeply interested in aspects of the human psyche that may indeed be referred to as 'spiritual': the development of empathy and altruism, and of a close bond with nature. So I ask the reader to accept that the words 'spiritual' and 'spirituality' are used in this translation in a non-religious sense and refer to the inner life and values of a human being. Sukhomlinsky saw this inner world as providing the motivating force for the outer manifestations of behaviour. He was wary of any methods that promoted good behaviour without addressing the psychological motives behind good behaviour, without paying

---

4 Sukhomlinsky, VA, *Dukhovnyi mir shkol'nika* [The spiritual world of a school student], in *Izbrannye proizvedeniya v pyati tomakh* [Selected works in five volumes], vol. 1, Kiev: Radianska shkola, 1979, p. 224.

attention to the development of empathy, compassion, the appreciation of beauty, and an aspiration for truth and justice.

Some other words I wrestled with are those used to describe various groupings of children within the Pioneer movement: the Soviet version of the Boy Scout and Girl Guide movements. During Sukhomlinsky's time this movement was based in every school and had a semi-military nomenclature. The equivalent of a scout troop was the *otryad* (отряд), which may be translated as 'detachment'. This normally included all the students in one class, from late in grade three up until about grade eight (children aged ten to fifteen). Within each class there were normally something like three groups of approximately a dozen students, each of which was called a *zveno* (звено), which can be translated as 'link' or 'group'. All the class detachments in a school combined to form the Pioneer *druzhina* (дружина). This term can also be translated as 'detachment', but I felt that would create some confusion. Given that the Pioneer movement had its origins in the Russian scouting movement and that English-speaking readers may be familiar with the structure of the scouting organisation, I have adopted English scouting terms to translate each group. The class detachment has been called a Pioneer 'troop'. The smaller groups within a class I have referred to as Pioneer 'patrols', and the gathering of all the class troops for a whole school is called a Pioneer 'group'.

Where a footnote is preceded by the words 'Translator's note', it is one I have added to explain something to the reader. Where no such words precede the footnote, it is a translation of Sukhomlinsky's own footnote.

I have tried to make my translation as accessible as possible, and to render Sukhomlinsky's attractive prose in a way that is fluent and readable. Sometimes I have divided very long sentences into two, and sometimes, when Sukhomlinsky has used a string of synonyms, I have omitted one of them. Sukhomlinsky makes very extensive use of the historic present tense. Where it was possible to do so without sounding unnatural, I have retained this use of the present tense to describe past events as it results in a more vivid narrative. Where Sukhomlinsky switches rather rapidly between past tense and historic present, I have opted for one or the other.

In Sukhomlinsky's time there was no consciousness of gender equality in the use of pronouns, either in his society or in ours. The situation is further exacerbated by the fact that in Russian all nouns—animate or inanimate—have grammatical gender and the words for 'person' and 'child' are masculine due to ending in a consonant. However, in making this translation I have tried to be gender-neutral in the use of pronouns. In many cases I have used the plural in place of the singular to avoid using a singular pronoun of one gender or the other. Where any remnants of older usage remain, I beg the reader's forgiveness and ask them to accept this work as a historical document that describes Sukhomlinsky's experience during the 1950s and 1960s.

In spirit, however, I believe the work to have been far ahead of its time. It addresses issues such as our relationship with nature, how to nurture children's souls in the face of the sometimes negative influences of mass media, how to help children develop empathy for others, how schools can develop strong relationships with families, how children's brains function and develop, and how to support children who struggle to acquire early literacy skills. These are all vital and contemporary issues.

I hope the reader will find Sukhomlinsky's narrative, and his accompanying reflections, both thought provoking and inspiring.

Vasily Sukhomlinsky

# *Preface*

DEAR READERS, COLLEAGUES, TEACHERS, EDUCATORS, school principals!

This work, consisting of three separate books,[5] is the result of thirty-two years working in schools: the result of reflection, concern, anxious moments, and times of deep emotion. My whole educational career has been spent in rural schools. I rarely travelled beyond my village, although I could have travelled a lot and seen more of the world both in my own country and abroad. Each time I had to leave my school for a few days my heart was troubled: what about the children? How could I leave them alone? And if it was at all possible to excuse myself from the trip, I would, and I would remain with the children. I would walk with the little ones to the forest, to the river bank, to a distant ravine in the steppe overgrown with bushes, or we would make our way in a boat to a quiet little island on the Dnieper … Something interesting would happen; some new facet of childhood would reveal itself and I would wonder to myself: perhaps I would never have become aware of this aspect of childhood if I had gone away and left you, my dear children, if I had not been with you at this moment.

I am not making any generalised conclusions, dear reader; I am not imposing my thoughts on anyone else. I only want to say that thirty-two years of uninterrupted work in rural schools has brought me great happiness, incomparable happiness. I have given my life to children, and after considerable reflection I have named this work

---

5 Translator's note: The three books Sukhomlinsky is referring to have been published under the following titles: *My heart I give to children*, *The birth of a citizen* and *Letters to my son*.

*My heart I give to children*, believing I have a right to do so. I want to tell teachers—both those who are working in schools now and those who will come after us—about a lengthy period in my life, a period of a decade. From the day when a little unwitting child arrives as a preschooler, to that solemn moment when a young man or woman receives their graduation certificate and embarks on an independent working life. This is a formative period for a human being, but for teachers it is also a huge part of their lives. What was the most important thing in my life? Without hesitation I reply: love for children. I repeat again, my dear reader: I am not imposing my thoughts on anyone else; I am not calling on teachers to work only as I have described in these books; I only want to share my thoughts about love for children. If my editor advised me to change the title of this book, I would call it *How I love children*.

Perhaps, dear reader, you will disagree with some things in this work; perhaps some things will seem strange or surprising. I beg you, in advance, not to view my work as some sort of universal manual for educating children, adolescents, young men and women. Schools have programs, lessons, students, teachers with their knowledge, and school routines … but there is also such a thing as a teacher's heart, the heart of a living human being who, like a mother or father, takes a keen interest in a child's every word, every step, every act and every change in expression. To use educational terminology, this book is devoted to extracurricular education (or education in the sense of character development). I did not attempt to describe regular lessons, or to detail the processes of instruction in the foundations of knowledge … To use the language of human relations this book is devoted to the heart of the teacher. I have attempted to show how to lead young people into the world of discovery of the reality around them; how to help them to study, lightening their intellectual load; how to awaken and establish noble feelings in their souls; how to educate human dignity, faith in fundamental human goodness, and boundless love for our native land; and how to sow the first seeds of lofty communist ideals in the sensitive heart and mind of a child.

The first book in this trilogy, the book you are holding in your hands, dear reader, is devoted to educational work with primary classes. In other words, it is devoted to the world of childhood. And childhood, a child's world, is a special world. Children live with their own conceptions of good and evil, honour and dishonour, and human worth. They have their own criteria of beauty and even their own perception of time. In childhood a day seems like a year and a year seems an eternity. Having access to that fairytale palace called 'childhood', I always considered it necessary, to some extent, to become a child myself. Only then will children not regard you as some creature who has accidentally found a way past the gates of their fairytale kingdom, as a watchman guarding that world, but indifferent to what goes on inside it.

Dostoevsky wrote some wonderful words: 'Let us enter a courtroom with the thought that we, too, are guilty.' Let us enter the fairytale palace of childhood with a child's ardent heart, a heart beating with the pulse of a child's life, with the thought that I too was a child. Children will trust you when they feel in their hearts that you understand this simplest, and at the same time wisest, of truths.

A child is a child.

Not all moral and political ideas comprehensible to a young man or woman, or even to an adolescent, are comprehensible to a young child. We should not rush to explain truths which, by virtue of a child's age, are incomprehensible. We should not approach a sacred matter like the patriotic education of children with concepts that would be fitting for an adult. I have always been firmly convinced, and will carry my conviction to the grave, that during the years of childhood, nature—the trees, flowers, birds and blue sky of our native land—and stories provide the most indispensable means for educating the sacred feeling of love for our homeland. On the pages that

I am offering to you there may not be any words about our homeland, communism or the Party—I value these words very highly, and do not wish to cheapen them with frequent use—but these texts in their essence teach how to educate real patriots.

I want to make one more cautionary comment about the content of this book and the nature of my experiment. The primary school depends first and foremost on the creative work of each individual classroom teacher. For that reason I have consciously avoided showing the collective work of the staff and the parents. If all of that were shown in this book, it would have grown to a huge size.

In a book about childhood it was impossible not to talk about the children's families, about their parents. The situation in some families, especially after the war, was dark and depressing. Some parents were quite incapable of being good role models for their children. I could not remain silent about that. If I did not give a full and honest description of the family situations, the orientation of my whole system of education would have made no sense. I firmly believe in the great power of education, as did Krupskaya and Makarenko. My motto is expressed in the words of Pisarev: 'Human nature is so rich, powerful, and elastic, that it can preserve its freshness and its beauty, even in the midst of the most oppressive and ugly environment.'[6]

The first book of my trilogy will appear in print, it seems, as I begin the thirty-third year of my educational work. The second book will come out at the end of the thirty-fourth year, and the third at the end of the thirty-fifth year.[7] I believe that one day I will have the

---

6  Pisarev, DI, *Works*, vol. 4, Moscow, 1956, p. 101.

7  Translator's note: The first book, *My heart I give to children*, was published in German in 1968 and in Russian in 1969. The second book, *The birth of a citizen*, was published in Ukrainian in 1970 and in Russian in 1971. The third book, *Letters to my son*, was published in abbreviated format (twenty-two letters) in Ukrainian in 1977 and appeared in Russian in 1979. A second edition was

opportunity to teach the grandchildren of the first students I taught in my native village. I want, once again, to make the journey from the 'school under the open sky', as I call the preschool year, to the graduation year. I believe that this will happen. The source of this faith is my love for children.

I invite you, dear readers, to write letters with your feedback about this book to the following address: Pavlysh, Onufriev District, Kirovograd Region, Ukrainian Socialist Soviet Republic, Sukhomlinsky, Vasily Aleksandrovich.

Come and visit us. During just three months of 1967 (February, March and April) we have been visited by teachers from the Primorsky, Krasnoyarsk, Krasnodar, Altai, Stavropol, Kirov, Kalinin, Kaliningrad, Sverdlovsk, Lipetsk, Kharkov, Dnepropetrovsk, Kiev, Poltava, Lvov, Odessa, Sumy, Cherkasy, Nikolaev, Crimea, Lugansk and Ivano-Frankovsk regions; from the Bashkir, Tatar, Mari, North Ossetian and Komi Autonomous Republics; from Moldavia, Armenia, Azerbaijan and Tajikistan.

Any teacher will be a welcome guest at our school. At our 'School of pedagogical culture' we want to meet anyone who is already working creatively and wants to discuss issues with us. We also want to meet those who aspire to work creatively.

---

published in Russian in 1987 containing thirty letters. Sukhomlinsky died in 1970.

PART ONE

*The School of Joy*

# *My educational convictions*

AFTER WORKING IN EDUCATION FOR ten years, I was appointed principal of Pavlysh Secondary School. Here my educational convictions, ten years in the making, finally crystallised. Here I wanted to see my convictions expressed in a living, creative endeavour.

The more I strove to give practical expression to my convictions, the clearer it became that management of educational work requires a judicious balance, between finding solutions to ideological and organisational challenges facing the whole school, and providing the personal example of a teacher at work. The role of the school principal as an organiser of the teaching staff is immeasurably enhanced if teachers see in his work an example of the highest pedagogical standards, as a direct educator of children.

Education is first and foremost a constant spiritual interaction between teacher and child. The great Russian educator KD Ushinsky called the principal the leading educator of the school. But under what conditions can the role of leading educator be realised?

To educate children through the teachers, to be a teacher of teachers, to study the art and science of education, is very important; but it is only one aspect of the multi-faceted process of managing a school. If the leading educator only teaches how to educate but has no direct interaction with children, he ceases to be an educator.

The very first weeks of my work as a principal showed me that the way to children's hearts would remain forever closed to me if I did not share with them common interests, passions and aspirations. I became convinced that without any direct, immediate educational influence on children, I, as principal, would lose an educator's most important quality—the ability to sense the spiritual world of a child. I envied the class teachers: they were always with the children. Now the class teacher is having a heart to heart chat, now he is making preparations to take his students to the forest, the river, to work in the fields. The children cannot wait for the day when they will go on their excursion, make porridge over an open fire, catch fish, spend the night under an open sky, and gaze at the twinkling stars. And I, the principal, am left on the sidelines. I can only organise, advise, note inadequacies and correct them, encourage what is necessary, and forbid the undesirable. Of course you cannot avoid these things, but I felt dissatisfaction with my work.

It seemed to me, and this conviction is now even deeper, that the highest degree of educational skill is to be found in the principal's direct, long term participation in the life of a class. I wanted to be with the children, to experience their joys and sorrows, to feel close to them, which is one of the greatest pleasures of an educator's creative work. From time to time I tried to include myself in the life of one class or another; I accompanied the children to a workplace or on a hike through our native country, travelled on excursions, and helped to create those unforgettable joys without which it is impossible to imagine a complete education.

But I and the children felt a certain artificiality in these relations. The contrived nature of the educational situation made me uncomfortable: the children could not forget that I was only with them for a short time. Genuine sharing of heartfelt interests comes about when, over a long period, the teacher becomes a friend, a like-minded companion to the child with common pursuits. I felt that such a sharing of common interests was necessary for me, not only to experience the joy that creative work brings, but in order to demonstrate to my colleagues the art and science of education. Direct, living contact with children on a daily basis is a source of ideas, educational discoveries, joys, sorrows and disappointments, without which creativity is unthinkable in our line of work. I came to the conclusion that the leading educator must be the educator of a class of children, a friend and companion to those children. This certainty was based on convictions that I had developed even before my work at the school in Pavlysh.

Above all, I was convinced that a genuine school is not only a place where children acquire knowledge and skills. Study is very important, but it is not the only important area in the spiritual life of a child. The more closely I examined what we are accustomed to referring to as the process of instruction and education, the more I became convinced that the real school is to be found in the multi-faceted spiritual life of a community of children, in which the educator and the student are connected by a multitude of interests and pursuits. Someone who only meets his students in the classroom, who remains on one side of the teacher's desk while the students sit on the other side, does not know a child's heart; and someone who does not know a child cannot be an educator. For such a person the thoughts, feelings and aspirations of children are hidden behind seven seals. Teachers' desks at times become like a stone wall, from behind which they mount an 'attack' on the 'enemy'—their students; but more often that desk becomes a besieged fortress, which the 'enemy' starves of sustenance, and the 'commander' taking shelter behind it feels tied hand and foot.

With great pain I saw that even for teachers who know their subject well, education sometimes becomes a bitter war, just because there are no spiritual threads connecting teacher and students, and the child's soul remains hidden, as if enclosed in a shirt buttoned right up to the neck. The main reason for these abnormal, intolerable relations between mentor and pupil, which occur in some schools, is mutual distrust and suspicion. Sometimes teachers simply do not feel the innermost movements of a child's soul, do not experience a child's joys and sorrows, do not strive mentally to put themselves in the child's place.

The eminent Polish educator Janusz Korczak refers in one of his letters to the need to ascend to the spiritual world of a child, rather than to descend to it. This is a very subtle thought, the essence of which we, as teachers, should strive to comprehend. Without idealising children, without attributing miraculous properties to them, a genuine educator cannot but take account of the fact that a child's perception of the world, and a child's emotional and moral reaction to the reality that surrounds them, are distinguished by a certain clarity, sensitivity and immediacy. Korczak's challenge to ascend to the spiritual world of the child should be understood to entail a sensitive understanding of, and empathy with, a child's perception of the world, a perception that involves both mind and heart.

I am firmly convinced that there are qualities of the soul without which a person cannot become a genuine educator, and among these qualities the ability to enter into the spiritual world of a child takes pride of place. Only those who never forget that they were once children can become genuine teachers. The problem for many teachers (children, especially adolescents, call them 'dry old sticks') is that they forget: the student is first and foremost a living person, entering into the world of cognition, creativity and human relationships.

In education there are no unconnected phenomena acting on people in isolation. Lessons are a most important organisational format in the overall process through which students get to know the world. The whole structure of their spiritual world depends on how they learn about the world and what convictions they develop. But getting to know the world does not equate only to study. The problem for many teachers is that they measure and evaluate the spiritual world of a child only with marks and grades, separating all students into two categories depending on whether or not they learn their lessons well.

But if teachers with a narrow understanding of the many facets of spiritual life find themselves in such an unenviable situation, what can be said of a principal who sees his mission only in controlling the work of teachers, in giving 'general directions' at the appropriate time, in granting or refusing permission? His position is even more unenviable.

I felt burdened by such a role. I suffered when I approached students who were enthusiastically involved with their teachers and tried to speak to them, and they did not pay any attention to me. The children were living a rich spiritual life with their teachers and I was not a part of it. Do we need such a school principal? No, we do not. The methods and forms of management that were established in pre-revolutionary schools when the principal was in essence an inspector supervising the teachers, a bureaucratic administrator who was obliged to monitor whether or not teachers were presenting the program correctly and whether or not they had said something superfluous or mistaken, has today become an anachronism.

Today the essence of school management is that in this most difficult job of education, the teachers should see, with their own eyes, the creation, development and establishment of best practice, incorporating the most progressive pedagogy. And whoever is the creator of that best practice, the person whose work is a model for other educators, should become the school principal. Without such a principal—the best educator—one cannot imagine a school in our time. Education is above all the study of human nature, the knowledge of human nature. Without knowledge of children's psyches—their intellectual development, thought processes, interests, passions, abilities, talents and inclinations—there is no education. Just as the head doctor in a hospital cannot be a true doctor without having his own patients, so a school principal cannot manage his teachers if he does not have his own students.

Who is the central figure in a school? In what sphere of the education process must a school principal provide an example that sets a standard for the other educators? The main figure in a school is the class teacher. She is both a teacher giving knowledge to the students, and a friend to the children and organiser of their many-faceted spiritual life. Study is only one petal of the flower that represents education in the wider sense. In education there is nothing major or minor, just as there is no main petal among the many petals that create the beauty of a flower. In education everything is important: the lessons, the children's development of diverse interests outside lessons, and the relationships between students in the school community.

After six years working as a school principal I became the educator of a class group. I would like to acknowledge that this is not the only way to develop direct, heartfelt communication between principal and students. There are other ways, with the choice depending on the creativity of the principal. But in my concrete circumstances, this way seemed to me to be the most promising. I consider work as the direct educator of a class group to be a long term experiment, conducted in natural conditions.

Before moving on to my tale of how our work developed over a period of several years, I will explain one other important conviction that, to a significant extent, determined the content and direction of my practical work.

The years of childhood play an especially important role in the formation of a human personality, particularly the preschool and early school years. The great writer and educator Leo Tolstoy was profoundly right when he asserted that from birth to the age of five, children acquire much more for the development of their intellect, feelings, will and character, than they do from the age of five to the end of their lives. 'Did I not live then, during those first years, when I learnt to see, hear and speak, slept, sucked, and kissed my mother's breast, and laughed, and gave joy to my mother?' wrote Tolstoy. 'I lived, and I lived blissfully. Was it not then that I acquired that by which I live now, and acquired so much, so quickly, that for the rest of my life I did not acquire one hundredth part of that. From the five-year-old child to what I am now is a single step. But from a new born babe to a five-year-old is a frightening distance.'[8] Tolstoy wrote these adolescent

---

8   Tolstoy, LN, *Collected works in 14 volumes*, Moscow, 1952, vol. 1, p. 330.

memoirs in 1878, with the wisdom of fifty years of life. The same idea was repeated by the Soviet educator Anton Makarenko: what a person will become is determined by the age of five.

The eminent Polish educator and writer Janusz Korczak, a national hero of the Polish people and a human being of extraordinary moral beauty, wrote in his book *When I am little again*, that nobody knows whether a student receives more when he looks at the blackboard or when an irresistible force (the force of the sun, turning the head of a sunflower) compels him to look out the window. What is more beneficial and important for him at that moment: the logical world, compressed to fit on the classroom blackboard, or the world sailing by on the other side of the window panes? Do not do violence to the soul of a human being. Examine closely the laws of natural development of each child, their peculiarities, aspirations and needs.

All my life I have remembered these words from a little grey-covered book in the Polish language. When, soon after the war, I learnt of Korczak's heroic sacrifice, his words became a guide for the rest of my life. Korczak was the director of an orphanage in the Warsaw Ghetto. The Nazis condemned the unfortunate children to death in the ovens of Treblinka. When Korczak was offered a choice between life without the children or death with the children, he chose death, without hesitation or doubt. 'Mr Goldsmith', the Gestapo officer told him, 'we know you are a good doctor. You do not have to go to Treblinka.' 'My conscience is not for sale', answered Korczak. The hero went to his death together with the children. He reassured them, taking care that the little ones' hearts were not pierced by the horror of knowing they were about to die. Janusz Korczak's life and his sacrifice of astounding moral strength and purity were an inspiration to me. I understood that to be a genuine educator of children you must give them your heart.

The great Russian educator Konstantin Ushinsky wrote that we may deeply love a person with whom we live constantly, but may not be aware of that love until some misfortune shows us the depth of our attachment. A person can live all his life and not know how much he loves his native land until some event, such as a prolonged absence, reveals to him all the strength of that love. I remember these words each time I go for a prolonged period without seeing the children, without feeling their joys and sorrows. With each year the conviction grew stronger in me, that one of the determining characteristics of pedagogical culture is a feeling of attachment to children. Konstantin Stanislavsky suggested that feelings 'cannot be produced on demand', but the cultivation of feelings by a teacher, an educator, is the very essence of pedagogical culture.

Without a constant spiritual exchange between teacher and child, without mutual sharing of thoughts, feelings and experiences, there can be no emotional culture, which in turn is the flesh and blood of pedagogical culture. Multifaceted emotional relationships with children in a single, friendly group, where the teacher is not only a mentor but a friend and companion, are extremely important in the cultivation of a teacher's feelings. Emotional relationships are inconceivable if a teacher only meets his students in lessons and children feel the influence of the teacher only in class.

Of course we should not consider 'the world, compressed into the blackboard' to be opposed to the 'world sailing past the window panes'. We should not think for a moment that compulsory instruction is an act of violence on the human soul, or that the blackboard is an enslavement of children's freedom and the world beyond the windows is the only true freedom.

During the years preceding my work at the school in Pavlysh, I was convinced many times of the enormous role that a primary school teacher plays in a child's life. The teacher must be as close and dear as a mother. A young pupil's faith in the teacher, the mutual trust between educator and educated, the ideal of humanity, which children see exemplified in their teachers—these are elementary, but at the same time complex and profound educational principles. The teacher who grasps these becomes a genuine spiritual mentor. One of the most valuable qualities in an educator is humanity, a deep love for children, a love which combines heart felt affection with the insightful strictness and expectations of a mother or father.

Childhood is an important stage in life, not a preparation for a future life but a genuine, bright, unique, unrepeatable stage in life. And how that childhood is spent, who leads children by the hand during their early years, what enters their hearts and minds from the surrounding world, determines what sort of people today's infants will become. The longer I worked in schools, the firmer this conviction became. In the preschool and early school years a person's character, way of thinking, and speech are formed. Perhaps everything that enters the minds and hearts of children from a book, from a textbook or a lesson, only enters because alongside the book is the surrounding world: nature, fields and meadows, the blue sky and the misty haze on the horizon, the song of the lark and rustling at night, the howling of a cold winter wind and the strange ice patterns on the window panes, the opening petals of a snowdrop and the scent of new leaf awakening; and because around them are the good and evil that little people see in the surrounding world. It is in this real world that they take their first difficult steps on the long road from birth to the day when they can open a book and read it independently.

Over a period of thirty-three years I studied the vocabulary of children in the early, middle and senior years, and also of adults. A striking picture was revealed. Seven-year-old children from the families of average collective farm workers (where the father and mother have graduated from high school and have a family library of 300–400 books), on entering primary school understand and feel the emotional colouring of 3,000 to 3,500 words, of which 1,500 are in their active vocabulary. Industrial or agricultural workers with a secondary education, at the age of 45–50, understand and feel the emotional colouring of 5,000 to 5,500 words, of which about 2,500 are in their active vocabulary. This fact provides clear evidence of the significance of the childhood years in a person's life.

A conviction that the preschool and early school years to a large extent determine a person's future, in no way denies the possibility of re-education at a more mature age. Anton Makarenko brilliantly demonstrated the power of re-education in his own experience. But it was to the early years that he gave particular significance. The right way to educate is not to correct the mistakes committed in early childhood, but to avoid those mistakes and remove the need for re-education.

Working as principal I noticed, with bitter disappointment, how the natural life of children is at times perverted when the teacher sees education only in the lessons, only in cramming as much knowledge as possible into children's heads. Children who, on their first, proud day at school, are deprived of all the joys that life in nature gave them, seem to me to be like slender stalks of wheat, with tender, soft, ears of grain not yet covered with light green pollen, opening up to meet the sun and the blue sky. And suddenly these stalks are transplanted into a stuffy room, into a wooden box, and carefully watered. Every forty-five minutes they are taken outside into the fresh air for ten minutes and then again installed in a hot-house, where there is enough light, but no sun and blue sky, enough moisture, but no limitless expanse of fields. From the sweet-scented flower that is a child's life, all the petals are carefully removed, leaving only one: study, books, lessons, a bell to start lessons, and a bell to end lessons.

It makes my heart ache to see how the natural life of a child is deformed, not only in school but in after school care. There are, unfortunately, some schools where after five to six hours of study children remain in school for another four to five hours, and instead of playing, resting and living in natural surroundings, they are sat down to a book. The child's time at school becomes an endless, exhausting lesson.

We cannot continue like this! After school activities are in essence an extremely valuable form of education. They provide favourable conditions for the continuous spiritual exchange between educator and children, without which the education of a high level of emotional culture is inconceivable. But unfortunately a wonderful idea is quite often perverted. After school care quite often turns into the same lessons, the same sitting at desks from one bell to another, exhausting a child's energy.

Why does this happen?

Because taking children to a clearing in the forest or spending time in a park is significantly more complicated than conducting a lesson. The most difficult and the most subtle education is that which is conducted in conditions that give children complete freedom to run, play, chase a butterfly or a sunbeam, call out in the forest and listen to their echoes. The whole secret of such an education, which is free in the best sense of the word, is to find a way of getting children to do what you need them to, without using compulsion.

We live in a time when without mastering scientific knowledge, it is not possible to work, to enjoy normal human relationships, or to carry out the duties of a citizen. Study cannot be a carefree game bringing only pleasure and satisfaction. The life journey of a young citizen will not be a walk in the park. We must educate knowledgeable, hardworking, resilient people, prepared to overcome difficulties no less significant than those overcome by their parents, grandparents and great-grandparents. The level of knowledge of a young person in the seventies, eighties and nineties will be much higher than the level of knowledge of previous decades. The greater the range of knowledge to be mastered, the more it is necessary to consider the nature of the human organism during childhood: that period of rapid growth, development and formation of the personality. People have always been, and will remain, children of nature, and that which connects them with nature must be utilised to bring them into communion with the riches of our spiritual culture. The world surrounding a child is first and foremost the world of nature, with its limitless abundance of phenomena, with its inexhaustible beauty. Here, in nature, is the eternal source of children's thought, speech and ideas. And at the same time, with each year there is a growth in the role of those elements of the environment that are connected with the social relations between people, and with work.

My years of work at the school in Pavlysh led to another educational conviction: the process of discovery of our surrounding environment provides an indispensable emotional stimulus for thought. For preschool children and during the early school years, this stimulus plays an exceptionally important role. A truth that generalises about objects and phenomena in the surrounding world becomes a personal conviction for children when it is brought to life by bright images that exert an influence on their feelings. How important it is that children discover their first scientific truths in the surrounding world, that the source of their thoughts should be the beauty and inexhaustible complexity of natural phenomena. Emotional sensitivity, subtle subjective reactions to the depth and wisdom of thoughts—these features of our spiritual world are unattainable if we are not educated from a young age in a natural environment.

From the very beginning of my work at the school in Pavlysh I gave special attention to children in the early years, especially the grade one students. During their first days of study they cross the threshold of the school with such trembling anticipation, and look into their teacher's eyes so trustingly! Why does it often happen that after a few months, and sometimes after a week, the light goes out in their eyes? Why does study for some students turn into torture? All the teachers sincerely want to preserve the children's spontaneity and facilitate their joyful perception and discovery of the world. They want the children to be inspired and enthused by their studies.

The main reason this does not happen is that the teacher knows little of the spiritual world of each child before they enrol in the school; and life within the school walls—limited to study, regulated by bells—seems to level the little ones, to reduce them to a single measure, not allowing the richness of each individual world to be revealed. Of course I gave advice and made recommendations to the teachers of the primary classes, suggesting ways to develop students' interests and to vary the spiritual life of the children; but advice was not enough. This important educational idea, which needed to be manifested in the relationship between the children and their teacher, would only become clear when it was clearly demonstrated for all our staff to see.

That is why I began my educational work with a class group, intending to work with them for ten years. I am writing about living, concrete children. Because in many cases I have to touch on deeply personal aspects of their family lives, I have changed the children's surnames.

The life of the class, described below, was not disconnected from the life of the school community. In many cases I will touch on forms and methods of education used throughout the school. But I do this only to show more clearly a single class, as it is precisely the educational work in each class that determines the success of education throughout the school.

# The first year — studying the children

IN THE AUTUMN OF 1951, three weeks before lessons began and at the same time as children were being accepted into grade one, the school enrolled six-year-old boys and girls; that is, those who were to begin studies a year later. I planned to work with these children for ten years.

When I gathered all the parents and children, and suggested sending the children to school a year before they were due to commence studies, opinions were divided. Some parents approved of my intention, considering that in the absence of a year-round kindergarten (at that time the kindergarten operated only in summer), having children attend school would provide useful support to families. Others were concerned that starting school early would have a negative impact on the children's health. 'They'll have time enough to sit in class,' said Lyuba's mother. 'Their childhood only lasts until they start school.' These words again forced me to consider how harmful the sudden disruption of a child's way of life can be at school, and how necessary it is to give children space for the natural development of their talents. I told the parents and grandparents that they need not fear, that visiting the school during the year prior to studies would not mean sitting in class and studying. How sensitive parents are. They feel with their hearts that all is not well with school education, and that sitting at a desk deprives little ones of the joy of childhood. To have to convince parents that their children will be spared the trials and tribulations of study: what a contradiction in terms, and how much human bitterness is in these words. That which should bring joy in fact takes joy away. Is that not a tragedy? It is to prevent such a tragedy that I have begun my educational work long before the children officially enrol in school.

By this time I had come to the deep educational conviction that the development of the mind is just as important as study.

The year preceding formal study was necessary for me to get to know each child well, to study in depth the individual characteristics of their perception, thought and intellectual work. Before imparting knowledge we have to teach children how to think, how to apprehend, how to observe. We must also have a thorough knowledge of the health of each student: without that it is impossible to teach properly.

Intellectual education is not the same thing as acquiring knowledge. Although it is impossible without formal schooling, just as a green leaf is impossible without the sun's rays, the education of the intellect is not identical with formal schooling any more than a green leaf is identical with the sun. The teacher is dealing with thinking matter, and the capacity of the nervous system to apprehend and gain knowledge of the surrounding world depends to a great extent on the health of the child. This dependency is very subtle and difficult to grasp. The study of children's inner, spiritual world, and especially of their thinking, is one of a teacher's most important tasks.

## *My students' parents*

IN ORDER TO KNOW CHILDREN well it is necessary to know the family: father, mother, brothers, sisters, grandfathers and grandmothers. In our school catchment area there were thirty-one children aged six: sixteen boys and fifteen girls. All the parents agreed to send their children to the 'School of Joy'—that is what the parents came to call our group of preschoolers. Of the thirty-one children, eleven did not have a father, and two had lost both parents. Those two boys, Vitya and Sashko, had both had tragic lives. Vitya's father, a resistance fighter during the Second World War, was killed by fascists after being cruelly tortured in front of his wife. Vitya's mother could not cope with her grief and lost her mind. The boy was born six months after these tragic events. The mother died after the birth and the baby was reared with great difficulty. Sashko's father died at the front, and his mother was killed during the battle to liberate the village from fascist occupation.

Several weeks before the opening of the School of Joy I met every family. I was disturbed to find that in some families there was no warmth between parents and children, between mother and father. The mutual respect, without which a child cannot have a happy life, was missing.

I can still see before me little blue-eyed Nina in a dark blue cotton dress. On her head she wears a white scarf with light blue flowers, which has been pulled over her forehead. Next to her stands her grandmother: her mother did not come with the child. I take the little girl by the hand and look into her eyes, and my heart aches.

She was an unwanted child: the mother did not want her to be born. During her pregnancy she bound her abdomen tightly and lifted heavy weights, but the child was born alive and healthy. In a disturbed psychological state, the mother wanted to end the child's life and commit suicide, and it was only due to a fortunate circumstance that the mother and child remained alive. The girl was born with a slight facial defect: with a flat, depressed forehead. The feelings of grief and loneliness with which the mother greeted the appearance of the child, gradually grew into compassion and then genuine maternal love. So that people would not notice the flat little forehead, Nina's mother tied a scarf round her head. The child became very dear to her and every illness brought her real grief. How could I lead this little girl into the world of childish joys? How could I protect her sensitive, impressionable heart from those troubles and disappointments that are inevitable for someone who feels that they are, to some extent, deprived of the happiness available to others? How can I educate, from this silent, timid little girl, a fine human being proud of her virtues? Looking into her beautiful eyes, as blue as cornflowers, I admire them and smile, and for the first time I see a smile in her eyes. My dear, little girl; how I wish that your beautiful eyes will be spared grief, that you will find happiness in life.

Here stands dark-eyed, dark-complexioned, snub-nosed Kolya. He has a wary expression. I smile at the boy and he frowns even more. I think of the abnormal situation in his family. (Before the war Kolya's father was in prison while his family lived in the Donets Basin. During the fascist occupation he was released from prison, and the family moved to our village. The mother and father profited from the misfortune of others by conducting shady business. They were involved in speculation. They hid goods stolen by police who were working for the fascists. During the difficult years after the war, the mother stole chickens from the collective farm and taught Kolya and his older brother how to catch crows. The children killed the birds so the mother could cook them and sell them at the market as chicken …) I look at the boy, wanting him to smile, but in his eyes I see reservation and fear. How can I awaken kindly, humane feelings in your heart, Kolya? What can I offer to counter the atmosphere of malice and cynicism in which you have been raised? I look into the indifferent, unseeing eyes of his mother, and that indifference makes me feel ill at heart.

I thought for a long time about whether it was worth including these details in my book. Dozens of times I crossed the words out, only to write them again. I could, of course, have given a more generalised description: the father and mother were not good examples for the child … But that would be smoothing things over too much. We should not ignore the existence of evil. In order to combat evil and overcome it, to cleanse young souls of the corruption inherited from the old world, we have to look truth in the face.

Tolya is thin and blond-haired, with eyes as blue as a spring sky. He stands next to his mother, holding her hand, and for some reason looks at the ground, only occasionally raising his eyes. The boy's father died a heroic death in the Carpathians: his mother was sent several medals. Tolya is proud of his father, but his mother has a bad reputation in the village: she leads a wild life and completely neglects the child ... What can I do to make sure the heart of this six-year-old is not crippled by this great misfortune? What can I think of to help the mother come to her senses, to awaken in her heart feelings of concern for her son?

The war has left deep scars, wounds that have not yet healed. These children were born in 1945, some in 1944. Some of them became orphans while still in their mother's womb. Take Yura: his father died on Czech land on the second last day of the war. His mother loves her son blindly and strives to satisfy his every whim. Yura's grandfather lives with them and he is also prepared to do anything to make sure the child has a carefree life. From what I have learnt of this family, it is clear that the boy could turn into a little tyrant. Blind maternal love is as dangerous as indifference.

Petrik has come with his mother and grandfather. I have heard a lot about his mother's difficult life. Her first husband left the family before the war. The woman remarried, but her second marriage was no happier: it turned out that Petrik's father had another family somewhere in Siberia. He left after the war. The proud woman convinced her son that his father had died at the front. The boy told other children about his father's imaginary feats. Other children his age did not believe him and said his father was a fraud. Petrik cried and went to his mother in tears. It is clear that unkind people have sown the seeds of distrust and bitterness in the child's soul. What needs to be done for the child to believe in goodness again?

Kostya is already seven but he has not enrolled in grade one. The boy has been brought to the school by his father, stepmother and grandfather. The lethal winds of war have burnt this child as well. A few weeks after our village was liberated from fascist occupation, Kostya's mother (she was expecting to give birth to him any day) found some metal objects and gave them to her first, seven-year-old son to play with. It turned out that one of the objects was a mine detonator. There was an explosion and the child died. The mother hanged herself. People rushed to help and remove her from the noose, and during her last moments of agony she gave birth to Kostya. It was a miracle the boy survived. He was saved by the fact that a neighbour was breast-feeding her own child at that time. The boy's father returned from the front. He doted on his son, cared for him and showed him affection. The boy was also loved by his stepmother—a wonderful woman—and his grandfather. But before Kostya was even five years old a new misfortune struck. The boy found a shiny metal object in the vegetable garden, began to tap it with a piece of iron, and there was an explosion. They took the child to hospital covered in blood. Kostya became disabled for the rest of his life. He lost his left hand and left eye, and his face is forever disfigured by blue specks of powder …

With merciless generosity the war has crammed our earth with all manner of mines and detonators, grenades and shells, boxes of bullets and bombs. In those days you would see wounded and crippled children in every school. No amount of advice, pleading or control could counter the insatiable curiosity of those little researchers and explorers of the world. It is now more than twenty-three years since the last shots of the war were fired in our district, and still, every year, an unexpected explosion somewhere in a field or in the forest rings out, a tragic echo of the war bearing sad news of another mother's grief.

How much kindness and affection will it take, Kostya, for you to become a happy person? How should I advise your father, stepmother and grandfather so that their love will be wise, and come with expectations? How will you study? Your family say you often have headaches. How can we make your study easier, strengthen your health, and dispel your depressed moods? Your father told me that you sometimes cry all by yourself, that you are not interested in playing with other children your age …

Sitting over there next to his mother is Slava, a thoughtful, grey-eyed boy. His mother is nearly fifty and has had the difficult life of a lonely woman. In her youth she dreamt of happiness, but she was not beautiful and no-one wanted to marry her. Her youth passed and she had not experienced happiness in her personal life. Then a man returned from the war lonely, like her, and covered in scars from his wounds. He fell in love with her and they married. But their happiness was short-lived: the husband soon died. All the strength of her love for her husband she transferred to her son, but she did not raise him properly. It was said that Slava avoided people, sitting at home for days at a time, and if you asked something of him, his eyes lit up with malice. When I looked at him just now, his eyes immediately prickled and became watchful.

The more I got to know my future pupils, the more I became convinced that one of my main objectives must be to return a proper childhood to those who had been deprived of it in their families.

The greatest trauma for many of these children's hearts was that they had been exposed to evil too early in life. Evil had entered into their cramped, still narrow, children's worlds, darkening their joys, hardening their souls, convincing them that people were bad and that there is no truth in the world. The most terrible thing an educator can encounter is a little child who has lost faith in people, goodness and justice.

During thirty-three years of working in schools I have met several dozen such children. Life has convinced me that if we fail to return faith in goodness and justice to little children, they will never feel the human being in themselves and never experience feelings of self-worth. During adolescence, such pupils become embittered. For them there is nothing sacred, and a teacher's words will not reach the depth of their hearts.

To heal the souls of such young people is one of the most difficult tasks facing an educator. This most subtle, painstaking work is essentially a test of our knowledge of human nature. To really understand human nature means not only to see and feel how children apprehend good and evil, but also to defend children's tender hearts from evil.

Galya has been brought by her father. She and her younger sister have experienced deep grief: their mother died. A year after their mother's death a stepmother came into their family: good, honest and sensitive. She understood what was going on in the children's hearts, was careful in expressing her feelings, and hoped to win the girls' affection. But weeks and months passed, and Galya and her little sister would not even speak to their stepmother. They seemed not to notice her. The woman cried, and sought advice from her husband and relatives about what she should do. She was even intending to leave the family but then gave birth to a boy. She thought the appearance of the child would warm the little girls' hearts, but her hopes were not realised. The children (especially Galya) ignored their little brother. How could I touch this proud heart? What advice should I give the father and stepmother? The father had already come up to the school and poured out his grief. I told him I could only advise them once I got to know Galya well.

Plump, grey-eyed, smiling Larisa is sitting next to her mother, holding a chrysanthemum in her hand. I know the mother's heart is burdened with grief. Her husband left her. The little girl had no recollection of the father but her mother told her that one day he would come. And then the woman married a good man, a worker at the tractor depot. She managed to convince the girl that this was her father. Larisa loves her new father but her mother's heart aches: what if someone's careless words should reveal her deception.

The girl is happy, but we must be vigilant to protect her heart from the impact of unkind words. Will we succeed in this? The stepfather … I wish every child had as good a natural father as Larisa's stepfather. The more I got to know this man the more I became convinced that the real father is the one who brings up the child. I often visited this family, and was amazed by an interesting phenomenon. The same kindness, affection and sensitivity that shone in the stepfather's eyes, shone in the little girl's eyes. Her eyes radiated the same delight and amazement at beauty as her stepfather's. Even her movements and facial expressions, the way she expressed wonder, alertness, or sternness—all these things Larisa had picked up from him.

Fedya … He does not have a father either, and the boy has heard caustic, insulting comments on several occasions, suggesting that his mother has not conducted herself properly. The child's soul has experienced confusion. How could what people say be true when Mum says that Dad died at the front? I have known Fedya's mother since before the war, during which her life took an unfortunate turn. How can I lead the boy into the complex world of human relationships in such a way that he will not be troubled by tormenting questions?

As educators we often forget that little children's knowledge of the world begins with knowledge of other human beings. Good and evil are revealed to children in the tone of voice their father uses with their mother, in the emotions that are expressed in his looks and gestures. I knew one little girl who went into a remote corner of the yard and quietly cried to herself after her father had come home from work silent and gloomy, and her mother had done everything she could to try and please him. Her heart was tearing itself apart with anger at her father and feelings of compassion for her mother.

But these are just the first, superficial signs that the child notices. What goes on in a child's heart when, from a casually dropped word, from an argument between mother and father, the child learns that their father and mother do not love each other and would divorce if they were not bound together by the child?

Nina and Sasha are twin sisters. Their father has brought them to school. This large family (there are four children apart from Nina and Sasha) has its own sorrow. The mother has been bed-ridden for several years with a serious illness. The twins are the eldest and do the housework. Nina and Sasha know what hard work is, and have very few joys in their family life. When the girls saw that one of the boys had a green rubber ball, their eyes lit up with delight, but the light in their eyes died as quickly as it had appeared and I saw such deep sorrow in its place that I got a lump in my throat. How can I give these little ones the bright, carefree joy of childhood? Will I be able to? The father has already reminded me that the girls will only be able to come to school for an hour at a time because they must help him at home.

We sit on the grass, in the shade of a tall, spreading, pear tree. I tell the parents how I plan to educate the children in the School of Joy. I talk about the things that can be discussed in front of the children, but cannot get out of my head the trials and tribulations in each family. Each family has its own grief, but to make it public, to give advice in the presence of other people, would be to turn other people's souls inside out and expose the deeply personal. No, I cannot talk about those things in front of all the parents. If I need to touch the innermost sanctum of a parent's heart, it must be in a private conversation with every word weighed a thousand times before it is spoken. The heartfelt wounds, the misfortunes, insults, sorrows, troubles and suffering of these mothers and fathers (the overwhelming majority of my pupils' parents are fine people), are so individual that it is impossible to have a general discussion about them. When I see the complex weave of good and bad in the people sitting next to each other, I realise that no parent would deliberately set a bad example for their children. I promise myself never to speak about deeply personal, intimate family matters at parent meetings.

The reader may feel that I have described too much grief and misfortune for a single class of children. You have to remember that these were the wounds of war. Many years have passed since those first, post-war years and the heartfelt wounds of those years have now healed. The children who learnt to read by the light of victory salutes in 1944 and 1945, have now grown up and become mothers and fathers. The children of those first post-war students have been studying at our school for some time; some are approaching young adulthood. You might think that today's young families would shine with happiness, but in real life it is not like that. We still have grief, unhappiness, tragedies … But in those years it was much worse. I was glad that amongst my parents, most mothers and fathers lived a good family life—lived in harmony, as they say, and brought up their children well.

Look at the father of sturdy little seven-year-old Vanya. He is a great worker, an agronomist, in love with the land and with his work for the community. Every year on his home plot he propagates dozens of apple trees and grape vines, and distributes them in the community. His wife is the leader of a silk production team, a master in her trade, a kind, empathetic, warm-hearted person, and a caring mother. During the difficult years of 1933 and 1934 she took four orphans in to her family and saved them from starvation, raising them as her own children. They still call her their mother.

Lyusya, a little girl with magnificent braids of dark hair, has a very decent, honest father. There are people of whom we say that they have beautiful souls. The vast majority of such people do not achieve anything spectacular, but the beauty of their souls is expressed in their relationships with other people. I doubt if Lyusya's father has ever told her that she should be sensitive and empathetic. He teaches his children sensitivity and humanity in the way he relates to his wife. Lyusya's mother has a heart condition, but in spite of that she works on the collective farm's beet plantation. Her father has taken on all the housework.

Katya's mother and father have turned their orchard into a kind of club for little children. From early spring to late autumn their own four children are joined by children from neighbouring yards to rest, play and frolic under a shower. Katya's father has turned the yard into a little sportsground. All the fruit harvested from their orchard is given to the children as treats.

Sanya is a little girl with dark blue, ever thoughtful eyes. Her parents are kind, warm-hearted people. Every summer three girls—the father's nieces—come from the city to stay with them. Sanya looks forward to the arrival of her cousins. Sanya's father has built a bathing shed for the little ones, next to a pond. Now he is building a motor boat to bring them even more joy.

Lida comes from a wonderful family. Her father, a worker at the train construction plant, is a musician and singer. He teaches children to sing and to play the violin, and organises impromptu concerts where about twenty children gather in his yard, listen to music, and learn folk songs.

Pavel comes from a happy family. The boy's mother was bedridden for more than four years. The boy's father managed to take her place, doing all the housework as well as working.

Seryozha is a dark-complexioned, dark-eyed little boy. In his family everyone gets on well: mother, father and two children. Whenever they have a day off they all go to the forest together. There is a clearing there where they have planted four little linden trees. At home the children have planted apple trees: one each for their mother, father, grandfather and grandmother. I have often wondered why the children in this family have such a strong love for their father, mother, grandfather and grandmother. It is probably because all the goodness poured into a child's heart comes back to the mother and father with a love a hundred times more powerful and more pure.

Lyuba has come to the school with her mother, father, grandmother, elder sister and younger brother. This little girl has five brothers and sisters, two grandmothers and a grandfather. In this family a spirit of unquestioning obedience to one's elders is based on mutual trust and respect. I have heard a lot about how the elders in this family respect their children and protect their feelings.

Good old folk traditions are observed in the family of the smallest boy, Danko. Three children, aged six, eight and nine, remain on the farm while their parents are at work. The little ones prepare dinner and supper, milk the cow and tend the vegetable garden. When the mother and father return from work on a summer's evening, the children have prepared them a shower, clean underwear, a hot supper and … a bunch of wild flowers on the table. Respect for work reigns in this family—you could say they worshipped work—but without any sense of rushing or haste.

Valya's father works at a car manufacturing plant in Kremenchuk and her mother works on the collective farm. In this happy family everyone studies: the parents and the three children. The respect for knowledge, for the school and for the teachers that reigns in their home, is very encouraging for our staff. When Valya enrolled in the School of Joy we learnt something remarkable about their family. It turned out that the old lady, who everyone thought was Valya's grandmother, was not related to them by birth. No-one remained of her own family—her two sons died at the front—so Valya's family took her in and the old lady became one of the family. Valya did not even know she was not her real grandmother.

Little, grey-eyed Lyuda's mother and father work on the collective farm, and have taught their children a deep respect for simple work on the land. Their family's honour is dear to them. 'Everything we do for others should be beautiful', says their father. During the summer holidays the older children work with their father in the fields at an outlying camp. Lyuda visits them with her mother several times a month, and these trips are a real treat.

Tanya's mother and father work in the collective farm's stockbreeding section. Their two daughters often spend time at their parents' workplace during summer. The mother and father have managed to inspire their children with a love of work. The teachers have admired, more than once, how the father has made a little enclosure in a corner of the farm, in which he has put a lamb or a calf. Tanya and her older sister carefully look after the animal. This is the children's favourite game, and it is made all the more inviting because mum and dad are playing it too.

Shura is a little boy with dark, searching, tender eyes. His father works for the railway and only comes home once a week. When his father arrives home it is a big event for Shura and his brother and sister, and leaves a deep impression. They cannot wait for their father to arrive home. He always brings a present, and his presents are quite unique. He is good at carving little figures of animals, people and imaginary creatures from wood, and brings each child a little wooden figure. The children also get enormous pleasure from his stories. He has a special gift for finding good people, and his stories about the fine people he has met provide the children with a window on the world.

Volodya's father is a bridge builder and his mother works on the collective farm. The young parents love their first-born passionately, but there is little wisdom in their love. They give their little boy too many toys of all descriptions, trying to satisfy their son's every whim as quickly as possible. Volodya is sitting next to his mother now, holding two rubber balls. He wants to say something to his mother, but she is not paying attention, and her son has puffed up his cheeks and has tears in his eyes.

Varya is a dark-complexioned, dark-eyed, curly-haired girl, as slender as a flower stem. Her mother works as a cleaner at the butter factory. Her father has been seriously ill since returning from the front, and while the whole family looks after him, his health has not improved. The three children feel that fate has placed a heavy burden on their mother's shoulders and try with all their hearts to lighten her load. The mother earns a modest income, and during the evenings she embroiders shirts and towels to earn the extra money she needs for her husband's treatment. Varya's elder sister, a ten-year-old who looks very much like Varya, has already learnt to embroider and helps her mother. Varya is also learning folk embroidery.

A child is a mirror of the moral life of their parents. I thought about the good and bad in each family. The most valuable moral attribute of good parents, which is passed on to children without any special effort, is the heartfelt kindness of mother and father, their ability to show kindness to others. In families where the mother and father give a little of themselves to others and take the joys and sorrows of others to heart, the children grow up kind, sensitive, and warm-hearted. The greatest evil is the egoism and individualism of some parents. Sometimes this evil is poured into a blind, instinctual love for their child, as in Volodya's case. If the mother and father give all the energy of their hearts to their children with no consideration for other people, this hypertrophied love ultimately leads to unhappiness.

I thought about this as I told the parents about my dreams for the School of Joy. It was a difficult conversation. With each word addressed to the parents I had to consider all the good and evil in each family. When I spoke of the spirit of honesty, truthfulness and mutual trust that would reign in the School of Joy, I could not stop thinking about Kolya's family. But I could not speak of the dishonesty permeating the life of that family in front of the other parents. That would drive the mother away from the school, and she was not likely to ever come back. Something else was needed here, but what? I thought about it for a long time and could not find an answer to that complex question.

I described the children's future education to the parents. Today the children were coming to school as little six-year-olds. In twelve years they would become adults: future mothers and fathers. The school staff would do everything they could to ensure that the children grew up to be patriotic citizens of their country with a love for their native land and for working people, to be honest, truthful, hardworking, kind and warm-hearted, responsive to the needs of others, rejecting evil and dishonesty, to be courageous and determined in overcoming difficulties, to be modest and morally beautiful, healthy and physically hardened. I wanted the children to become people with clear minds, noble hearts, golden hands and lofty feelings. The child is a mirror of the family: just as the sun is reflected in a drop of water, so a mother and father's moral qualities are reflected in their children. The ultimate goal for both school and parents is to help each child find happiness. Happiness is many-facetted. It comes from discovering one's talents, from developing a love of work and finding creativity in it, from appreciating the beauty of the surrounding world and creating beauty for others, from loving another person and from being loved, from raising children to be fine people. It is only through cooperating with parents that teachers can help children find true human happiness.

The children and parents go home and I say to myself, 'Tomorrow, 31 August, the life of our School of Joy will begin'.

What will tomorrow bring? Today the children are holding their mothers' hands but tomorrow they will come by themselves. Each one will bring their own joys. Each one will experience the sunny morning. Each one will have an eternity of living in front of them. On the eve of that day my main concern was that the school would not take away the little ones' childish joys. On the contrary, I must introduce them to the world of school in such a way that they continually discover new joys, so that the discovery of the world does not turn into boring study. At the same time school should not turn in to a continuous, outwardly attractive but empty game. Each day must enrich the children's minds and feelings and strengthen their wills.

# *A school under the open sky*

I WAITED FOR THE LITTLE ones with trepidation. At eight o'clock twenty-nine children came. Sasha did not come (her mother was probably not well) and Volodya was not there—it appeared he had slept in and his mother had not wanted to wake him.

Nearly all the children were dressed in their best clothes with new shoes. That concerned me: village children have always gone barefoot when it is warm. It is an excellent way of building resistance to colds. Why do parents try to protect children's feet from the earth, from the morning dew and the sun-baked soil? It is all done with good intentions, but the result is bad. Every year more village children come down with influenza, tonsillitis and whooping-cough. We should bring up our children to brave heat and cold.

'Let's go to school, children', I said to the little ones, and headed for the orchard. The children looked at me with confusion.

'Yes children, we are going to school. Our school will be under the open sky, on the green grass, under a spreading pear tree, by the grape vines, or in the green meadows. Let's take our shoes off and walk barefoot, as you are used to doing.' The children started chattering joyfully. They were not used to wearing shoes in hot weather and found them uncomfortable. 'And tomorrow, come barefoot. That will be best at our school.'

We headed along a path to the grapes. In a quiet corner hidden by trees, grape vines were growing. Spread over a metal frame, they formed a green shelter. Inside the shelter the ground was covered with soft, green grass. Peace reigned in there, and from the shelter's green twilight the whole world looked green. We spread out on the grass.

'This is where our school begins. From here we will look out at the blue sky, the orchard, the village and the sun.'

The children fell silent, spellbound by the beauty of nature. Between the leaves hung bunches of ripe, amber-coloured grapes. The children wanted to sample the tasty fruit. 'There will be time for that children, but first let us admire the beauty.' Drops of morning dew were still hanging on the leaves like diamonds.

'Look children, and see how the orchard appears when seen through a drop of dew.'

Carefully, so as not to touch the leaves, the children spread themselves around the green wall. Each found a drop of dew and looked through it at the orchard. Exclamations of wonder rang out. Through a drop of water the orchard looked amazingly beautiful: each tree was ringed with a rainbow-coloured halo. It seemed that from the limitless depths of the blue sky little sparks were raining down on the trees. Like blinding embers, like ringing shards of crystal, they settled on the leaves and trunks. The children expressed their admiration in quiet gasps: 'How beautiful!' Someone looked through a transparent grape and saw an even more amazing scene: the world was wrapped in green mist, as if in some fairytale underwater kingdom. The surface of the earth—the fields, meadows and roads—seemed to shimmer in a malachite mist, while sparks of sunlight rained down on the shining trees.

'The sun is scattering sparks', said Katya softly. The children could not tear their eyes away from that enchanting world, and I began to tell them a story about the sun.

'Yes children, Katya has put it very well. The sun is scattering sparks. It lives high up in the sky where there are two giant blacksmiths and a golden anvil. Just before dawn, the blacksmiths with fiery beards go to the sun, who gives them two bundles of silver threads. The blacksmiths take their iron hammers, put the silver threads on their golden anvil, and hammer away. They forge a silver garland for the sun, and from under their hammers silver sparks are scattered all over the world. The sparks fall to the ground and you can see them now. In the evening the tired blacksmiths go to the sun and give him the garland. The sun puts the garland on his golden hair and goes into his magic garden to rest.'

I tell the story and draw it at the same time. On the white page of my notebook fantastic images appear: two giant blacksmiths labour at the golden anvil and silver sparks are scattered by their iron hammers.

The children listen to the tale, enchanted by this magic world. They seem afraid to break the silence, not wanting the spell to be broken. Then suddenly they deluge me with questions. What do the blacksmiths do at night? Why does the sun need a new garland every day? Where do all the silver sparks that fall to earth every day go?

'Dear children, I will tell you all that another time. We will have plenty of time for that; but now, I want to give you some grapes.' The children wait impatiently while the basket is filled with grapes. I give each child two bunches. I advise them to eat one and to take the other bunch home for their mother, so she can try them. The children show amazing restraint and wrap the grapes in paper. But I cannot help wondering: will that restraint last all the way from school to their homes? Will Tolya and Kolya bring grapes for their mothers? I give Nina several bunches: for her sick mother, for her sisters and for her grandmother. Varya takes three bunches for her father. I have a thought: as soon as the children are strong enough, each child can plant their own grape vine at home … Varya needs to plant ten cuttings this autumn so they can bear fruit next year. That will be good for her father's health …

We leave the magic green light of the grape bower. I tell the children, 'Tomorrow come in the evening at six o'clock. Don't forget.'

I can see the children do not want to leave, but they disperse, clutching their white bundles to their chests. How I would love to know who will reach home with the grapes! But I must not question the children about this; if some tell me themselves, that will be good.

And so ended the first day of our school under the open sky … I will remember that day for the rest of my life; as I will remember my own first day at school when my first teacher, Praskovia Alekseyevna, took us to the meadow and showed us an amazing world—the life of an anthill; as I will remember the day I became a father; as I will remember the day I presented a graduation certificate to my first student, whom I had led by the hand for ten years—from the first attempt to write letters in an exercise book to thoughts about the future of humanity.

That night I dreamt of silver sparks of sunlight, and when I woke early in the morning, I thought for a long time about what to do next. I had not compiled a detailed plan of what to say to the children each day or where to take them. The life of our school developed from an idea that had inspired me: children by their very nature are inquisitive researchers, explorers of the world. So let a world of wonder reveal itself to them in living colours, in clear and vibrant sounds, in stories and games, in their own creativity, in beauty that uplifts the heart, in the urge to do good deeds for others. Through stories, imagination and play, through children's unique creativity: that was the sure way to a child's heart. I would introduce the little ones to the surrounding world in such a way that every day they discovered something new in it, so that every step led us on a journey to the wellsprings of thought and speech, to the wondrous beauty of nature. I would take care that each of my pupils grew up to become a wise thinker and researcher, that each step on the path to knowledge enriched the heart and tempered the will.

On the second day the children came to school in the evening. A quiet September day was fading. We left the village and found a place to sit high on an ancient burial mound. Spread out in front of us was a wonderful view of a wide meadow that seemed to glow in the evening sunlight, of tall, slender poplars, and, on the horizon, distant burial mounds. We had come to the very wellsprings of thought and words. Stories and fantasy—these provide a key to unlock those springs, and life-giving streams will bubble from them.

I remembered how, on the day before, Katya had said, 'The sun is scattering sparks …' Twelve years later, when graduating from school, Katya wrote an essay about her native land and repeated that image when expressing her love for nature. Such is the power of a fairytale image to influence a child's thought. A thousand times I have been convinced that when they populate the world with fantastic images and when they create these images, children discover not only beauty, but truth. Without stories, without the play of imagination, a child cannot live. Without stories the surrounding world is just a beautiful picture painted on a canvas. Stories bring that picture to life.

Figuratively speaking, a story is a fresh wind fanning the fire of a child's thought and speech. Children not only love to hear stories, they create them. When I showed the children the world though the leaves of a grapevine, I knew I would tell them a story, but did not know exactly which one. Katya's words—the sun is scattering sparks—provided a stimulus for my flight of fancy. What truthful, precise, artistically expressive images children create; how striking and colourful their language is. We must not hide the surrounding world from them with a classroom's walls, a blackboard and the pages of a textbook.

Before opening a book, before sounding out their first word, I wanted the children to read the pages of the most wonderful book in the world—the book of nature.

Here, in the midst of nature, it was particularly clear to me that, as teachers, we are dealing with the most tender, most delicate, most sensitive thing in nature—a child's brain. When you think of a child's brain, you must imagine a tender rose on which a drop of dew is quivering. How much care and tenderness is needed to pick the rose without spilling the drop of dew. That is how much care we need each minute of the day, as we touch the most delicate thing in nature—the thinking matter of a growing organism.

Children think in images. This means, for example, that while listening to a teacher's story about the journey of a drop of water, in their imaginations they paint silver waves of morning mist, a dark storm cloud, peals of thunder, and a spring shower. The clearer these pictures are in their imaginations, the more deeply they comprehend the laws of nature. The tender, sensitive neurons of their brains have not yet reached their full strength: they need to be developed and strengthened. For this to happen, children's thinking processes must be in accord with the natural demands of their brains. Most importantly, children must be taught to think in the midst of nature, at that life-giving wellspring of thought from which streams of living water constantly flow.

Children think ... That means that a certain group of neurons in the cortex of their brains perceives images (pictures, objects, phenomena, words) from the surrounding world, and that signals pass through the sensitive nerve cells, as if through communication channels. The neurons 'process' this information—catalogue it, group it, juxtapose it, compare it—all while continuing to receive new information, which in turn must be taken in and processed. In order to cope with the volume of constantly arriving images, and with processing the information, the nervous energy of the neurons constantly switches between perceiving images and processing them.

This astonishingly rapid switching of the nervous energy of neurons is the phenomenon we call thought—a child is thinking ... Children's brain cells are so delicate and react so sensitively to the objects of perception that they can only function normally when the object of perception they are making sense of is an image they can see, hear and touch. This switching of thought, which is the essence of the thinking process, is only possible when children are presented with either a real, visual image, or a verbal image that is created so vividly they are able to see, hear and sense what is being described. That is why children love stories so much.

The nature of children's brains dictates that their minds should be educated at the wellsprings of thought—amongst visual images and mainly in natural settings, so that thought can switch from a visual image to the processing of information about that image. If children are isolated from nature, if all that a child is exposed to from the first days of school is words, the brain cells are quickly exhausted and cannot cope with the work set by the teacher. These cells need to be allowed to develop, to get stronger, to gather energy. Here we find an explanation for a phenomenon that many teachers encounter in primary classes: children are sitting quietly, looking you in the eyes, apparently listening attentively, but not understanding a single word, because the teacher talks and talks, because they have to understand rules, to solve problems, to follow examples. Without living images there is too much abstraction and generalisation, and the brain gets tired … That is why children fall behind. That is why it is necessary to develop children's thinking, to increase their mental capacity in the midst of nature—this is dictated by the natural laws governing a child's development. That is why every excursion into nature is a lesson in thought, a lesson in developing the mind.

We sit on the ancient burial mound while a chorus of grasshoppers rings out harmoniously all around and the scent of steppe grasses hangs in the air. We are silent. You do not have to say a lot to children or cram their heads with stories. Words are not an idle pursuit, and overconsumption of words is one of the most harmful forms of overconsumption. As well as needing to hear their teacher's words, children need time for silence. During such moments they think and make sense of what they have seen and heard. It is very important for teachers to show restraint when explaining things to children. We must not turn children into passive receptors of words. In order to make sense of each bright image—visual or verbal—time and nervous energy are required. Knowing when to give children time to think is one of the most refined attributes of a teacher. In the midst of nature children must be given the chance to listen, to see and to feel …

We listen attentively to the chorus of grasshoppers and I am glad the children are absorbed in this enchanting music. May this quiet evening, overflowing with the scent of fields and with wonderful modulating sounds, live in their memories forever. One day, they will make up a story about a grasshopper.

But for now the children gaze thoughtfully at the sunset. The sun has disappeared beyond the horizon and delicate shades of sunset spread across the sky.

'Now the sun has gone to rest', says Larisa, and her face becomes sad.

'The blacksmiths have brought the sun its silver garland … Where does it put yesterday's garland?' asks Lida.

The children look at me expecting a continuation of the story, but I have not decided which image to use. Fedya helps me.

'The garland has melted across the sky', he says quietly.

There is an expectant silence as we all wait to see what Fedya will say next. The boy has obviously composed a continuation to the story and his silence is probably due to shyness. I help Fedya:

'Yes, the garland has melted across the sky. During the day it gets white hot on the sun's fiery hair, and becomes as soft as wax. The sun has only to touch it with his burning hand, and it pours in a golden stream across the evening sky. The last rays of the sun, as it goes to rest, light up that stream. You can see the play of its pink colours, ever changing, growing darker as the sun moves away. Soon the sun will enter its magic garden, and the stars will come out.'

'What are stars? Why do they come out? Where do they come from? Why can't you see them during the day?' ask the children. But I should not overwhelm the children's minds with too many images. We have had enough for today, and I divert their attention to something else.

'Look at the steppe. Can you see how it is getting dark in the valleys, in the meadow, in the lowlands? Look at those hills: they look soft, as if they are floating in the evening gloom. The hills are turning grey. Look at their surface. What do you see?'

'A forest ... Bushes ... A herd of cattle ... Sheep and a shepherd ... People are spending the night in the fields, lighting campfires; but you can't see the campfires, only the smoke rising into the air ...'
These are the images born of the children's imaginations as they watch the rapidly darkening hills. I suggest returning home but the children do not want to. They ask if they can sit a little longer. At dusk, when the world seems to clothe itself in a veil of mystery, children's imaginations run wild. I have only to suggest that the evening dusk and the darkness of the night were flowing like rivers from distant valleys and forests, and the children's imaginations give birth to two fairytale creatures: Darkness and Dusk. Sanya tells a story about these creatures. They live in a distant cave, beyond the primordial forest. During the day they sink into a dark, bottomless pit, where they sleep and sigh in their dreams (why they sigh, only the author of the story knows). But as soon as the sun leaves for its magic garden, they come out of their hiding place. Their huge paws are covered in soft hair, so no-one hears their steps. Dusk and Darkness are kind, peaceful, gentle creatures, and do not hurt anyone.

The children are ready to make up a story about how Darkness and Dusk put children to sleep, but we have had enough for today. We go home and the children ask if tomorrow they can come in the evening again, when, as Varya states, 'it is easy to make up stories'.

Why do children listen so willingly to stories, why do they so love the evening twilight, when the atmosphere facilitates children's flights of fancy? Why do stories develop speech and thought more powerfully than any other means? It is because story images are so laden with emotional colouring. The words from a story live in a child's consciousness. Children's hearts stop beating when they hear or pronounce words that create a world of fantasy. I cannot imagine school instruction that does not include making up and listening to stories. I still have stories composed by the little children during those first two months of the School of Joy. They reveal a world of children's thoughts, feelings, desires and attitudes:

### The hare (Shura)

Mum gave me a little plush hare. It was just before New Year. I put it on the Christmas tree in the middle of the branches. Everyone went to bed. On the tree a tiny little lamp was shining. I saw the hare jump from its branch and run around the tree. It jumped around for a while and then climbed back onto the tree.

### The sunflower (Katya)

The sun rose. The birds woke up and a lark rose up into the sky. A sunflower woke up as well. It roused itself and shook some dew from its petals. It turned to the sun: 'Hello, sun. I have been waiting for you all night. See how my yellow petals have drooped without your warmth. Now they have perked up and are happy again. I am round and golden, just like you, sun.'

### How they ploughed the field (Yura)

A combine harvester has cut the wheat. A hedgehog crawls out of its burrow and sees: there is no wheat, the seed heads are not rustling any more. It rolls through the stubble like a ball. Suddenly it sees a huge monster crawling towards it: a metal beetle that rumbles and roars. After it comes a plough. Behind it is a black, ploughed field. The hedgehog sits in his burrow and looks out with amazement. 'Where did that giant beetle come from?' it wonders. But it is really a tractor.

## *The acorn (Zina)*

A wind sprang up. An acorn fell from an oak tree, yellow and shiny, as if forged from copper. It fell down and thought, 'It was so nice in the branches, but now I am on the ground. From here I cannot see the river or the forest.' The acorn became sad. 'Oak tree, please take me back onto your branch', it begged. But the oak tree replied, 'Don't be stupid. Look at me. I also grew from the earth. You should quickly put down roots and grow. Then you will turn into a tall oak tree.'

Children are not only concerned about what happens in nature. They want the world to be at peace. They know there are forces contemplating war. Here is a story in which these dark forces are depicted in the image of a snake:

## *How we defeated the Iron Snake (Seryozha)*

He lived in a swamp, far, far away, beyond the ocean. He hated our people. He made atomic bombs. He made lots and lots of them, loaded his wings with them, and took off. He wanted to throw them at the sun. He wanted to put the sun out, so we would perish in darkness. I sent the swallows out against the Iron Snake. The swallows took sparks from the sun's fire in their beaks and chased after the Snake. They threw the fire on its wings. The Iron Snake fell into the swamp and burnt up together with its bombs. The sun shone, and the swallows were glad and twittered happily.

This story demonstrates the peculiarities of a child's view of the world. A child cannot imagine the triumph of good over evil without the participation of birds and animals. The children's writer Arkady

Gaidar once said that a story should end like this: 'The red army defeated the white army, and a hare rejoices'. The hares and swallows that are so dear to children's hearts are not just story characters; they are the embodiment of goodness.

We sit on the ancient burial mound admiring the colours of the sunset and listening to the chorus of grasshoppers. We are about to open a new page in the story of the sun. As the fiery globe touches the horizon I say to the children, 'Look at the village. What do you see in the windows of the homes?'

In the windows of the homes fires are burning. The last rays of the departing sun are reflected in the window panes, shining like crimson flames. Captivated, amazed, the children are silent. The crimson flames gradually die down in some windows, only to flare up in others.

The sun is lighting fires in the windows. 'Oh, how beautiful!' We admire the crimson fires until the sun disappears beyond the horizon.

Each day brought some new discovery in the surrounding world. Each discovery was transformed into a story created by the children. Story images helped the little ones to feel the beauty of their native land. The beauty of our countryside—revealed through stories, imagination and creativity—inspires a love for our homeland.

The beauty of nature, of our native tongue, and the beauty of the kind people surrounding a child, feed a child's heart with patriotic feelings. With little children you do not need to speak high-flown words about the greatness and might of our native land (high-flown because these words are still incomprehensible to them). That can wait for another time.

Let children feel beauty, and delight in it. Let images of their homeland remain forever in their hearts and memories. Beauty is the flesh and blood of humanity, of kindly feelings, of warm-hearted relationships. I was glad to see how the hardened hearts of Tolya, Slava, Kolya, Vitya and Sashko were gradually melting. Smiles, enthusiasm, wonder at the beauty of nature—I saw these as providing a path to the children's hearts.

The life of our School of Joy was not cramped by strict regulations. It was not stipulated how much time the children should spend under the open sky. The main thing was that the children should not tire of it, that they should never long for the teacher to tell them it was time to go home. I tried to end our lessons when the children showed heightened interest in what we were observing or doing. I wanted the little ones to look forward to the next day with anticipation of new joys. I wanted them to see the sun scattering silver sparks in their dreams. One day the children might spend an hour or an hour and a half, the next day four hours. It all depended on how much joy the teacher was able to bring the children on that day. It was also very important that each child not only experienced joy, but also created it, making their own little contribution to the life of the class.

During that autumn we enjoyed prolonged warm, dry weather. The leaves on the trees had still not turned yellow in the middle of October. Several times thunder rolled through the sky as if summer had returned, and in the mornings, drops of dew sparkled on the grass. This created favourable conditions for our work. Several times we returned to our burial mound and 'travelled' through the clouds. These hours left indelible impressions on the children's memories with the white, fluffy clouds providing a world of amazing discoveries. In their strange, constantly changing outlines, the children saw wild animals and fairytale giants. Their childish imaginations flew, like speeding birds, beyond the clouds, beyond seas and forests, to distant unknown lands. In these flights of fancy the children's individual worlds were clearly revealed. A strange cloud would float into view.

'What do you see in it, children?'

'An old shepherd in a straw hat, leaning on a stick', says Varya. 'Look, you can see his flock of sheep next to him. In the front there's a ram with curly horns, and behind him are lambs ... And the old man has a bag over his shoulder, and something is poking out of the bag.'

'That's not an old man', objects Pavlo. 'It's a snowman like we made in winter. Look, he's even got a broom in his hand. And that's not a straw hat on his head; that's a bucket.'

'That's not a snowman', says Yura. 'That's a haystack. There are two shepherds with pitchforks on the haystack. You can see they're tossing the hay down on to a cart. What sort of a ram is that? It's not a ram, it's a cart. Those aren't horns; that's a harness ...'

'It's a huge, enormous hare. I saw one like that in my dream. And that isn't a cart down the bottom; that's the hare's tail.'

I would like all the children to use their imaginations, but for some reason Kolya, Slava, Tolya and Misha remain silent. My heart aches when I see an expression of condescension on Kolya's face, such as one might come across on the face of an adult who considers childish pursuits beneath his dignity. I wonder why, when I have already seen the boy's eyes light up with delight at beauty ... (At that time I had not thought about it much, but I had a gut feeling that until I succeeded in drawing such children into the enjoyment of childish pleasures, until their eyes lit up with unfeigned delight, until they enjoyed childish mischief, I had no right to speak of any educational influence over them. Children need to be children. If they are not involved in the battle between good and evil when listening to a story, if instead of delight you see indifference in their eyes, that means something is damaged in the child's soul and you need to invest a lot of energy to heal it.)

Another strange cloud appears on the horizon. This one looks like a wonderful palace surrounded by tall walls and watchtowers. The children's imaginations fill in any gaps in the outline of the palace, and Yura is already telling us a fairytale about a magic kingdom beyond the seven seas, about a cruel witch and a brave knight who saves a beautiful princess. Vitya's imagination has created a different story. Somewhere far beyond the borders of our country, a terrifying creature lives in the mountains and plans war. The wings of fancy take the boy on a flying ship, capable of taking him in an instant to the cave where the dark force lives, destroying the evil and establishing eternal peace on Earth.

Then I tell the children about distant tropical lands, about endless summer and unusual constellations, about sky-blue oceans and tall palms. Here fairytale is interwoven with reality and I open a small window onto a distant world. I talk about the earth and its peoples, about seas and oceans, about the abundance of the plant and animal worlds, about natural phenomena.

\* \* \*

Experience has convinced me that if children are to fully develop their intellects and have a rich spiritual life, they must hear stories and explanations from a teacher who shares their joys and sorrows. The educational significance of these stories comes from the fact that children hear them in a setting that encourages creative imagination: on a quiet evening when the first stars are coming out; in the forest by a campfire; or in a cosy hut by the light of smouldering coals, while autumn rain beats on the window pane and a cold wind sings its melancholy song. Explanations should be clear, vivid and concise. We should not load children with too many facts, with a host of impressions, or their sensitivity to the teacher's words will be blunted and it will be hard to interest them in anything.

I advise educators: work with children's feelings and imaginations; open a window on the boundless world very gradually; do not swing it open wide; do not turn it into a wide door towards which the little ones, carried away by everything you have told them, will hurtle, rolling out like marbles ... First they will feel lost in the face of so many strange objects; and then those objects, about which they essentially know nothing, will seem familiar to them and become no more than empty sounds.

The school under the open sky taught me how to open a window on the world for children, and I tried to pass on this lesson to all the other teachers. I advised them: do not overwhelm children with an avalanche of knowledge. In your lessons do not try to explain everything you know about the subject, as the children's curiosity and thirst for knowledge may be buried under that avalanche. Learn to expose children to some single phenomenon in the natural world, but in such a way that this little part of the world comes to life with all the colours of the rainbow. Always leave something unsaid, so that children want to return again and again to what they have learnt.

The achievements of human thought are limitless. Amongst other things, people have created a multitude of books. Show children the beauty, wisdom and depth of thought in a single book, but show it in such a way that each child forever falls in love with reading, and is ready to swim independently in the ocean of books. I shared with the other teachers my thoughts about our 'journeys' to the wellsprings of living words—that is what I called the little children's short, graphic, emotionally charged stories about objects and phenomena from the surrounding world that they had seen with their own eyes. Teachers in the primary classes began to make similar 'journeys', following my example. The doors of the classrooms were flung open and children began to go out on to the green grass in the fresh breeze. Reading and arithmetic lessons, especially in grades one and two, began to be conducted more and more frequently under the open sky. This was no abdication of lessons or retreat from books and learning into the world of nature. On the contrary, this enriched lessons, and brought books and learning to life.

# Our Nook of Dreams

NOT FAR FROM THE SCHOOL, beyond the village, is a deep ravine overgrown with bushes and trees. For little children this is a dense forest, full of undiscovered mysteries. One day I notice the entrance to a cave in the side of the ravine. The cave is spacious inside, with solid, dry walls. This is a real treasure trove! This will be our 'Nook of Dreams'. It is hard to convey the delight of the children when I first take them to the cave. The children squeal, sing, call out to each other, and play hide and seek. That very day we spread dry grass over the floor.

At first we simply enjoy our secret nook, and make it cosy and habitable. We attach some pictures to the walls, widen the entrance and make a table. The children are delighted with a proposal to build a stove there so we can light a fire from time to time.

We dig out a place for the stove and knock through an opening for the chimney pipe. We remove the excavated soil and bring in clay and bricks. It is hard work but we have a dream: a stove. We build it for two weeks. The work inspires everybody. Even Kolya, Slava and Tolya, whose indifference to everything has so disturbed me, cannot remain on the sidelines. Their eyes light up more and more often, and their enthusiasm lingers. Our interesting work also inspires shy, timid, indecisive children like Sashko, Lyuda and Valya. I become more and more convinced that the emotional feeling in a group—the collective joy and enthusiasm—is a significant spiritual force, capable of uniting children and awakening interest in what the group is doing, even in previously indifferent hearts.

At last we are able to light a fire in our stove. The dry kindling merrily bursts into flame. Evening descends on the land. In our dwelling it is light and cosy. We look at the trees and bushes covering the slope of the ravine, and from a mysterious thicket opposite, fairytale images march towards us. They seem to invite us to make up stories about them. The trees and bushes are enveloped in the evening haze, bluish-grey at first and then lilac-coloured. In this haze the trees take on the most unexpected shapes.

At such times children willingly exercise their imaginations and create stories.

'What do those trees scattered on the slope of the ravine look like?' I ask, not so much addressing the children as my own thoughts. To me they look like a green waterfall, rushing headlong from a precipice, only to freeze and turn into giant statues of basalt or malachite. I wonder if any child's thoughts will develop in the same direction as mine. During this evening there will be an opportunity to observe how the children think.

I learn that while one child's thoughts bubble along rapidly, giving birth to more and more images, another's flow like a mighty river—slow, full, wide and mysterious in its depths. You cannot even tell if that river is flowing, but it is strong, irresistible, and cannot be diverted. The rapid, effervescent, impetuous thoughts of other children can more easily be diverted when they meet an obstruction. Shura sees a herd of cows in the crowns of the trees, but Seryozha has only to ask, 'And what are they going to feed on? There is no grass there' for Shura's thoughts to fly off in another direction. Now it is not cows, but clouds, coming down to earth to rest for the night. Yura's thoughts soar just as quickly and impetuously. But Misha and Nina are watching silently, intently—what are they seeing? Already dozens of images born of the children's imaginations have flashed past, but Misha and Nina are silent. So is Slava. Is it possible not a single idea has come to them? It is already time to go home when Misha, the quietest of all the boys, suddenly says:

'It is a wild bull who has charged with its horns at the cliff, and unable to overcome it, has stopped in its tracks. Look, he is straining, almost pushing back the precipice …'

And suddenly all the other images that had crowded our minds fly away. We see that the mass of trees does in fact look amazingly like a bull, frozen in impotent rage. The children start chattering: look how his feet are gripping the bottom of the ravine, see how his neck is swelling—probably his sinews are straining, and his horns are stuck in the ground …

So that is what Misha was thinking about! While bright, living images were flashing through our minds, the river of his thoughts followed its own course. He listened carefully to his friends but not one image distracted him. The boy's imagination was the most lucid and the most down to earth. The child saw something that he had probably seen in real life, and that had made a deep impression on his consciousness. And silent, slow thinkers like him suffer so much during lessons. Teachers want a student to answer as quickly as possible. They are not interested in how a child thinks; they just want the child to answer so they can give him a grade. It does not occur to them that you cannot speed the flow of a slow but mighty river. That river should be allowed to flow as nature intended. Its waters will definitely reach their intended destination, but please do not hurry, do not be anxious, do not lash the mighty river with the birch rod of your grades—that will not help.

I wonder if every teacher has reflected on the fact that the development of the human organism—from birth to maturity—is longer in humans than in any other representative of the animal kingdom. The human organism grows, develops and strengthens for twenty years or more. A great secret of nature hides in the lengthy duration of this period of human development. Nature has allocated this lengthy period for the development, strengthening and education of the nervous system, including the cortex of the brain. Human beings only become human because over a very lengthy period they live through the infancy of the nervous system, the childhood of the brain.

A child enters the world with billions of nerve cells that react sensitively to the surrounding world and, given certain conditions, are capable of carrying out the functions of thought. These cells constitute the material basis for consciousness. Nature does not provide a single extra nerve cell during the period from birth to maturity, or from maturity to old age. During the childhood stage in the development of human thought, deep inner processes occur in the cells of the cerebral cortex: these cells are strengthened during the process of active thinking and gradually accumulate impressions, images and concepts. During the infancy of the nervous system the cells of thinking matter must exercise every day, and the main forms this exercise takes are perception, observation and contemplation.

Before embarking upon any deep study of cause and effect relationships in the surrounding world, children need to pass through a period of cognitive exercises. These exercises involve the observation of objects and phenomena. Children see living images and then imaginatively recreate those images in their own representations. The viewing of real objects and the creation of imaginative representations of those objects: there is no contradiction in these two stages of the cognitive process. The fantasy image in a story is interpreted by a child, and created by that same child as a vivid reality. The creation of fantasy images provides fertile ground for the vigorous development of thought processes.

During childhood, thought processes should be connected as closely as possible with bright, living, concrete objects in the surrounding world. In the beginning, do not expect children to think about cause and effect relationships. Let them simply inspect an object and discover something new about it. A boy saw an enraged bull in a mass of trees wrapped in the evening dusk. This is not simply the play of a child's imagination, but an artistic, poetic way of thinking. In the same trees other children see something different, unique to themselves—they invest the image with the individual characteristics of their own perception, imagination and thought. Each child not only perceives, but draws, creates and constructs. A child's perception of the world is a unique form of artistic creation. The image perceived and, at the same time, created by the child is charged with striking emotional colouring. Children experience an elemental joy when they perceive an object from the surrounding world and add something to it from their imagination. The emotional richness of perception provides the spiritual energy for children's creativity. I am deeply convinced that without emotional stimulation the normal development of a child's brain cells is impossible. There are physiological processes taking place in a child's brain that are connected with emotion. During moments of enthusiasm and intense stimulation, additional nutrition is supplied to the cells of the cerebral cortex. At such times the brain cells consume a lot of energy, but they simultaneously receive a lot from the organism. After observing the intellectual work of children in the primary classes for many years, I came to the conclusion that at times of great emotional stimulation, children's thoughts become particularly clear and more intensive memorisation takes place.

These observations threw new light on the process of educating children. The thinking processes of children in the primary classes are inseparable from their feelings and emotions. The process of instruction, and especially children's perception of the surrounding world, should be charged with emotion. The laws of development of a child's thought processes demand this.

The wonderfully warm days of an Indian summer began. We did not stay in one place, but roamed the fields and woodlands, only occasionally looking into our Nook of Dreams. Two kilometres from the village the children found a little hill from which we had a breathtaking view of the village nestled among orchards, distant fields, dark blue burial mounds and forest belts. The air became amazingly clear and transparent. Fine silver cobwebs floated above the ground and formations of migratory birds appeared more and more often in the blue sky. Not far from our little hill was a grove of trees, on the edge of which grew many briar bushes. We admired the bead-like, purple berries, and the silver webs hanging from the branches. The outline of each bush was engraved in our memories, and we gazed at the orchards and rows of tall poplars on the edge of the village. Each day the children discovered something new. Before our very eyes the green grove clothed itself in crimson, the leaves displaying an amazing array of colours. These discoveries brought the children great joy.

Here the wellsprings of living language and creative thought were so rich and abundant that had we made one discovery each hour there would have been enough to last for many years. In front of us was a briar bush, laden with bunches of purple berries. From berry to berry were strung silver webs, sparkling with trembling drops of morning dew. The dew drops seemed to be made of amber. Spellbound, we stood by a bush and witnessed amazing things. From the edges of the webs drops of dew were moving, as if alive, crawling to the sagging centres and merging with each other; but why did they not get bigger and fall to the ground? We were completely absorbed in our observations. It turned out that the dewdrops quickly evaporated, diminishing in size as we watched and then disappearing completely.

'The sun is drinking the dewdrops', whispered Larisa. The image created by Larisa's imagination caught the children's interest and a new story was born. Here, beside the briar bush, at one of the wellsprings of living language, a new stream began to flow. Perhaps it was just chance, but it had to happen sooner or later. Larisa noticed the similarity between the rhyming words *rosinki* (dewdrops), *pautinki* (spider webs) and *businki* (beads). This striking coincidence seemed to light up the children's minds. Until now they had only heard poems from older brothers and sisters who had read them in books, but suddenly verse was born from living words, from the surrounding world. Her eyes sparkling with joy, Larisa said:

'*Dewdrops fell at night,
On the silver spider webs.*'[9]

Everyone was silent but I could see that each child's thoughts had taken flight like a bird, with a feeling of wonder at the power of words.
'*And began to shake and tremble, like amber beads*', continued Yura.
This is what happens when we approach the original source of all things, when a word incorporates not only the designation of an object, but the aroma of flowers, the scent of the earth, the music of our native steppe and forests, and our own feelings and emotions.
Had I followed pedagogical guidelines I probably should have invited the children to continue the poem, but such guidelines flew out of my head and, inspired by the children's creativity, I blurted out:

'*The sun drank the dewdrops,
The silver webs were washed
And the purple berries smiled ...*'

We shouted, ran around the bush, and repeated the poem we had made up. I wanted to tell the other teachers about this surge of inspiration and how it flowed from the surrounding world as soon as possible. I wanted to advise them: the first lessons in thought should not be in the classroom in front of a blackboard, but in in the midst of nature. I wanted to tell them that genuine thought is always permeated with thrilling emotion. If children can only sense

---

9 Translator's note: Here, and in the lines that follow, the children and their teacher compose several lines of rhyming verse. The rhyme and metre are lost in translation.

the flavour of a word, their hearts will be inspired. Go to the fields or the park, drink from the wellsprings of thought, and that living water will turn your pupils into insightful researchers, inquisitive, curious people and poets. I have been convinced over and over again: without a poetic, emotional and aesthetic impetus, a child's intellect cannot fully develop. The very nature of a child's thought demands poetic creativity. Beauty and living thought are connected as organically as the sun and the flowers. Poetic creativity begins with a vision of beauty. The beauty of nature heightens perception, awakens creative thought, and endows words with unique associations. Why do people acquire such a large vocabulary during childhood? Because that is when they first discover the beauty of the surrounding world. Because in each word they not only find meaning, they sense the most subtle shades of beauty.

## *Nature—the source of health*

EXPERIENCE HAS CONVINCED ME THAT for approximately 85% of students who fall behind in their studies, the main reason is a poor state of health: some indisposition or illness, more often than not unnoticed, which is only cured through the joint efforts of mother, father, doctor and teacher. Such hidden conditions, masked by children's vitality and animation, may affect the circulatory, respiratory and digestive systems, and are often not fully blown illnesses but rather deviations from a normal state of health. The observations of many years have convinced me that in many cases, so-called mental retardation is due to some general indisposition that children themselves are not aware of, rather than to any physiological changes or impairment to the function of the cells of the cerebral cortex. In some children you can observe an unhealthy pallor, a lack of appetite. The slightest attempts to improve nutrition provoke a reaction: pimples appear on the body. Exhaustive pathology tests reveal nothing: everything seems okay. In most cases it turns out that the problem is a disturbance of the metabolism, resulting from spending too much time indoors. Due to this disturbance, the child loses the capacity for concentrated intellectual work. The occurrence of such problems increases during periods of rapid growth and sexual maturation.

The only radical treatment in such cases is a change in the routines of work and rest: prolonged periods in the fresh air, sleeping with an open window, going to bed early and getting up early, and good nutrition.

Some children appear healthy, but when you study their work closely you discover some hidden ailment. And here is what is interesting: these hidden ailments and indispositions become much more noticeable when the teacher tries to fill every minute of the lesson with intense intellectual work. Some children cannot cope at all when a teacher tries to ensure that 'not a single minute of the lesson will be wasted'. I am convinced that this accelerated tempo is harmful, even for completely healthy children. Excessive intellectual exertion leads to children's eyes growing listless; their wits are dulled and their movements become sluggish. Before long children are not capable of anything; they just want to get out in the fresh air; but the teacher keeps them 'in harness' and urges them on: giddy-up, giddy-up …

During the first weeks of the School of Joy I carefully studied the children's health. Although all the children had grown up in the countryside in the lap of nature, some of them were pale with weak chests. And Volodya, Katya and Sanya were just skin and bones. They nearly all had good nutrition at home. The main reason that some children were weak and sickly was that they lived in a hothouse environment, where mothers protected them from the slightest draft. These children tired quickly. During the first days of the School of

Joy they had trouble walking a kilometre. Their mothers complained that they had poor appetites.

I convinced the parents that the more they protected their children from catching cold, the weaker they would become. All agreed to my insistent request that on hot days they should send the children to school with bare feet. This delighted the children. One day we were caught in a field during a warm downpour. The children had to walk home through puddles. In spite of the parents' fears, no-one fell ill. With great difficulty I managed to convince the parents not to dress their children in a hundred garments, piling on jumpers and tops 'just in case'. It became our rule that during autumn, spring and summer, the children should not spend a single minute indoors. During the first three or four weeks of the School of Joy the children walked two or three kilometres every day; during the second month, four or five kilometres; and during the third month, six kilometres. And all this walking took place in fields and meadows, in woodlands and forests. The children did not notice the distance covered each day because we did not set ourselves the aim of covering a certain number of kilometres. Walking was a means for achieving other goals. The children wanted to walk because they were exploring the world. The children came home tired, but happy and cheerful. Health is impossible without tiredness. Health flows into a child's organism with life-giving energy when, after difficult exertion, a child rests. After walking several kilometres in the fresh air the children developed, in their parents' words, 'the appetite of a wolf'. On days when we planned a trip to the forest I advised the little ones to bring bread, an onion, salt, water and a few raw potatoes. At first the parents were doubtful: would the children really eat that? But it turned out that in the forest, bread, onion and potatoes were the most delicious food. Moreover, the children's appetites developed and when they got home they ate the soup they were offered with pleasure. After a month even the palest children had rosy cheeks, and the mothers could not speak highly enough of their children's appetites. Their fussiness had disappeared and they ate whatever they were offered.

Movement is one of the most important factors contributing to physical conditioning. Children love to run and to play. We made a playground for them. Here they had everything necessary for playing and having fun in the fresh air, but I dreamt of more. I wanted to make a merry-go-round and some swings. I wanted the children's lively games to be connected with fairytales, to be fed by fantasy. I already imagined the figures of Konyok-Gorbunok (a magic horse from a fairytale), an elephant, a grey wolf, and a cunning fox standing on the wooden circle of our merry-go-round. The children would not only ride on them, but experience the excitement of saddling Konyok-Gorbunok or a grey wolf. So far these were no more than ideas, but I was sure that in six months or a year I would make them a reality. I obtained the materials for building a merry-go-round. I was also thinking about how to prepare the children for winter so they could spend as much time as possible in the fresh air.

Many years observing the physical development of young school children has convinced me of the major role played by a complete, healthy diet. In the diet of many of the children there was a lack of important nutrients essential for strengthening the organism, and for preventing colds and metabolic disorders. Only eight families had honey, and honey is sunshine on a plate, figuratively speaking. I chatted with the parents and convinced them of the importance of honey for their children's health. By the end of September, thirteen families had acquired one or two hives of bees. By springtime there were bees in twenty-three families.

During autumn I advised the mothers to build up winter supplies of jam made from the fruit of briars, blackthorn and other vitamin rich fruits. I discussed the need for each family to have enough fruit trees, especially apples. All winter there should be fresh fruit. In a village that is very easy; you just need to put in a bit of work.

Air saturated with the phytoncides of grasses (wheat, rye, barley, buckwheat and meadow grasses), is an elixir of health. I often took the children to the fields and meadows so they could breathe air infused with the scent of cereal plants. I advised parents to plant several nut trees near their children's bedroom windows. Nut trees fill the air with phytoncides, killing many pathogenic microbes. Harmful insects such as flies and mosquitoes cannot stand the smell of nut trees and keep away from them. I also tried to make sure every family had a summer shower in their yard.

For several years I pondered why so many children had poor eyesight. Why does a grade three child already need glasses? Observation of many young children led me to the conclusion that the problem lay not so much in exhaustion from too much reading as in irregular routines—especially diets lacking in vitamins—and in the fact that children are not physically resilient and easily catch colds. Some childhood illnesses affect the eyesight. Regular routines, a complete diet, physical conditioning: these protect children from illness and allow them to enjoy the beauty of the surrounding world.

Years of observation of children revealed a disturbing phenomenon: in spring, from March onwards, all children experience deteriorating health. The children seem to run out of steam. Their resistance to respiratory infections is weakened and their capacity for work is lower. It is especially noticeable that eyesight deteriorates in the spring months.

I found an explanation for this phenomenon in medical and psychological works. By spring, the reduction in solar radiation over the winter months makes itself felt and there is a fall in the level of vitamins in the body. This leads to changes in the interactions between the body's systems, and continuous, intense mental activity brings the nervous system to a state of fatigue.

I thought about how to reduce the impact of these factors. The parents began to take measures to stock up on vitamin rich foods for the spring months. We tried to maximise our use of each sunny day in winter and spring with walks in the fresh air. I could not help thinking that we ought to reduce the intensity of intellectual work during the spring months, and saw a way to do this through introducing more variety in our intellectual activities. As much as possible, intellectual activity should take place outdoors, and it should be combined with physical work. Gradually this became one of our guidelines for study during the spring months.

During the years immediately after the war, many children were clearly predisposed to neurosis. With some of my pupils (especially Tolya, Kolya, Slava and Fedya) this found expression in depression and an aloofness from life. I tried not to allow children's inhibitions, timidity, indecisiveness or excessive shyness to develop into neurosis. I tried to make sure that our collective life brought them joy, and that their daily interactions with friends required active involvement. It was especially important, in my view, to use our school environment to soften the impact of any disappointments and conflicts children encountered in their families. I tried to make sure that, in our school group at least, children's troubles and sorrows were forgotten. For me it was very important to know what was going on in each child's soul, so as not to allow children's sensitive hearts to be hurt.

Children whose souls had been damaged by traumatic experiences required special attention. Sometimes the nerves of Kolya, Sashko, Tolya, Petrik and Slava, were stretched to the limit. You had only to touch one of them and they would 'flare up' and 'explode'. On some days you could not question these children. Procedures that were effective when educating others were completely inappropriate for these children. I came across the term 'medical pedagogy' in medical works, and this seemed to best describe the approach that was required when educating children whose unhealthy state of mind left its stamp on their behaviour. The main principles of medical pedagogy are: 1) spare the child's sick and vulnerable psyche; 2) the ethos and organisation of school life should be such as to distract children from dark thoughts and experiences, and to awaken their enjoyment of life; and 3) under no circumstances should children be given to understand that they are being treated as ill.

One of the boys in our school who was predisposed to hysterical neurosis was Volodya. I was very concerned that the boy's mother and father were so proud of him. They had convinced themselves that their son was an exceptional child. I was afraid that when the inevitable disillusionment came, the boy could develop hatred for his parents and for adults generally. The main treatment for such children, in my view, is the education of modesty and respect for others. I tried to help Volodya see the human being in all those close to him.

Medical pedagogy devotes particular attention to children with delayed, inhibited thinking processes. Sluggishness and inertness of the cells of the cerebral cortex should be treated just as thoughtfully and patiently as a disease of the heart muscle or the intestines. But such treatment requires a thousand times more care and educational skill, and a deep knowledge of the individual characteristics of each child.

## *Each child is an artist*

A WEEK AFTER LESSONS AT the School of Joy began I told the little ones, 'Tomorrow, bring sketch books and pencils. We are going to draw.' The next day we spread out on a lawn in the school grounds. I suggested to the children, 'Look around you. What can you see that is beautiful? Draw whatever you like the most.'

We could see the school orchard and our experimental plot lit up by the autumn sun. The children started chattering. One liked the red and yellow pumpkins, another liked the heads of sunflowers bent to the ground, a third liked the dovecote, and a fourth the grapevines.

Shura admired the light fluffy clouds floating in the sky. Seryozha liked the geese on the mirror-like surface of the pond. Danko wanted to draw a fish: he told us with excitement how he had once gone fishing with his uncle. They did not catch anything, but they saw how the fish 'played'.

'I want to draw the sun', said Tina.

Silence descended. The children were absorbed in their drawing. I had read a lot about the methodology of conducting a drawing lesson, but now I had living children in front of me. I saw that a child's drawing—the process of drawing—is part of a child's spiritual life. Children do not simply transfer something from the surrounding world to the page. They live in that world and enter into it as creators of beauty, taking pleasure in that beauty. Consider Vanya, completely absorbed in his work. He is drawing a bee hive. Next to the hive is a tree with huge flowers. Above a flower is a bee, almost as big as the hive. The boy's cheeks are flushed and his eyes shine with the fire of inspiration, and this brings great joy to his teacher. Is it really possible to squeeze such a creative process into the framework of lessons, homework, grades and a teacher's directions about what to draw?

Children's creativity is a deeply individual sphere of their spiritual life, involving a self-expression and self-affirmation that reveals the unique individuality of each child. This uniqueness cannot be encompassed by any one set of rules, compulsory for everyone.

Kolya has not said what he likes and I am very concerned to see what he will draw. In the boy's sketch book I see a spreading tree with large round fruit—that must be an apple tree. The tree is surrounded by a swarm of little stars in a halo of light beams. High above the tree is a crescent moon. How I would like to read the child's secret thoughts and feelings in this interesting drawing. I see the same spark of inspiration in his eyes that I saw when we looked at the world through a drop of dew.

'What are those stars above the apple tree?' I ask Kolya.

'Those aren't stars', says the boy. 'Those are the silver sparks which fall on the orchard from the moon. The moon has giant blacksmiths too, doesn't it?'

'Of course it does', I answer, astounded at the thoughts that had excited the child on some quiet evening. He must have looked at the night sky, admired the moon's radiance and noticed a trembling halo of pale light over the apple trees.

'But what threads do those giant blacksmiths hammer at night?' wonders the child; and it seems to me that he is not so much addressing his teacher as his own recollections of the night sky, the pale moonlight and the round dance of the stars. I did not want to disturb the child's creative inspiration. My heart beat more strongly from a joyful discovery: creativity opens those secret corners of a child's soul where kindly feelings lie dormant. In helping a child to feel the beauty of the surrounding world, a teacher unobtrusively releases those hidden springs from which humanity and kindness flow, washing away all the evil that is alien to a child's nature.

Following Larisa's example, I begin to draw the giant blacksmiths. I think I am drawing pretty well. My blacksmiths look like real blacksmith's strikers, and my anvil looks just like the one in the collective farm's smithy. Forgetting that I am an adult, I experience feelings of joy: of course my blacksmiths will be better than Larisa's. But the children are not particularly interested in my blacksmiths and a little crowd gathers around Larisa. 'What has she drawn?' I wonder. I look over the children's heads. There does not appear to be anything special about her drawing, so why are they all admiring it and not paying attention to mine? The more I study the little girl's picture, the clearer it becomes that little ones have their own vision of the world, and their own artistic language with its own imagery. You cannot imitate that language however much you try. My blacksmiths are wearing normal caps and aprons, with long beards and boots. But in her picture, a halo of sparks blazes around the luxuriant hair on the heads of the mighty blacksmiths. And the beards are not just beards, but swirling fire. The huge hammers are almost twice the size of their heads … For a child this is not a departure from the truth but a most vivid representation of truth—of the truth about the fantastic strength and skill of humankind, and their fairytale connection with the element of fire. We should not try to make this wonderful language of children's imaginations conform to our adult language. Let children speak to each other in their own language. I advised teachers of the primary classes: teach children the laws of proportion, perspective and proportionality—that is all right—but at the same time allow room for children's imaginations; do not destroy children's artistic language and their fairytale vision of the world …

All the children wanted to talk about what they had drawn. In their accounts, bright images and similes sparkled like gemstones. Drawing helped children to develop their oral language.

From that day on, we nearly always took sketch books and pencils on our walks to the fields and forests. The older students made small sketch books for the little ones to put in their pockets. In the spring, several months after the life of our school began, I made a big album in which each child drew their favourite part of the surrounding world. I wrote little stories in that album. It constituted a whole page in the life and spiritual development of our class.

## *Caring for the living and the beautiful*

I WAS VERY CONCERNED ABOUT the indifference of some children towards living things and to beauty in the surrounding world. I worried about actions that seemed, at first glance, to provide evidence of children's senseless cruelty. Once we were walking through a meadow. Butterflies, bumblebees and beetles were flying above the grass. Yura caught a beetle and, taking a shard of glass from his pocket, cut the insect in half and 'researched' its internal organs. In a remote corner of the school grounds, several families of swallows had been nesting for many years. On one visit there, before I had time to say anything about the swallows' nests, Shura had thrown a stone at the nesting box. All our school students looked after the beautiful canna flowers growing in the grounds, but Lyusya went over to a flower bed and pulled up a plant. All of these things happened during the first few days of our School of Joy. I was struck by the fact that even though children took delight in beauty, they could be indifferent to the fate of the beautiful. Long before I met my pupils, I was convinced that admiration for beauty is only the first green shoot of kindness, and that it needs to be further developed into a practical urge to act. I was especially troubled by the actions of Kolya and Tolya. Kolya had some sort of obsession with the destruction of sparrow nests. I heard that he had thrown unfledged nestlings, which had fallen from a disturbed nest, into a sewage pipe at the butter factory. The baby sparrows cheeped for a long time, but Kolya just put his ear to the pipe and listened. Children's cruelty was demonstrated not only by Kolya, who had witnessed evil in his family, but by children living in normal surroundings. And the most troubling thing was that the children did not see anything wrong with those 'minor' displays of evil, of indifference to beauty and to life, from which crude heartlessness gradually develops.

How could I awaken pure, kindly feelings? How could I encourage heartfelt benevolence, a caring attitude towards the living and the beautiful? On one of our walks in the fields we found a lark with a damaged wing. The bird was fluttering from one spot to another but could not fly. The children caught the lark. The little bundle of life shivered in their hands. Its frightened eyes, like beads, looked up at the blue sky. Kolya squeezed it in his hand and the bird cheeped pitifully. 'Is it really possible that none of them feel compassion for this bird left behind in an empty field?' I wondered, and looked at the children. Tears appeared in the eyes of Lida, Tanya, Danko, Seryozha and Nina.

'Why are you tormenting the bird?' Lida asked Kolya, with pity in her voice.

'Do you feel sorry for it?' asked the boy. 'Then take it and look after it.' And he threw the bird to Lida.

'I do feel sorry for it, and I will look after it', said the girl, caressing the lark.

We sat down on the edge of the forest. I told the children how, in autumn, migratory birds head off on a long flight. In the empty fields a few lonely birds remain. One might have a clipped wing; another might be crippled, having escaped from the claws of a predator ... 'A harsh winter awaits them, with blizzards and frosts. What will happen to this lark? The poor thing will freeze. And it sings so beautifully in spring and summer, filling the steppe with enchanting music. The lark is a child of the sun. It says in the fairytale that this bird was born from the sun's fire. That is why our people call it *zhavoronok*: *zhar* means "fire", and *voronok* means "little raven". And we all know how much it hurts when a heavy frost makes your fingers numb and a searing wind chokes your breath. You hurry home, to a warm hearth, to a friendly fire ... But where will this bird go? Who will give it shelter? It will turn into a frozen ball.'

'But we won't let the lark die', says Varya. 'We will find a warm place for it and make it a nest. Then it can wait for the spring ...'

The children began to vie with each other, suggesting how to build a shelter for the lark. Each one wanted to take the bird home for the winter. Only Kolya, Tolya and a few other boys remained silent.

'Why take the lark home, children? We can make a warm nest for it at the school. We will feed it and treat it, and in spring we will set it free.'

We took the lark to school, put it in a cage, and placed it in a room we had set aside for the little ones. Each morning one of the children came to feed the lark.

A few days later Katya brought a woodpecker. Her father had found it in the forest. It looked as if, by some miracle, it had escaped from the paws of a predator. The woodpecker's wings hung limply, and dried blood was caked on its back. No-one knew what food to give a woodpecker—little beetles, perhaps? Where would you look for them? Under bark?

'I know', boasted Kolya. 'They don't just eat beetles and flies. They like willow buds and grass seeds. I've seen …'—the boy wanted to say something else but he was embarrassed. He had probably hunted woodpeckers.

'Well, seeing as you know how to feed woodpeckers, you could collect his food. You can see how pitifully he is looking at us.'

Kolya began to bring food for the bird every day. He still did not have any feeling of pity for the living creature. He was simply pleased to earn the admiration of his friends: look at our Kolya, he knows how to feed birds. But it does not matter if the awakening of kindly feelings begins with vanity. Once good deeds become habitual, they will awaken the heart.

I remembered hundreds of boys' answers to the question: what sort of person do you want to become?—strong, brave, courageous, intelligent, resourceful, fearless … But not one said kind. Why is kindness not considered to be on a par with such virtues as courage and bravery? Why are boys even embarrassed by their kindness? Without kindness—genuine warmth of heart which one person shows to another—beauty of the soul is impossible. Without kindness a human being turns into an intelligent animal, and a group of people turns into a herd. Kindness is humanity's salvation; indifference treads humanity underfoot. I reflected on why boys show less kindness than girls. Perhaps it only seems that way? No, it really is so. A girl is kinder, more empathetic and affectionate, probably because an unconscious maternal instinct lives in her from an early age. A feeling of concern for life is established in her heart long before she becomes the creator of new life. The root, the source of kindness, is in creation, in creativity, in the affirmation of life and beauty. Kindness is inextricably linked to beauty.

It was a day for celebration when Fedya brought an oriole to school one morning. This bird was also unable to fly for some reason. The boy had found it in a bush near the animal breeding farm. The children could not tear their eyes from the oriole's beautiful, many-coloured feathers. We came to the 'bird clinic' (the children's name for a corner of their room) to greet each new day, and to say goodbye at the end of the day. Kostya brought a weak and sickly sparrow he had picked up from the side of the road. The bird did not want to peck at grains or bread crumbs. The boy took the bird's illness to heart. We all grieved when our sparrow died. Kostya cried. The girls cried. Kolya became silent and gloomy.

I remembered the words of Janusz Korczak:

> Children's pure democracy knows no hierarchy. A child is quickly saddened by a labourer's toil, a hungry child, the cruel fate of a village horse, or a slaughtered hen. A dog or a bird is close to him. A butterfly and a flower are his equals. A pebble and a cockleshell are his brothers. The arrogance of the upstart is foreign to him. A child does not know that only a human has a soul.[10]

Yes, that is all true, but kind children do not fall from the sky. They have to be educated.

During a walk along a dried up river bed the children found a baby hare with a crippled leg. We brought him to our room and put him in a new cage. Now we had a new clinic—for animals. A week later Larisa brought a scraggy kitten, shivering from the cold. We put

---

10 Korczak, Janusz, *Selected educational works*, Moscow: Prosveshchenie, 1966, p. 271.

it in the same cage as the hare. The children now had a lot to think about. They brought carrot for the hare and milk for the kitten. It is hard to convey in words the children's delight when, one morning, we found the kitten and hare cuddling up to each other, fast asleep. The children talked in whispers, afraid of waking the animals …

In winter, several tomtits arrived at our bird clinic. The children had picked them up near some bird feeders set up for the winter … And something else gave me great joy: some of the little ones set up their own bird clinics and living corners at home. After we set up an aquarium with little fish in our room, the children started to beg their parents to set up aquariums at home. Many parents came to the school and asked how to go about it. It was difficult to find plants and fish for the aquariums, and not easy to find food. But all these difficulties were overcome thanks to the persistence of the children. They gave no peace either to their parents or to me. Slava's and Tina's mothers came to me. Their children would not give them a moment's peace: the others had goldfish and they did not. We had to turn to the older students for help. In those days we did not yet have school workshops, and the need to construct aquariums forced us to set up our first workshop for the older students.[11]

I will never forget those evenings, when we sat by an aquarium illuminated with a little lamp and admired the goldfish. I told the children about the depths of the ocean, about the fascinating life of sea creatures. My pupils, who have long graduated from school, still remember those evenings, even as adults. Kolya recently said to me:

---

11 Translator's note: The original says: 'for the Pioneers and members of the Young Communist League'. In soviet schools, all children joined the Pioneers at about ten years of age. Pioneers were a bit like boy scouts and girl guides, and every school class was something like a scout troop. When children were about fifteen years old, they graduated from the Pioneers to the Young Communist League (the Komsomol).

'I used to dream about that lamp. Its light was my first source of knowledge. I wanted to know more about the depths of the sea, about exotic fish.'

If a twenty-four-year-old man remembers fish with such warmth, it means it is no trivial matter. Kindly feelings flowed from that experience. With bated breath I waited for the time when the beauty of the surrounding world would awaken kindly feelings—affection and compassion—in the most indifferent hearts. I will never forget the first autumn frosts of that year. We went to a rose bush in the garden and saw a brilliantly flowering bloom. On its tender petals were drops of dew. It was a miracle the flower had survived that cold night, and as we looked at it we all felt sad: soon the frost would destroy this beauty. My eyes met Kolya's, and for the first time I saw in his eyes sadness and anxiety—the pure feelings of a child. Then we went to the greenhouse, where there were several pots containing flowers that were rare in our locality—rhododendrons and cactuses. We sat down and for a long time we admired a little scarlet flower, the flower of a cactus.

Caring for the living and the beautiful gradually became part of the children's lives. In the late autumn of 1951, when the leaves had fallen from the trees, we went into the forest, dug up a little linden tree, brought it to the school grounds, and planted it. The little tree became our friend. We dreamt about it, fantasised, and made up stories about it, as if it were a living creature capable of feeling and responding to our care and concern. The children were glad when warm rain fell: our friend needed lots of moisture. We were worried when the earth was frost bound and a piercing wind blew over the fields: our friend would be cold. The children gathered snow and piled it around the linden tree. The girls brought some reeds, and bound them round the trunk of the tree. As spring approached we often visited our friend and looked with excitement to see if any buds had opened. The children were in raptures when the first green leaves appeared: the tree was alive. In summer we watered our linden tree.

A collective feeling of affection and kindness, a collective benevolence, is a mighty force. Like a raging torrent it carries along even the most indifferent. I was overjoyed to see how Kolya, Tolya, Slava and Petrik went excitedly to see our friend, the green linden tree; how their eyes shone when they fed the fish in the aquarium. Again and again I was convinced how much easier it is to educate a person during early childhood, rather than during adolescence or early adulthood. The earlier we plant the roots of kindness in a child's soul, the more brightly the flowers of humanity will bloom.

Those children, whose hearts trembled at the thought that the little linden tree was cold during a winter chill, are now adults. Our friend has become a large, spreading tree; and even now young men and women, mothers and fathers, come to it, and a wave of kindness fills their hearts when they remember that golden autumn of their childhood.

Experience confirms that the roots of kindly feelings reach back into childhood, and that humanity, kindness, affection and good will are born in work, care and concern for the beauty of the surrounding world.

Kindly feelings, emotional culture, these are the core of humanity. If kindly feelings are not educated in childhood you will never educate them, because this essence of humanity takes root in the soul along with the discovery of the earliest and most important truths, along with experiencing and feeling the subtlest nuances of one's native language. In childhood a person must pass through an emotional school: a school educating kindly feelings. Just as one cannot catch up during young adulthood that which is missed in intellectual education during childhood, so one cannot catch up what is missed in the sphere of emotional education. Kindly, humane feelings and motives will never excite people's souls, and will not motivate their actions, if they have not passed through a school in kindly feelings.

# *We listen to the music of nature*

MUSIC, MELODY, A FEELING FOR the beauty of musical sounds—these provide an important means for educating a person, morally and intellectually, for ennobling the heart and purifying the soul. Imagine that a harmoniously developed personality—richly endowed both morally and spiritually—is represented by a beautiful flower. Now imagine that the petal of that flower that has grown from musical appreciation is removed. The flower will immediately fade and lose its beauty. The experience of many years has convinced me that without the development of feelings—moral feelings, aesthetic feelings, intellectual feelings—there is no human being; and it is impossible to awaken, develop and refine feelings without musical appreciation. Music opens a person's eyes to beauty: the beauty of nature, the beauty of a human being, the beauty of moral relationships, and the beauty of work. And this vision and awareness of beauty facilitated by music begins during the preschool years. Music is a powerful means for educating the heart, for awakening kindly, humane feelings, for self-education. Thanks to music, people become aware of that which is sublime, majestic and beautiful, not only in the surrounding world, but within themselves.

Many years observing the spiritual development of the same students, from the early school years to maturity, have convinced me that the uncontrolled, uncoordinated influence on children of cinema, radio and television hinders rather than assists a proper aesthetic education, giving rise to a superficial reaction to beauty, cultivating ignoble, primitive aesthetic expectations of the surrounding world, people and art. A chaotic abundance and 'overconsumption' of musical impressions is particularly harmful. I considered it important that exposure to musical works should alternate with exposure to the background against which a person can understand and feel the beauty of music: the tranquillity of fields and meadows, the rustling of an oak forest, the song of the lark in a blue sky, the whisper of ripening ears of wheat, the drone of bees. This is the music of nature, the source from which a person draws inspiration when creating a musical melody.

In aesthetic education in general, and musical education in particular, the psychological objectives of the teacher who is acquainting children with the world of the beautiful are important. For me the main objective was to educate a capacity to relate emotionally to beauty and to instil a thirst for impressions of an aesthetic nature. In my view, the main aim of our whole system of education was to teach people to live in the world of the beautiful, so that they could not live without beauty, so that the beauty of the world created an inner beauty.

In the School of Joy a lot of attention was given to listening to music: both musical works and the music of nature. The first task was to awaken an emotional reaction to a melody, and then to gradually convince the children that the beauty of the music had its origins in the beauty of the surrounding world. It is as if a musical melody throws out a challenge to people: stop and listen to the music of nature; drink in the beauty of the world; preserve that beauty and increase it. The experience of many years has convinced me that a human being acquires both their native language and the rudiments of musical appreciation—the ability to grasp, understand, feel and experience the beauty of a melody—only during childhood. That which is missed in childhood is very difficult, almost impossible to make up as an adult. A child's soul is equally sensitive to its native language, the beauty of nature and a musical melody. If the beauty of a musical work touches the heart in early childhood, if children sense the many nuances of human feeling in its sounds, they reach a level of refinement that cannot be reached through any other means.

The beauty of a musical melody reveals to children their own beauty. They become conscious of their own virtue. Musical education does not mean educating musicians; it means educating human beings.

In early autumn, when in the clear air every sound can be heard distinctly, I sit on the grass with the children just before dusk. I suggest listening to 'The flight of the bumblebee', from Rimsky-Korsakov's opera *The tale of Tsar Saltan*. This accessible music draws an emotional response from the children. The little ones say, 'You can hear the bumblebee getting closer and then further away. You can hear the twittering of the little birds …' We listen to the melody again. Then we walk to a flowering meadow, rich in nectar. The children hear the chorus of the bees and then the buzzing of a bumblebee. There it is, big and furry, rising and now settling on a flower. The children are in raptures: it is almost exactly the melody recorded on the tape, but in the musical work there is a unique beauty that the composer has discerned in nature, and conveyed to us. The children want to listen to the recorded music again.

The next day we visit the sweet-flowering meadow in the morning. The children listen to the chorus of bees and try to detect the sound of the furry bumblebee. Something which previously seemed ordinary to them now reveals its beauty. Such is the power of music.

I selected melodies whose vivid images were accessible to the children and conveyed sounds that they could hear around them: the twittering of birds, the rustling of leaves, the rumble of thunder, the babbling of a brook, and the howling of the wind … At the same time I did not overwhelm the children. I repeat: a surfeit of musical images is harmful for children. It can provoke confusion and then completely blunt emotional responsiveness. I used no more than two melodies per month, but with each melody I conducted a lot of work, with the aim of awakening in the children a desire to listen to the music again and again, so that on each occasion they would discover new beauty. It is very important that between listening sessions, which are devoted to melodies that you consider significant in acquiring the rudiments of musical appreciation, there should not be other chaotic, confusing impressions. After listening to a melody children should listen to the quiet of the fields. Between listening to two melodies, they should come to know the beauty of nature.

We walk to a grove of oak trees. It is a quiet, sunny day of our Indian summer. The trees, decked in many colours, glitter in the sun's rays. We can hear the songs of the autumn birds and the distant roar of a tractor engine. A formation of departing geese crosses the blue sky. We listen to Tchaikovsky's 'Autumn song (October)' from *The seasons*. The melody helps the children to feel the unique beauty of things that they had previously not noticed in their natural surroundings: the quiet trembling of the leaves on the yellowing oak trees; the scent of the clear air; the fading camomile flowers by the side of the road.

The children are in a bright, happy mood, but the music, in a minor key, brings on a light sadness. The children sense the approach of overcast, rainy days, cold blizzards, and early dusk. Under the influence of the music, they talk about the beauty of summer and the first golden days of autumn. Each child remembers something striking, something significant, and now the images of summer and autumn appear before them in all their beauty. For instance Larisa says, 'I walked with my father to a ravine. On the slopes of the ravine was a green wall: forest, forest everywhere, flooded with sunlight. Somewhere a turtle-dove started cooing. And it was so beautiful in the forest, so beautiful ... I wanted to walk and walk, and for the sun to shine forever. When the turtle-dove cooed, the leaves on the trees seemed to freeze and to listen.'

Shura remembers: 'Mum took me into the field. She was working near the combine harvester. I rode with my uncle on the harvester. And then I got sleepy. Mum laid me on a pile of fresh straw. I looked at the sky and my pile of hay started floating high above the earth. Sometimes I got very close to a little bird flitting in the sky; sometimes

I was further away from it. And the grasshoppers were floating with me, singing in a chorus and flying to meet the bird. That is how I fell asleep. When I woke up the bird was still flitting in the sky and the grasshoppers were singing even louder.'

We listen once again to Tchaikovsky's melody and I sense that in the music children find memories dear to their hearts: of the beauty of unforgettable summer and autumn days. The children listen to more memories.

'Dad and I were carting a load of hay. I lay on the hay and the stars were twinkling in the sky. A quail was calling in the field. And the stars seemed so close, it was as if I could reach up and take one, like a little lamp.'

This is Zina's recollection. I listen to the girl and am amazed. Zina has always remained silent. You cannot drag a word out of her. But the music has prompted her to speak.

How pleased I am that music heightens emotional responsiveness and awakens thoughts brought on by the beauty of musical images. I would like every child to dream and fantasise under the influence of music. How good it is that music has the power to intensify the poetic, dreamy element in children's natures. I am glad that Kolya and Tolya, listening to Tanya and Larisa's excited accounts, are sitting thoughtfully. They are also remembering something.

Music is a powerful stimulus for thought. Without musical education a child's intellectual development will be incomplete. The origins of music lie not only in the surrounding world but in people themselves, in their inner worlds, in thought and speech. A musical image reveals new qualities in the objects and phenomena of the surrounding world. Children's attention is concentrated on the objects and phenomena on which music has shed new light, and their minds draw vivid pictures. These pictures beg to be described in words. Children use words creatively, drawing upon their experience of the world for new concepts and for reflection.

Music—imagination—fantasy—stories—creativity—this is the pathway children follow to develop their inner capabilities. Music awakens vivid images in children. As a means of awakening the creative abilities of the mind, it is without equal. Listening to the music of Grieg, the children imagined fairytale caves, impenetrable forests, and good and evil creatures. Even the most silent child wanted to speak. Children's hands reached for their pencils and sketch books—they wanted to record those fairytale images on paper. Music aroused the thinking of even the most sluggish children. It was as if it bestowed some miraculous force on the brain cells. In this increase in mental energy under the influence of music I saw evidence of the emotional stimulation of thought.

On winter days when all our summer paths were covered in snow, I sat in a school room with the children and we listened to the music of Tchaikovsky, Grieg, Schubert and Schumann. In the twilight hours the children especially liked listening to fairytale music. I told the children a Ukrainian folk tale about the witch Baba-Yaga and then we listened to Tchaikovsky's music inspired by that tale. It is difficult to convey in words the richness of the fantastic images and ideas born under the influence of that music. In their dreams, the children soared beyond distant mountains, beyond the primordial forest, beyond blue seas, to mysterious caves and ravines. With amazement I listened to the children's remarkable stories. Some of them I remembered for the rest of my life. In Yura's imagination, Baba-Yaga was transformed into someone who hated humanity, who attempted to destroy people's joy, to destroy the gift of song. 'She took a big pot, sat in her mortar, and flew around the world. As soon as she heard a song, she flew to the place where people were singing and having fun, and struck her pot against the mortar. The people fell silent, forgetting how to sing because she had trapped the song in her pot. In this way Baba-Yaga hid all the songs. Only one singing shepherd boy remained, all by himself. He played on his pipe and sang songs. No matter how much the witch struck her pot on the mortar she could not stop him singing. His pipe was magic. The wicked, wicked Baba-Yaga sat in her misery, on her pot with all the songs. The whole world was quiet and nobody sang or was happy, except for the shepherd boy. The boy went to sleep. Baba-Yaga stole his pipe. The boy woke up. He gathered other brave boys around him and went in search of Baba-Yaga …' Yura went on to imagine how the shepherd boy freed all the songs and returned joy to all the people. It is an amazing phenomenon. Under the influence of music children create in their imaginations such vivid images of fairytale creatures, incarnating good and evil, that it is as if they are participants in a battle for what is right. Music fills fairytale images with a living heartbeat, with vibrant thought. Music leads children into the world of goodness.

Each time I noticed that the children's thinking had become sluggish I took them to the oak grove or the orchard, and we listened to music that awakened vivid images of good and evil. Music stimulated the flow of thoughts. During those winter days more and more dreamers were revealed in our school. Little Danko was so shy that you rarely heard a word from him, but then he told his tale about Baba-Yaga. It is true that it was quite like Yura's tale. In Danko's version Baba-Yaga flew around the world and picked all the flowers. She flew to her diabolical kitchen, put her pot in the oven, and all the flowers were destroyed. 'But I (children often put themselves in the role of the fairytale hero) gathered the seeds of all the flowers and sowed them all over the earth. The flowers bloomed again. When Baba-Yaga found out about it she was so angry she smashed her mortar and her bony leg, and now she cannot harm people anymore.'

After these amazing stories I talked to the other teachers about the difficulties encountered in educating children. We came to a unanimous conclusion: our pedagogy forgets that for a good half of their years of study in school, students remain children. Teachers are so busy cramming facts, generalisations and conclusions into children's heads, that we sometimes do not give children the opportunity to visit the wellsprings of thought and living language. We bind the wings of their dreams, imagination and creativity. From a living, active being, the child is frequently turned into a memorising machine. No, it should not be like that. We should not separate children from the world with a brick wall. We should not deprive them of a spiritual life. To live full spiritual lives children need to live in a world of play, stories, music, imagination and creativity. Without that they are dried flowers.

Of course study cannot be an easy game that provides continuous and constant pleasure. Above all, it is work. But when we organise that work, we need to consider the characteristics of a child's inner world at each stage of their intellectual, moral, emotional and aesthetic development. The intellectual work of a child differs from the intellectual work of an adult. For a child the ultimate goal of acquiring knowledge cannot be the main stimulus for their intellectual work, as it is in the case of an adult. The source of the desire to study is in the very nature of children's intellectual work, in the emotional colouring of their thoughts, in the way children live through their intellectual experiences. If this source dries up there is no way you can force a child to read a book.

I will never forget the first winter of the School of Joy. If not for the music, fantasy and creativity, that warm classroom would soon have grown wearisome. Music filled our surrounding world with amazing charm. In the gloom of cold January evenings our imaginations led us to perceive fairytale creatures everywhere: on the silver carpet gleaming in the moonlight, in the swirls of blizzard snow, and in the cracking sound of a frozen pond.

The first spring of our School of Joy arrived. The streams began to murmur, the snowdrops flowered, and the chorus of the bees rang out in a sea of apple and pear blossom. During those days we listened to the music of the spring forest, the blue sky, the meadows and steppe.

One quiet evening we went to a meadow. There we saw thoughtful willows covered in tender new foliage. The fathomless firmament was reflected in a pond, and formations of swans flew across the pure blue sky. We listened to the music of that beautiful evening. Somewhere in the pond a marvellous sound could be heard, as if someone had lightly touched the keyboard of a piano, and the pond, its banks and the sky seemed to resonate. 'What is that?' whispered Vanya. 'That is the music of the spring meadows', I told the children. 'In the pond you can see the reflection of the deep blue sky. At a great depth there is a huge bell made of crystal. There, in a magic palace, lives a beautiful princess called Spring. She touches the crystal bell with a little golden hammer and the echo pours over the meadows.'

The sound rang out again. Kolya smiled. 'That's just the frogs calling.' I was afraid the children would laugh and the spell would be broken, but no-one even stirred. 'Perhaps it's a frog and perhaps it isn't', said Sashko. 'But even if it is a frog, the meadow is singing.'

As if in response to his words, the sound rang out above a neighbouring pond. A few moments later a distant meadow replied. We stood, charmed by the wonderful music of the spring meadows. This music is a life-giving source of optimism. It helped the children to understand and experience the joy of existence in a world of beauty. The harmony of that beauty seemed to me like a radiant halo, which, for the rest of our lives, surrounds our unforgettable memories of childhood.

On the first sunny day of April, when the ancient burial mounds shimmered in the hot air, we went into the steppe to listen to the song of the lark. A little grey ball of life flashed in the azure sky and the delicate ring of a silver bell carried to our ears. Suddenly the bell fell silent and the grey ball plummeted to Earth. Above the tender green shoots of winter wheat, the bird stretched its wings, and slowly, as if stretching an invisible thread, rose higher and higher. Now it was not the ring of a bell that we heard but the sound of a silver string … I wanted this wonderful music to reach the children's hearts, to open their eyes to the beauty of the surrounding world. I told them a story about the lark.

'It is a child of the sun. In winter the sun travels far, far away from us, and the earth is covered with snow and bound with frost. Slowly, slowly the sun comes back to us, but it is hard for it to melt the snow. It throws burning sparks at the snow drifts. Thawed patches appear where the sparks land, a lump of earth comes to life and a wonderful bird is born: a firebird, a lark. It rises into the blue sky and flies towards the sun. It flies and sings, and the sun scatters its silver sparks. The lark hangs in the blue sky, watching the earth, looking for the brightest spark it can see. Then it flies like a stone to the earth and picks up the spark, which instantly turns into a fine silver thread. The lark lowers one end of the thread and ties it to a stalk of wheat. It pulls the other end higher and higher towards the sun, into the bright blue sky. You can see it is not easy for it to climb so high. Look how its little grey wings are beating. The silver thread rings out like the string of a musical instrument, and the higher the lark flies, the higher the sound that string makes. The lark stretches the silver thread all the way to the sun, and then returns to Earth again to look for another spark.'

Will such stories make it more difficult to learn the real laws of nature? No, on the contrary, they will make it easier. The children understand perfectly well that a ball of earth cannot become a living creature, just as they understand that there is no such thing as the giant blacksmiths, Baba-Yaga or Koshchei the Immortal (a wizard in Russian and Ukrainian folklore). But if children did not have fairytales, if they did not experience the battle between good and evil, if they did not feel the human notions of truth, honour and beauty reflected in those stories, their world would be cramped and uncomfortable.

The story of the lark helped children to understand the music of nature and prepared them for listening to a musical composition. We returned to the school and listened to Tchaikovsky's 'Song of the lark (March)'. The children were delighted. In the wonderful sounds of the music they could hear the ring of the silver bell, and the overflowing sound of the fine silver string joining the green field with the sun. We listened to this piece on many occasions: on fine, clear mornings, and on grey, cloudy days. And on each occasion the children remembered that wonderful world flooded in sunlight, the blue heavens, the little grey ball of life, and the limitless expanse of the fields. The little ones wanted to embody their visions of the fairytale bird in bright images. They drew pictures of the lark, the silver spark, and the string stretching from the earth to the sun.

Gradually we created an album of the children's favourite musical works. From time to time we came to our room and listened to music. I called the album our 'music box'. The children liked that. They would say with pride, 'We have a music box'. I had an idea. From year to year we would choose the best works we could find from the treasures of musical culture and create a music room. There we would be able to appreciate the beauty created by nature and by humanity. We would sing, and learn to play on the violin and the piano. But that would be in the future. First we could learn to play our humble country pipe.

One overcast day we went to a grove and cut a pipe from an elder tree. We polished it and cut holes in it. I played a Ukrainian folk song about a happy shepherd. It is difficult to convey in words the children's delight. Each child wanted to try their abilities, each dreamt of their own musical instrument. Each one made their own pipe. Lida, Larisa, Yura, Tina, Seryozha and Kostya all turned out to have a keen musical ear and an ability to pick up a tune. Within a few weeks the children were playing the tunes of folk songs and dances. I will never forget that quiet evening when Tina played the Ukrainian folk song 'All over the hill the reapers are reaping'. The girl's eyes shone and her cheeks were flushed. Her mother told me that Tina sat for ages in the garden with her pipe, 'thinking up' something, playing tunes, and sometimes gazing dreamily at the sky and the trees.

One day I came to school early in the morning. All around was quiet. Suddenly, from the depths of the orchard, the quiet sounds of a pipe could be heard. I followed the sounds. Somebody was making up their own tune: the melody was clearly an improvisation. The whole melody breathed a pure, light sadness. Carefully, so as not to disturb the musician, I approached a rose bush. On the grass sat Tina. It was as if the pipe was part of her body. The girl was looking at a flowering rose, and her eyes were soft and tender. Now I understood the melody: the girl was playing about the beautiful flower and the blue spring sky. That which had seemed to me to be sadness was concern: the girl was using sounds to communicate her thoughts about the future.

Kostya also became absorbed in his pipe playing. It was difficult for him to play with only one hand but he quickly learnt to play several folk songs, and then began to improvise: to fantasise and to communicate his thoughts, feelings and experiences through music. Once, during a summer storm, we were sitting in our Nook of Dreams. The last peals of thunder faded into the distance and a rainbow hung over the earth. We were all silent, admiring the beauty of this scene. Then we heard a quiet melody—Kostya was playing. In his music you could hear the murmur of a stream, which was replaced by an agitated rumbling as a storm cloud approached and distant thunder growled. The boy had forgotten that we were listening to him. He was completely absorbed in his creation. Then he suddenly noticed his friends' thoughtful faces and was embarrassed … Not everyone can become a musician, but I deeply believe that everyone can develop an appreciation for music.

Our involvement in this simple folk music was a deeply personal matter. Sometimes the children were in a musical mood and wanted to sit down and play. More often than not, this happened in the evenings after sunset, while the earth was still illuminated by the dying light of the sun. We felt very fortunate that music could give us such joy and pleasure.

Kolya had a sensitive musical ear and the boy quickly learnt to reproduce the melodies of folk songs. Once when we were returning home from the forest, I said to Kolya, 'Do you remember how you drew the blacksmiths forging the silver garland? Try to tell the story of the blacksmiths on your pipe: how they hammer and how the cold sparks scatter on the earth.'

'Those sparks aren't cold, oh, no', objected the boy heatedly. 'They're hot, oh, so hot.'

'Yes of course they're hot.' It is impossible for something cold to fly from a hammer and anvil. I also tried to tell the story of the blacksmiths on my pipe: the story of the sunny blacksmiths.

The next day, in the morning, we came to the school orchard. With the simple melodies of our pipes we told the story of the wonderful blacksmiths. We not only understood each other, we felt the mood underlying each melody. I listened to the music of Kolya's blacksmiths. The boy not only conveyed the ringing dialogue of their hammering, but took delight in their strength. He was amazed at the beauty of the silver sparks falling on the fields and orchards, and saddened that his gaze could not take in the whole earth. He wanted to see the beauty that he vaguely felt to be in everything.

Yes, I could see a path to this child's heart. Music educates the soul; it humanises feelings. Like language, music reflects what is truly human. In developing children's sensitivity to music we ennoble their thoughts and aspirations. Music can open up in each heart a life-giving stream of human feelings. Children can discover the beauty of the surrounding world in the living, vibrant words of their native language, and in a musical melody. But music—the language of human feeling—does more than convey to a child's soul the beauty of the world. It reveals human greatness and virtue. While enjoying music a child feels truly human. The soul of a child is the soul of a sensitive musician. Within a child's soul are tightly-stretched strings, and if you know how to touch them you will hear enchanting music: not only in a figurative sense, but in a literal sense. Childhood is impossible without music, just as it is impossible without play or stories.

Experience confirms that music provides a most favourable setting for developing spiritual ties between children and their teacher. It seems to open people's hearts. Listening to a beautiful melody, experiencing and admiring its beauty, teacher and pupil become closer, more like family.

During those moments of common feeling, which are achievable only through music, educators see things in a child that they would never see without music. Under the magical influence of musical sounds, when the soul is enchanted with lofty feelings, children will entrust their troubles and concerns to you. On one of those occasions Kolya told me that he had a sketch book where he drew everything that excited, delighted and troubled him. Then the boy showed me his drawings. I saw the world of his dreams. Kolya wanted to drive a tractor and to be a frontier guard.

## *Our winter joys and concerns*

WINTER ... WHAT WONDERFUL OPPORTUNITIES for children's education and development there are in this remarkable season! Those who consider that summer is the only time for strengthening children's health are deeply mistaken. If winter is not used to strengthen children's health, with its moderate frosts and soft, abundant snow, summer will not provide benefits either. I taught the little ones to spend time out in the frost and to breathe the pure, frosty air.

In the morning we would go to the school glasshouse to greet the sunrise, which lent a scarlet colour to the strange patterns on its frozen panes. Each pane inspired our imaginations: we saw fantastic animals, mysterious mountain ravines, clouds and flowers. Here, looking at the frozen panes, the children created many stories. Here they learnt to read, of which I will have more to say later.

After greeting the sun, the children opened the door from the passage into the glasshouse and entered a world of flowers. Chrysanthemums flower in one of our glasshouses during winter. Each child had their own flower—their friend. The children watered the flowers. These were joyful moments, as rainbows appeared in the water droplets, and the children admired them and dreamt of summer … This is where we made up the story about a bridge to the sun—a golden rainbow.

After each blizzard when the earth's white carpet was renewed, we went to look at the snowdrifts in the school yard. Snowdrifts are an amazing world: just as mysterious and unexpected as clouds. In the strangely shaped snowdrifts the children found fairytale towers on the tops of inaccessible mountains, ocean waves, a white swan, a grey wolf and a cunning fox. On one occasion nature seemed to create, just for us, a fairytale ship with sails and a captain's bridge, with an anchor and pirates gazing into the distance. For several days in a row, until the wind and sun levelled it, we went and inspected the ship. In the evenings the children gathered at the school and listened to my stories about pirates, and about the good people who freed the weak and the unjustly injured, about the battle between good and evil, about the triumph of truth over injustice.

We did not go for walks when it was really cold, but if the frost was only light, the children spent time in the fresh air. And when the thaw came we really celebrated. The Pioneers helped us to build a snow city. They made a shelter from blocks of snow resulting in something like a cave. Here, too, rest and work were accompanied by stories and play. We pretended to be travellers to the North Pole. I told the children stories about the great white silence. In my stories fantasy was interwoven with people's real, heroic accomplishments. With sadness, the children said goodbye to their shelter as it melted in the sun's rays.

We travelled into the forest twice during the winter: once in cars and once on horses. The light frost burnt our cheeks but no-one complained about the cold. Those days spent in the winter forest remained in the children's memories forever. We listened to the music of the winter forest and observed the life of the birds. In a forest ravine, we found a spring that had not frozen over. We warmed ourselves by a campfire and made porridge. We admired the beauty of the evening sunset, as before our eyes the snow-covered branches changed colour: first pale pink, then orange, crimson and violet-blue. Our story about the sun was enriched with new images, thrilling the children with their fantastic strangeness and beauty. Here we composed a poem in which the children conveyed their impression of the winter forest. Katya, admiring the beauty of a pine tree dressed in snow, said:

'The pine tree is sleeping.'

Zina drew a more striking image:

'The pine tree has gone to sleep till summer …'

'The pine tree slumbers until spring', said Seryozha, and everyone felt the melodiousness of those words.[12] The children wanted to continue their friend's line of thought.

'So many dreams its slumber brings', said one of the children.

---

12 Translator's note: In this scene, the children create a rhyming couplet. I have not translated it literally, but have tried to recreate its rhythm and approximate meaning.

*The pine tree slumbers until spring,*
*So many dreams its slumber brings,*

… sang the boys and girls, experiencing a feeling of pride that they had composed a song all by themselves.

That winter evening revealed to me the rich inner world of a child. I was further convinced that we should teach children to think and develop their intellectual capabilities at the direct source of thoughts and language.

What little child does not like to make a snowman or ride on a sled! On still days, when the frost was moderate and the sun was shining brightly, we spent whole days in the open air. On the edge of the village we constructed an ice slide. We were not satisfied with wooden and metal sleds—they did not slide quickly enough—so we made twenty ice sleds. We took some straw, mixed it with manure and poured water over it, making the sleds in the shape of a nest. The sleds were completely safe.

I remembered an idea from my own childhood … We found a cartwheel and stuck its axle through a hole in the ice of a pond. The ice froze around the axle, and the wheel turned into an ice carousel. Holding on to a stick fastened to the wheel, the children slid over the mirror smooth surface of the pond. We spent whole days playing games like that. The weaker children—Sanya, Volodya, Katya and Kostya—became rosy cheeked.

The distinctive beauty of nature in winter revealed itself especially strikingly to the children on quiet, cloudless, frosty evenings. We would stand somewhere in the orchard, looking at the scarlet sunset and waiting for the first stars to come out. In the evening light the snowdrifts shone pink, then pale violet. At such moments the feelings that overcame the children found expression in words and in music. The children recalled the melodies of folk songs that were in keeping with the unique beauty. Enchanted, we walked to the school, lit a fire in the stove and sang songs.

On quiet winter mornings the children admired the sunrise. They stood silently, contemplating the beauty. They wanted to find words to express their admiration. I helped them when they were searching for a word. Each discovery not only awakened joy, but was at the same time a stimulus for thought.

## *Our first Day of the Lark*

AS WE STOOD BY THE cages of our bird and animal clinics during the winter, we dreamt of a warm spring day when our little friends could once again fly in the blue sky or hop through a grove. At last, the long awaited day of celebration arrived. A day after the first lark appeared in the sky we took our cages of birds and animals to the top of an ancient burial mound. The steppe was ringing with the calls of birds. The children opened the cages and the lark, the woodpecker, the oriole and the hare were free. There was our lark, singing in the sky; and there it was, plummeting to earth … We stood, enchanted by the beauty, and experiencing joy from the knowledge that we had preserved the life of living creatures.

At that moment I saw the future in my mind's eye: each year we would climb this burial mound and celebrate the Day of the Lark.

The Day of the Lark came to mark the boundary between spring and summer. The children considered it a personal honour to have saved the life of a bird. Each child had their own 'corner of life and beauty'. The image of the lark, with its unique song ringing above the sun-drenched fields—all of this entered the children's spiritual world forever. The children also looked forward to the Day of the Lark because that day was associated with the excitement of artistic creation. Together with their mothers, the children fashioned little larks, swallows, starlings, bullfinches, magpies, nightingales and tomtits from bread dough and brought them to school. The children's little creations embodied their love of nature and each child expressed their own notions of beauty.

In autumn the children sorrowfully said goodbye to the migratory birds. Such sorrow ennobles the human heart. Without it there is no kindness.

## *How we learnt to read and write*

I WILL TELL YOU HOW the little ones learnt to read and write. Dear reader, please do not consider what I am about to describe to be a new method for teaching literacy. I did not think about the scientific basis for our creativity—and that is what I am describing: children's creativity, extra-curricular work supporting formal studies. I am far from thinking that it can replace methods for teaching literacy that have been tried and tested for decades. I am describing the creativity that was born in the midst of fields and meadows, in the shade of oak trees, in the hot wind of the steppe, at the dawn of a summer day and during the dusk of winter.

For many years I had thought what a difficult, exhausting and uninteresting business reading and writing become during a child's first days of school life, and how many failures children meet on the thorny path to knowledge—all because study turns into a purely bookish affair. I saw how children struggled during the lesson to distinguish the letters, how those letters danced before their eyes, melting into a pattern that was impossible to decipher. At the same time I saw how easily children memorise letters and make words from them when the activity is lit with some interest, is connected with play and, most importantly, when nobody is telling them that if they do not learn their lessons, it will be the worse for them.

From the first days of their school lives an idol appears on children's thorny path to knowledge—the grade. For some children it is kind and considerate, for others it is cruel, merciless and relentless. Children simply do not understand why the grade is a patron for some and a tyrant for others. Seven-year-old children cannot comprehend the relationship between a grade and their work, their personal efforts. They try to satisfy or, in the worst case, to deceive the idol, and gradually learn to study not for the joy it brings but for the grade. I am not suggesting we completely banish grades from school life. We cannot manage without grades. But children should only receive grades when they are capable of understanding that the quality of their intellectual work depends on the personal effort they invest in study.

In my view, the most important thing that is required of assessment in the primary school is that it should be a source of optimism and joy. A grade should be a reward for hard work, not a punishment for laziness and carelessness. If the teacher sees failing grades as a whip with which to urge on a lazy horse and good grades as a carrot, children will soon learn to hate both the whip and the carrot. Failing grades are a very sharp and subtle instrument, which a wise primary school teacher always keeps in reserve but never uses. To tell the truth, in the primary school that instrument should only exist so as never to be used. The pedagogical wisdom of the educator lies in never allowing children to lose faith in their abilities, in never allowing them to feel that they cannot succeed. Each task must be at least a tiny step forward. Seven-year-old children, who have only just crossed the school's threshold and can barely distinguish between A and B, suddenly receive failing grades. They do not understand what is going on. At first they do not even experience bitterness or anxiety. They are simply stunned. 'Sometimes a reasonable child stops short in amazement when confronted by the aggression of malicious, grey-haired stupidity', wrote Janusz Korczak. 'Respect a child's ignorance.' These words of the Polish educator have stayed with me all my life. Only when a teacher achieves the highest wisdom in the study of human nature—the ability to respect a child's ignorance—will a failing grade become the sharpest, most subtle instrument, which is, however, never used in the primary school.

Several years before we opened the School of Joy the following incident occurred. I took some young children—six-year-old pre-schoolers—to a grove. We sat down on the edge of the grove and I began to tell them about butterflies and beetles. Our attention was attracted by a large, horned beetle crawling on the grass. Several times it tried to take off into the air, but could not escape from the grass. The little ones studied the insect in all its detail. I had a sketch book in front of me and I drew the beetle. I wrote underneath in big block letters: ЖУК [Ukrainian for 'beetle'—pronounced 'zhook', where 'zh' is like the sound of the 's' in 'pleasure']. The curious little children began to repeat the word and to examine the letters, which for them were little drawings. Some copied these letter-drawings in the sand, while others wove the word out of grass stems. Each letter reminded the children of something. For example, the letter 'Ж' reminded them of our luckless beetle spreading its wings as it attempted to fly.

A few months later I visited a lesson with the very same children, who were now studying at the school. The teacher complained that she was having trouble teaching them to read. And what a coincidence, at that very lesson they were studying the letter 'Ж'. The children's faces lit up with smiles and the classroom was filled with a buzzing, as the children repeated the word 'ЖУК', emphasising the letter 'Ж'. All their hands went up, and the teacher heard with bewilderment that all the children knew how to write the word 'ЖУК'. What a happy lesson that was. For me it was one of the lessons that life taught to pedagogy.

I remembered that occasion years later, in the School of Joy. Children should live in a world of beauty, of games, stories, music, drawing, fantasy and creativity. That same world should also surround children when we want to teach them to read and write. After all, how children feel when they take their first steps up the ladder of knowledge, what they experience, will influence the rest of their climb. It is simply frightening to think that, for many children, that first step becomes a stumbling-block. Look at school life and you will see that it is precisely during the period when children are developing literacy skills that many of them lose faith in their abilities. Dear colleagues, let us climb that first step in such a way that children do not experience tiredness; in such a way that each step towards knowledge is the proud flight of a bird, and not the weary plod of an exhausted traveller staggering under a heavy burden.

From the first weeks of the School of Joy I had taken the children on journeys to the source of words. I opened the children's eyes to the beauty of the world, and at the same time attempted to convey to their hearts the music of words. I strove to ensure that for each child a word was not simply the designation of an object or phenomenon, but carried within it an emotional colouring—its own fragrance, its own subtle nuances. It was important for children to listen to each word as if to a beautiful melody, so that the beauty of the word, and the beauty of that part of the world that the word reflected, should awaken interest in those drawings that convey the music of human speech—in letters. Until children sense the fragrance of a word, until they are aware of its subtle nuances, we should not begin instruction in literacy, and if teachers do, they condemn children to hard labour. (In the end the children will overcome that burden, but at a heavy cost!)

The process of learning to read and write will be facilitated if literacy is presented to the children as a bright, engaging part of life that is full of living images, sounds and melodies. Things that children have to memorise must be interesting in the first place. Instruction in literacy should be closely connected with drawing.

We went on journeys to the sources of words with sketch books and pencils. Here is one of our first journeys. My aim was to show the children the beauty and the subtle shades of meaning of the word 'ЛУГ' [Ukrainian for 'meadow'—pronounced approximately as 'loogh', where 'gh' is like a voiced version of 'ch' in the Scottish word 'loch']. We settled ourselves under a willow that leant over a pond. In the distance a green meadow was bathed in sunlight. I said to the children, 'Look at the beauty before us. Above the grass, butterflies are flying and bees are buzzing. In the distance is a herd of cattle that look like toys. It seems as if the meadow is a light green river and the trees are its dark green banks. The herd is bathing in the river. Look how many beautiful flowers early autumn has sprinkled around. And as we listen to the music of the meadow, can you hear the soft drone of the flies and the song of a grasshopper?'

I draw the meadow in my sketch book. I draw the cows, the geese scattered about like white fluff, and a barely perceptible puff of smoke and white cloud on the horizon. The children are spellbound by the beauty of the quiet morning and they are also drawing. I write underneath the drawing: 'ЛУГ'. For the majority of children, letters are drawings. And each drawing reminds them of something. Of what? Of a blade of grass? Bend the blade over and you have an 'Л'. Put two blades together and you have a new drawing, an 'У'. The children write the word 'ЛУГ' below their drawings. Then we read the word. Sensitivity to the music of nature helps the children to sense the meaning of the word. The outline of each letter is memorised. The children impart to each letter a living sound, and each letter is easily memorised. The drawing of the word is perceived as a whole. The word is read, and this reading is not the result of lengthy exercises in phonic analysis and synthesis, but a conscious reproduction of a phonic, musical image, which corresponds to the visual image of the word that has just been drawn by the children. When there is such an integration of visual and auditory perception, infused with a wealth of emotional colouring—which is contained both in the visual image and in the musical sound of the word—the letters and the small word are memorised simultaneously. Dear reader, this is not a discovery of some new method for teaching literacy. It is the practical realisation of that which has been proven by science: that it is easier to memorise something one is not obliged to memorise, and that the emotional colouring of perceived images plays a crucial role in memorisation.

This integration of the visual image, the sound and the emotional colouring of a word, does not exclude independent, discrete phonic analysis. On the contrary, while attending to the pronunciation of the word 'ЛУГ', the children distinguish each sound in it, and understand that the word consists of separate sounds, each with a corresponding letter.

A few days later we go on a new journey to the source of words. We come in the morning to the school yard to greet the sun. The grass on the lawn, the leaves on the trees, the bunches of grapes, the yellow pears and the dove-blue plums—everything is sprinkled with drops of dew. In every drop a spark of sunlight burns. The sparks disappear from one place and reappear in another. It is as if the sun is drinking some drops and sprinkling others. But that is just the way it seems. A spark appears in a drop of dew when the sun shines on it. But where does the dew go? Some drops evaporate, others slowly roll down the grass stems and are drunk by the earth. Without the dew, the grass and flowers would dry out.

Then we look at the shining dew drops on the asters, nasturtiums, canna flowers and roses. I draw a blade of grass, a nasturtium, the sun, and drops of dew with burning sparks. The children also draw. Under our pictures we write the caption 'РОСА' [Ukrainian for 'dew', pronounced approximately as 'rossáh']. These letters remind the children of the sun and the dew drops. We read our letter pictures. Each child draws the letters in their own way, revealing their understanding of the world in what they have drawn. Seryozha says to his friends, 'This drop of dew is hanging on a blade of grass. Soon it will roll down to the earth'—that is how he interprets the letter 'P'. 'This drop is still waiting for the sun'—that is how he sees the letter 'O'. 'And in this drop a spark of sunlight is already burning'—Seryozha runs his pencil once more over the outline of the letter 'C'.

I invite each child to draw a blade of grass with drops of dew in a big sketch book. The children write the word 'dew' under their pictures. It may seem easy to say that the children drew and wrote a caption, but for them the drawing and the caption contain a whole world of images, sounds, colours and feelings. Each letter is connected in the child's consciousness with concrete images. That is why it is easy to memorise the whole word, and each letter.

Over the course of several days we again and again admire the dew drops, and again and again we draw and write captions. And each new drawing is not a routine exercise but a creation. Our creativity is associated with the word 'dew' for two or three weeks. Each child creates several drawings of a blade of grass or a twig that takes their fancy, listens to the sound of the word, distinguishes the separate sounds in it and designates the sounds with letters. Finding a similarity between the letters and the objects of the surrounding world—that is in essence fantasy, fairytale, children's creativity.

I write a title on the cover of the sketch book: 'Our native language'. 'We will keep this sketch book for many years', I tell the children, 'Until you finish school and become adults. You will each have your own sketch book with drawings and words, but this will be our shared sketch book.'

The days and weeks passed, and we made more and more new journeys to the sources of living words. It was especially interesting to become acquainted with the words 'village', 'coniferous forest' [a single syllable word in Ukrainian], 'oak tree', 'willow', 'forest', 'smoke', 'ice', 'mountain', 'ear of grain', 'sky', 'hay', 'grove', 'linden tree', 'ash tree', 'apple tree', 'cloud', 'burial mound', 'acorn' and 'autumn leaf-fall'. In spring we devoted our journeys to the words 'flowers', 'lilac', 'lily', 'acacia', 'grape', 'pond', 'river', 'lake', 'forest edge', 'mist', 'rain', 'thunder storm', 'dawn', 'doves', 'poplar' and 'cherry tree'. On each occasion a picture was drawn in the 'Our native language' sketch book by the child in whom the word awakened the most striking images, feelings and recollections. Nobody remained indifferent to the beauty of our native language. By the spring of 1952, about eight months after we began our work, the children knew all the letters, and could write and read words.

I must issue a word of caution here about attempts to mechanically duplicate my experience. Teaching reading and writing by this method is a creative process and creativity does not fit within the confines of a template. To borrow something new one must be creative. The most important element in the method I have described is the richness of children's spiritual life, the integration of intellectual work, play, stories, fantasy, music and creativity.

It is very important that children should not be set the compulsory task of memorising the letters or of learning to read. Our children climbed their first step up the ladder of knowledge in the process of play. Their intellectual life was inspired by beauty, stories, music, fantasy, creativity and the play of their imaginations. The images that excited their feelings and enchanted them with their beauty sunk deep into their memories. I was struck by the burning desire of many children not only to express their feelings in words, but to write words.

One day we took shelter from the rain in a forest hut. Thunder rumbled and forks of lightening flashed. Small hailstones peppered the earth. The hailstones lay on the grass for some time after it stopped raining. The sun peered out from behind the storm cloud and the little hailstones turned green. The children squealed with delight: how beautiful! The next day the little ones wanted to draw what they had seen. Yura, Seryozha, Shura and Galya even wrote captions to their pictures. They already read quite well and now I got to see their first compositions. Here they are: 'The storm cloud sprinkled hail on the grass'; 'White hailstones on the green grass'; 'The sun melted the white hailstones'; 'The thunder sent white hailstones'.

This example showed me once again: the closer children are to the primary source of thought and language—to the surrounding world—the richer and more expressive their language will be. I believed that my little ones would soon be writing miniature compositions. My confidence was vindicated in the summer of 1952. In one corner of the school grounds we had sown poppies. I took the children there when the poppies had exploded with a myriad of colours. The astounding beauty stirred a wave of joyful feelings in the children's hearts. We admired the flowers for a long time, listening to the drone of the bees. The next day we came to the same place with sketch books and coloured pencils. The children drew and I told them a story about a poppy seed, and how the rainbow had given it the beauty of seven colours. Many children wanted to express their admiration in words and wrote vivid, expressive captions: 'A carpet of poppies is flowering' (Tanya); 'A carpet of poppies has covered the earth' (Nina); 'The poppies have flowered, the sun rejoices' (Zina); 'The bees are buzzing over a carpet of poppies' (Galya); 'The sun has sprinkled flowers over the earth: dark blue, pink, red, light blue' (Larisa); 'A furry bumblebee on light blue petals' (Seryozha); 'The flowers are swaying on delicate stems' (Shura); 'The sun is playing in the poppy flowers' (Kolya); 'Light blue petals have fallen from the sky, a carpet has flowered on the earth' (Katya). The children copied these drawings and captions from their sketch books to the shared sketch book of 'Our native language'.

The lively wellsprings of the children's imaginations bubbled with bright images during our journeys to the sunflowers and to a field of flowering buckwheat. The more the children were excited by the beauty of the surrounding world, the more deeply the letters were embedded in their memories—although this goal was never made obvious. I became more and more convinced that the heart and soul of children's thinking is an artistic vision of the world that impels them to express their appreciation of beauty in words. Children's thinking is artistic, figurative and emotionally charged. For children to become intelligent and quick-witted, they need to experience the happiness of an artistic vision of the world in early childhood.

Inexhaustible springs of fantasy, creativity and living thought open up in a child's consciousness when they see and feel beauty! I will never forget one of our journeys to the source of living words. One summer day we went to the collective farm's apiary. The old beekeeper treated us to fresh honey and cold spring water. The children sat under an apple tree and admired the beauty of a field of flowering buckwheat. The bees, returning to their hive after a flight into the steppe, circled above a little stream of cold spring water and quietly hummed. 'They are telling each other about the flowers and the groves, about the buckwheat and the sunflowers, about the bright poppy heads and the blue clover flowers', said the children.

Five years later, when my little ones had become grade four students, I suggested they write a fairytale composition on the topic 'What the bees are buzzing about', and the unforgettable impressions of that June day came pouring out in vivid images and vigorous streams of thought. The things one falls in love with in early childhood are never forgotten. Let the beauty of our native language and of the surrounding world be forever impressed on the consciousness of children during the years of childhood. May the first steps up the steep ladder of knowledge be inspired by beauty!

As the children gradually mastered reading and writing, books became more and more part of their spiritual life. We created a little library of picture books. Unfortunately, I could not find good picture books in the book shops, and had to write and illustrate little books myself. The first little picture book I illustrated was a Ukrainian folk tale about Grandpa Frost, a wicked stepmother, a kind stepdaughter, and a lazy daughter. The book turned out to be a fair length—over thirty pages—with an illustration and a few sentences (sometimes only one sentence) on each page. By the spring of 1952 most of the children could read it fluently. Varya, Kolya, Galya, Larisa, Seryozha and Lida read particularly well.

We would sit on the grass and one of the children would open the picture book and read … It is not just a matter of reading words and putting together sentences. It is a creative act. When reading a fairytale, a child enters the world illustrated in the pictures. The intonation of the child's reading conveys the slightest nuances in the emotions and intentions of the kindly Grandpa Frost, of the wicked stepmother, the industrious and warm-hearted stepdaughter, and the lazy heartless daughter. The children are deeply involved in the story: they hate evil and delight in the triumph of goodness.

And the interesting thing is that children read the same story dozens of times, but still listen with great interest. I remember the teachers' concerns: why do the children read so monotonously, with so little expression? Why is it so rare to hear emotion expressed in the children's reading? It is because, in many cases, the reading is not connected to the children's spiritual life, to their thoughts, feelings and ideas. The child is interested in one thing, but has to read about something else. Reading only enriches children's lives when the words touch secret recesses of their hearts.

We began to create new picture books. The pictures were drawn by Yura, Seryozha, Katya, Lida, Lyuba and Larisa. There was not a single child who did not want to draw. Difficulties in mastering literacy were overcome thanks mainly to their interest in drawing.

In the summer of 1952 the children began to read short published books: folk tales retold by Leo Tolstoy, short stories from Konstantin Ushinsky's *Native language*, and poems by Pushkin, Lermontov,

Nekrasov, Shevchenko, Lesya Ukrainka and Ivan Franko. When we read the poem 'Children, let's get ready for school' from Ushinsky's *Native language*, the little ones memorised it instantly. Delighted by that, I thought with concern about the many awkward poems found in children's readers, starting with our alphabet text book. Dry and written in artificial language, such verses are more likely to kill any feeling for poetry than to educate a love of words.

## *You live amongst other people*

IN A REMOTE CORNER OF the school yard the Pioneers had planted some chrysanthemums. As autumn approached, white, blue and pink flowers bloomed. On a warm, clear day I took the little ones to see them. The children were in raptures at the abundance of flowers. However, bitter experience had convinced me that children's admiration of beauty is often egoistic. A child can pick a flower and think nothing of it. And so it was on this occasion. Soon I saw one, two, three flowers in the children's hands. When no more than half the flowers were left, Katya shouted, 'Is it really all right to pick the chrysanthemums?'

There was no note of surprise or indignation in her words; she was simply asking.

I did not reply. Let this day provide a lesson for the children. The children picked a few more flowers; the beauty of that corner disappeared, the clearing appeared orphaned. The rush of delight at beauty, which had flared for a moment in the children's hearts, died down. The little ones did not know what to do with the flowers.

'What do you think children, is this place beautiful?' I asked. 'Are these stalks, from which you have picked the flowers, beautiful?'

The children were silent. Then several children spoke at once: 'No, they're not beautiful.'

'And where will we go now to admire the flowers?'

'These flowers were planted by the Pioneers', I told the children. 'They will come here to admire the beauty and what will they see? Don't forget that you live amongst other people. Everyone wants to admire beauty. We have lots of flowers at our school, but what will happen if every student picks one flower? There will be nothing left. People will have nothing to admire. We must create beauty and not destroy it. Autumn will come and with it the cold weather. We will transplant these chrysanthemums to the greenhouse. We will admire their beauty. To pick one flower, you must grow ten.'

A few days later we went to another clearing. Here there were even more chrysanthemums. This time the children did not pick the flowers. They admired the beauty.

A child's heart is sensitive to appeals to create beauty and joy for others, but it is important that such appeals are followed by work. If children feel that there are other people next to them and that they can bring others joy through their actions, they learn from a young age to bring their own desires in line with the interests of others. And this is very important for educating kindness and humanity. People who do not know how to limit their desires will never become good citizens. Egoists, self-seeking people who are indifferent to the grief and suffering of others, grow from those who are only aware of their own desires and pay no attention to the interests of the group during childhood. The ability to control one's desires—in this apparently simple, but in fact very complex human habit—is the source of humanity, sensitivity, warmth and self-discipline, without which there can be no conscience and no genuine human being.

And here again it is necessary to emphasise the significance of the early years in educating humanity. Moral convictions, attitudes and habits are all closely connected with feelings. Feelings provide, figuratively speaking, the life-giving soil for altruistic moral actions. Where there is no sensitivity, no acute perception of the surrounding world, people grow up soulless and heartless. Sensitivity and impressionability of soul are formed in childhood. If the childhood years are missed, you will never make up the lost ground.

To lead a child into the complex world of human relationships is one of the most important tasks of education. Children cannot live without joy. Our society does everything to ensure that childhood is happy but a child's joys should not be carefree. When a little child picks the fruit of joy from a tree carefully grown by their elders, without thinking about what is left for others, they lose an important human characteristic: a conscience. Before children become aware of being future citizens of a socialist country, they must learn to repay kindness with kindness, to create happiness and joy for others with their own hands.

For several years before the creation of the School of Joy I had been concerned that many parents, blinded by an instinctual love for their children, see only the beautiful in their child and do not notice negative characteristics. I remember one incident. Instead of using the toilet, a four-year-old boy relieved himself in the yard in full view of his mother and their neighbour. The mother was not indignant, but was touched: 'What a fine son we have; he is not afraid of anything'. In his wilful eyes, in his puffed up cheeks, in the scornful grin of the foolish four-year-old, you could already catch glimpses of a disgusting creature who could easily grow into a scoundrel if no-one straightened him out and made him look at himself through the eyes of others.

I had to speak with Volodya's mother several times. As soon as the mother began to say something her son pulled at her dress and grabbed her hand—he always needed attention immediately. In children, individualism takes the form of persistent attention-seeking and a lack of respect, the origins of which are indulgence, condescension and the absence of any punishment. Some parents (and unfortunately the occasional teacher) consider that when talking with children it is necessary to adopt a childish tone of voice. The sensitive ear of a child detects condescension in such a tone. When an adult uses baby talk, the unsophisticated heart of a child responds with wilful behaviour. I was always wary of slipping into that tone of voice and, without for a moment forgetting that I had children in front of me, I saw in each little person a future adult citizen. I thought it was particularly important to keep that in mind when talking about working for others. The worst thing that can accompany children's work is the thought that they are doing adults a big favour, and therefore deserve lavish praise, even rewards.

In autumn we dug up the chrysanthemums and transferred them to the greenhouse. For village children that is not an onerous task. The children watered the transplanted bushes each day and waited impatiently for the appearance of the first flowers. The greenhouse became a wonderful place. 'Now let's invite some guests here', I advised the children. 'Who shall we invite?' Many of the children had little brothers and sisters, and brought them to the greenhouse. The little boys' and girls' hands stretched towards the chrysanthemums, but my pupils would not let them pick the flowers.

'If we manage to grow lots of flowers, on 8 March [International Women's Day] we will give all our mothers a chrysanthemum each', I told the children. This goal inspired the children and by 8 March we had enough flowers. We invited all the mothers to the celebration, showed them the greenhouse and presented each of them with a beautiful flower. Galya's mother came to the school and the girl handed over her chrysanthemum. I had spoken to Galya many times about her relationship with her stepmother, convincing her that she was a kind person, and my words had reached the child's heart. I was delighted that Kolya's and Tolya's mothers, Sashko's grandmother, and Kostya's stepmother also came to the celebration.

There are many things that are impossible to explain to small children. Beautiful words about nobility are unlikely to touch their hearts. But even little ones are capable of feeling the beauty of kindness with their hearts. From the first days of the School of Joy I tried to ensure that each little child experienced the joy, the grief, the sorrow and the misfortunes of other people. During autumn and spring we often visited the old collective farm beekeeper, Grandpa Andrei. The old man did not have any family. Loneliness was his great sorrow. The children sensed that Grandpa Andrei rejoiced in every one of our visits. Before each visit to the apiary I advised the children: let us take Grandpa some apples, grapes or plums—he will be pleased. Let us pick some wildflowers—that will give him joy. The children's hearts became more and more sensitive to the moods, emotions and feelings of other people. The children themselves began to look for ways to bring the old man joy. One day we were cooking some porridge in the forest. The moment when the campfire burst into flames brought so many joyful feelings to the children ... And right at that joyful moment Varya said thoughtfully, 'But Grandpa Andrei is all by himself now'.

The children all became thoughtful. Perhaps this picture will seem sentimental to some adults. Some may wonder: are seven-year-old children really capable of such spiritual impulses? Yes, dear fellow teachers. If you take the opportunity at this early age to hone children's sensitivity, if you instil in their hearts the great truth that 'you live amongst other people, my children', they will want to share their joys with others, and will experience great pain at the thought that they are having fun while their friend is alone.

The children decided to share their joy with Grandpa Andrei. 'Let's take him some porridge and lard', said Kostya. These words were met with enthusiasm. The little ones put so much porridge in the pot that even the hungriest man could hardly have eaten it all. At the apiary we had supper a second time, together with the old man.

Sensitivity to the joys and sorrows of others is educated only in childhood. At this age the heart is especially sensitive to human suffering, misfortune, grief and loneliness. It is as if children are transformed when they put themselves in another's place. I remember how one day, on the way back from the forest, we passed a lonely hut exposed to the four winds. I told them that a disabled war veteran lived there. He was sick and could not plant apple trees or grape vines. Tears appeared in the children's eyes. Each child experienced the loneliness of that sick man. We planted two apple trees and two grape vines: that was our present to the man. And in return we received the most precious gift—the joy of creating happiness for another human being.

In this very subtle matter there should be as little talk as possible about good and evil. In such cases it is completely inappropriate to lavish praise or give rewards to encourage industriousness, when that industriousness comes from an impulse to do good deeds. The education of sensitivity, of empathy for the grief and suffering of others, is the very essence of communist education. A person can only be a friend, comrade and brother to another person if that other person's grief is experienced as their own grief.

Children should learn to sense other people with their hearts: that is one of the main educational goals that I set myself. I consider this goal to be exceptionally important. Without success in this direction there can be no success in education, and, if this is not done, everything else you do is a façade.

If a child does not care what is going on in the heart of his friend, mother, father or any fellow citizen with whom he comes in contact, he will never become a real human being. I tried to hone the heartfelt sensitivity of my pupils so that they could read feelings of joy or sorrow in the eyes of others, not only those with whom they had contact every day, but even those whom they met by chance.

One day we were returning from the forest. We saw an old man sitting on the grass by the side of the road. He was upset by something and his eyes were full of sorrow. 'Something has happened to that man', I told the children. 'Can you see how much sadness there is in his eyes ... Perhaps he has fallen ill on the road? Perhaps he has lost something?' We walk up to the old man and ask him, 'How can we help you grandpa?' The old man sighs heavily. 'Thank you children', he says. 'However much you want to help me you will not be able to. I am grieving. My dear old wife is dying in hospital. I am going to be with her now and am waiting for the bus. You cannot help me, but I feel a little better because there are good people in the world.' The children fell silent. Their carefree childish chatter stopped. They were all affected by the old man's sad words. They had been planning to play a little longer, but somehow they forgot any thought of play and each went their own way.

To teach how to feel is the most difficult task in education. The best school for learning warmth, sensitivity, empathy and sympathy is friendship and comradeship, treating others as your brothers and sisters. Children are very sensitive to the emotions of others when they do things for their happiness, joy and peace of mind. If not inspired by the creation of goodness, little children's love for their mothers, fathers, grandmothers or grandfathers can easily turn into an egotistical feeling. Children may love their mothers because they are the source of their joys and are necessary to them. We need to educate in a child's heart genuine human love: feelings of care and concern for the fate of another human being. True love is only born in a heart that experiences concern for the fate of another human being. It is important for children to have a friend to take care of. Grandpa Andrei became such a friend to my pupils. I became convinced that the more children care for another person, the more sensitive their hearts become to their friends and parents. I told the children about Grandpa Andrei's difficult life. His two sons had perished in the war; his wife had died. He felt alone.

'We will go to see Grandpa Andrei more often. Each time we must find a way to make him happy.'

When we were getting ready to visit him, each child was trying to think of a way to bring him happiness. The children presented him with a sketch book, in which each of us had drawn a picture. On the bank of the river we collected pebbles of many colours and gave them to Grandpa Andrei. He made a special wooden box to keep the pebbles in and gave it to us ... The boys wove a straw hat for their friend. Grandpa Andrei carved several animal figures for us from wood: a hare, a fox and a sheep ...

The more heartfelt concern the children showed to their friend, the more they noticed troubles and sadness around them. They noticed that Nina and Sasha sometimes came to school with sad, preoccupied eyes. The children asked the sisters how their mother was. The mother was feeling poorly—that was why the girls were sad. Kindly feelings take root in the heart when children do something to lighten the sorrow of their friends. Several times we visited Nina and Sasha's family. We pulled up the weeds in their yard and helped harvest the potatoes in their vegetable garden. Every time we made preparations to go to the forest we wondered if Nina and Sasha would be able to come with us. Sometimes they stayed at home because they had to help their father. So we would visit Nina and Sasha the day before our special outing and help in whatever way we could.

To live in society means to be able to forgo one's own joys for the benefit and peace of mind of other people. We have probably all come across cases where children are confronted with grief, unhappiness and tears, but continue to enjoy their own pleasures. Sometimes a mother will try to distract her child from anything dark or sad, concerned that not a single drop should spill from her child's cup of joy. This is a blatant school for egoism. Do not lead a child away from the darker sides of human life. Let children know that there is sorrow in our life as well as joy. Let the grief experienced by others enter a child's heart.

A person's spiritual world, their moral calibre, depends ultimately on the sources from which they derived joy in childhood. If those joys were the thoughtless joys of a consumer, if children did not know what grief or hurt or suffering were, they will grow up to be egoists who are blind to the needs of others. It is very important that our students should know the highest joy—the joy of those stirring emotions that arise from concern for another human being.

## *Our class is a friendly family*

FROM THE VERY FIRST DAYS of our School of Joy, I tried to foster a spirit of family warmth, intimacy, empathy, mutual trust and assistance. Three children had birthdays in September: Vitya, Valya and Kolya. We celebrated their birthdays collectively: the school cafeteria baked them a tart and we gave them drawings and books. I was amazed to learn that in Kolya's family they never celebrated birthdays for children or adults. This was the very first celebration in the boy's life, and he was moved by the attention of his friends.

In childhood every person needs love and affection. If children grow up in a heartless environment they will become indifferent to goodness and beauty. A school cannot completely take the place of a family, especially the mother, but if children are deprived of affection, warmth and care at home, we, as educators, must be particularly attentive to them.

Our little group began to accumulate its own property, secrets, cares and disappointments. We kept toys, pencils and notebooks in a cupboard. In our Nook of Dreams we had a 'pantry', in which we kept potatoes, grain, butter and onions—for those autumn evenings when it was raining outside. All the members of our family were little children, but some were especially small: Danko, Tina and Valya. When walking on roads and in the forest we considered it our duty to help the littlest ones.

If individual children stayed home for some unknown reason, their friends would visit them in the evening to see if they had fallen ill. This became a valued tradition.

A feeling of attachment forms the basis for an important spiritual imperative, without which one cannot imaging communist relations between people—the need for human fellowship. I tried to ensure that each child found happiness and a rich emotional life in communicating with their friends through a mutual spiritual exchange. Each child must bring something unique to the group, and create happiness and joy for others.

## *We live in the garden of health*

ONLY ONE MONTH REMAINED UNTIL my pupils would become school students. August—that wonderful month of summer—was approaching. On hot July days the children came to school early in the morning or towards evening. Some of them had a long way to walk home for lunch and sometimes six or seven children remained at school to dine in the school cafeteria. I had an idea: the little ones could live for a month away from home, somewhere in the orchard. We chose a spot on the bank of the pond. The Pioneers helped us build several shelters among some thickets. The watchmen guarding the melon plantations live in such shelters all summer. We put hay in the shelters and made little tables for drawing. A large collective farm orchard was located nearby and the orchardist gave us permission to use the orchard as our main recreation area. We built a kitchen next to the shelters, and the collective farm gave us supplies and allocated a cook to help us. Sanya's father constructed a bathing shed, and next to it was a motor boat that made the boys' eyes light up.

And so began our life together in the Garden of Health—that is what the parents called our living quarters and place of recreation. We lived in the open air for a whole month. We woke at dawn before the sun rose. We bathed in the pond, did some exercises, had breakfast, and set off on a walk somewhere—to the forest, the orchard or the fields. During that month we had our most interesting journeys to the sources of words. We watched the sunrise and sunset from our burial mound in the steppe. We saw how hundreds of swallows gathered in flocks to fly to warmer climes, and how the sun and the morning breeze chased away the white shroud of mist that covered the river. The children had their lunch in the fields and meadows or in the forest, eating apples, pears, plums, new potatoes boiled in their jackets, fresh cucumbers, watermelon, rockmelon, boiled sweet corn and tomatoes. August is the month for fruit and vegetables. During these days each child ate at least two kilograms of apples and pears. Each day Grandpa Andrei brought us honey. In the mornings and evenings the children drank fresh milk. The cook prepared us a delicious beetroot soup with vegetables.

Suntanned in shorts, singlets and bare feet, the children set off each day for a hike or ride in the motor boat.

Good nutrition, sunlight, fresh air, water, appropriate work and rest—all of these things combined to restore and strengthen the children's health.

## *Thoughts on the eve of the first school year*

THE LIFE OF OUR SCHOOL of Joy was coming to an end. Soon my pupils would become school students—a thought that brought me both joy and anxiety. Joy because for many years I would lead my little ones on the path of life, work and knowledge, and because in the course of a year my little ones had become strong and suntanned.

At the end of our time together in the School of Joy I compared how Volodya, Katya, Sanya, Tolya, Varya and Kostya were a year ago to how they were now. They had been pale and weak with dark circles under their eyes. And now they were all rosy and suntanned. People say such children look like 'peaches and cream'. I was also joyful because without a stuffy classroom, without a blackboard and chalk, without pale drawings and cut-out letters, the children had climbed the first step up the staircase of knowledge—they had learnt to read and write. Now it would be so much easier for them than if that first step had begun with the rectangular frame of a classroom blackboard.

I have the greatest respect for pedagogy and hate hair-brained schemes. But life itself requires that the acquisition of knowledge should begin gently, that study—a child's most serious and painstaking work—should at the same time be joyful work that strengthens children spiritually and physically. This is especially important for little ones who cannot yet understand the aim of the work or the nature of their difficulties.

It has been said a thousand times: study is work and you cannot turn it into a game. But we do not need to construct a Great Wall of China to separate work and play. Let us closely examine the significance of play in the life of a child, especially during the preschool years. Play is a most serious business for a child. Children discover the world through play and reveal their creative abilities. Without play, full intellectual development is impossible. Play is a huge open window through which a life-giving stream of concepts and ideas pours into the child's spiritual world. Play is a spark, igniting the fires of inquisitiveness and curiosity. So what is so terrible about a child learning to write through play? Or combining work and play during a particular stage in their intellectual development so that the teacher rarely has to say, 'Well you've had a play. Now it's time to work.'

Play is a very broad and multifaceted concept. Children play not only when they are running and competing to see who is the fastest and the friskiest. Play may take the form of intense creative effort and imagination. Without the play of mental energy, without the creative use of the imagination, instruction will be lacking something—especially in the preschool years. In the broadest sense, play begins wherever there is beauty. And since a little child's work is inconceivable without an aesthetic foundation, it follows that in the early years work must be closely connected with play. On the ceremonial first day of the harvest in our school grounds, all the children come dressed in their best clothes. The first harvested ears of grain stand in a vase on a table with a tablecloth. In this there is an element of play full of deep meaning. But the play will lose its educational value if it is artificially added on to work, and if the beauty does not express a human evaluation of the surrounding world and of oneself.

One issue remains unresolved: when is the most expedient time to begin instruction in literacy? Is it when a child first sits at a desk in grade one, or perhaps a little earlier during the preschool years? Experience has convinced our staff that school should not mark a dramatic turning point in a child's life. When children become students they should be able to continue doing the things they did previously. Let new things enter their lives gradually and not overwhelm them with an avalanche of new impressions.

I am convinced that instruction in literacy that is closely connected with drawing and with play could provide an excellent bridge linking preschool education with studies in school. In their drawings of letters my pupils discovered the beauty of sunlit dewdrops, a mighty hundred-year oak tree, a willow leaning over a pond, a formation of cranes in the blue sky, and a meadow that had fallen asleep after a hot July day. The children might not be able to draw their letters beautifully yet—that is not the most important thing—but they felt the beat of life in every drawing. It also gave me joy that the children had begun to appreciate the nuances and music of words. The foundations of vivid, poetic thought, rich in images, were laid in their minds. Drawing had become part of the children's spiritual life. In their drawings the children tried to express their feelings, thoughts and experiences. For my pupils, listening to music had become a spiritual imperative.

I was delighted that the children had taken the first steps in their moral development. They had begun to appreciate the beauty in human acts of kindness. Sensitivity to the joys and sorrows of other people had awakened in their hearts. They already knew the happiness of creating beauty and joy for another person. As I understand it, the process of education over many years—from the time when children first cross the school's threshold to the time when they experience life as a mature, fully developed personality—is above all a process of educating human feelings. The people we are educating must genuinely feel that the people living around them experience the same grief, suffering, disappointment and difficulties that they do. I tried to ensure that during the childhood years the kindly actions of my pupils were based primarily on the ability to feel for another person. It gave me joy to see that the little ones had learnt compassion, and were quick to sense the feelings of their friends, older children, parents and adults in general. The greatest joy was to see that in everyone they met in life, they saw a human being first and foremost.

Along with my feelings of joy I experienced some anxiety. Daily intellectual work would now become the children's prime responsibility. Would I be able to maintain their lively interest in the surrounding world? Each child sees the surrounding world in their own way, perceives objects and phenomena in their own way, and thinks in their own way. Would I be able to introduce the world of knowledge to a child who thinks like a rushing, bubbling stream, and at the same time to one who thinks like a quiet, full river whose flow is barely perceptible?

I experienced even more anxiety when I thought about the spiritual world of each child. I was dealing with sensitive, tender, impressionable hearts. The more contact I had with the children, the more clearly I saw that their impressionable hearts and minds were becoming ever more receptive to my words, looks, and the tone of my advice and comments. In front of me were thirty-one children—thirty-one worlds. I remembered the words of Heinrich Heine: 'Each person is a world that with him is born and with him dies. Under each gravestone lies the history of the world.' How different they are even now, in the preschool years: Kolya and Kostya, Varya and Tina, Danko and Larisa, Volodya and Slava … But those deeply personal things that make each one unique will stand out more clearly and noticeably with every day and every week. Somewhere in the hidden recesses of every child's heart is a string that resonates with its own tone, and in order for that heart to respond to my words I needed to tune myself to that string. On more than one occasion I have observed what painful emotions awaken in a child's heart when the child is upset about something, is hurt, and the teacher does not notice. Will I be aware of what is going on in each child's heart each day? Will I always be fair with the children?

Fairness is the basis for a child's trust in the teacher; but not some abstract fairness, taking no account of individual differences, interests, passions and impulses. To be fair you need intimate knowledge of the spiritual world of each child. That is why I saw our continuing educational work as a process of coming to know each child ever more deeply.

PART TWO

*The Years of Childhood*

# *What is primary school?*

ON A QUIET, SUNNY MORNING on the last day of August 1952, all the students, teachers and parents gather on a green lawn in front of the school building. This ceremonial day, on the eve of the first day of studies, has long been a traditional day to celebrate school and books. It is especially moving on this occasion.

Just as an explorer who is setting out for distant, unknown lands looks into the eyes of his companions, so I look into the eyes of my little ones. There they stand: sixteen boys and fifteen girls in traditional embroidered Ukrainian shirts, the girls with scarlet and blue ribbons plaited into their hair, the boys in new caps. They are embarrassed by the solemn occasion, and if not for the mothers and fathers standing behind them, they would feel even worse. The parents and many of the grandparents have come with the children. I can see Kolya's and Tolya's mothers. Galya's stepmother has her hand on the girl's shoulder and Galya is not frowning like she did a year ago. Everyone is congratulating us and wishing us a happy journey together. The grade ten students approach the little ones and present each child with a gift in memory of the occasion—a book with the inscription: 'I wish you a happy journey my little friend. Look after this book. For the rest of your life may it remind you of the festive day when you became a student. May it always be kept in your family library.' (The years have passed, my pupils have become adults and every one of them keeps this book as a sacred gift, as a priceless reminder of a golden childhood.)

We enter the school grounds, the little ones accompanied by their parents, teachers and the grade ten students. The senior students have carefully dug up an apple tree, carried it with a large clump of earth to this place and lowered it into a hole. Each little child takes a handful of earth and fills in the hole. The children water the little tree and disperse to their homes. Tomorrow they will come to school and begin their first lesson. For four years they will be students of the primary school, and for four years I will teach and educate them. On the eve of that day I am disturbed by the question: 'What is primary school?' Many teachers speak of the major, decisive role of the primary school: 'A firm foundation for all knowledge is laid in the primary classes'; 'The primary classes proved the cornerstone for all that follows'. You often hear these words in discussions about problems in the middle and upper classes, discussions about gaps in knowledge and superficial or shaky knowledge. The primary school is often blamed for not giving students the knowledge and skills required for further study.

And indeed, experience shows that above all the primary school needs to teach students how to study. Outstanding educators have written about this: John Amos Comenius, Konstantin Ushinsky and Adolph Diesterweg. This is confirmed by the practical experience of teachers. The most important function of the primary school is to give students an essential body of sound knowledge and skills. The ability to study includes a range of skills essential for the acquisition of knowledge: the ability to read, to write, to observe the phenomena of the surrounding world, to think, and to express one's thoughts in words. These skills are, figuratively speaking, the tools without which it is impossible to acquire knowledge.

As I prepared to teach children in the primary classes, I tried to define precisely what the children needed to memorise and hold firmly in their long term memories, and what skills they needed to have.

But that is not all that a primary school needs to achieve. We must not forget for a moment that in the primary school we are dealing with children.

During their studies in grades one to four, from the age of seven to the age of eleven, the foundation of character is laid. Of course the process is not completed by the end of the primary classes, but during these years a person lives through a most intense period in their lives. During this time children need to not only acquire knowledge and skills essential for further studies, they also need to live a rich spiritual life. The years of study in the primary school correspond to a whole stage of moral, intellectual, emotional, physical and aesthetic development. This will only become a reality, and not just empty words, if the child lives a rich life today, and is not just preparing for the acquisition of knowledge tomorrow.

There are thousands and thousands of wonderful primary teachers in schools throughout our nation. For the children in their care, each one of them is not only a luminary of knowledge but a mentor, a teacher of life in the full sense of the word. Primary school in the Soviet Union provides a firm foundation for compulsory secondary education. But we cannot ignore the fact that many primary schools, and especially primary classes in eight-year schools and full secondary schools, suffer from serious defects. The fate of a primary school student in some schools seems to me to be sad indeed: the child has a bag on his back into which the teacher tries to cram the heaviest possible load. To carry this load up to a certain point in time—until they begin studies in the middle and upper classes—is quite often seen by the teacher as being the sole purpose of the student's life and activity.

A boy or girl in school is seen first and foremost as a student, and not as a child. (In schools people seem to be ashamed to use the word 'child'; the word 'student' is emphasised all the time.) Children carry their burden, bathed in perspiration, and do not see God's wide world. They have no idea of the joys of free time, and along the way more and more weight is added.

The primary school does need to give students a sound knowledge in certain defined areas. Any lack of clarity or lack of definition about this weakens not only the primary school, but all the stages of study that follow. Without a clear definition of the range of knowledge, skills and practical experience that children must acquire, there is no school. One of the serious defects in the primary stage of instruction is that all too often the teacher loses sight of which rules and definitions the child must deeply understand and memorise during each year, and which words children need to learn to write correctly so that they never forget how to spell them. In an effort to lighten children's intellectual load as much as possible, some teachers forget that a child needs to not only learn about something and find it interesting, but memorise it and retain it in their memory forever. There is currently a lot of talk about general development in the primary school. Of course, general development is an exceptionally important element of instruction and education, but just as important a role is played by that elementary knowledge, without which there can be no general development. General development entails the constant acquisition of knowledge, and to acquire knowledge you need to be able to study.

While not forgetting the exceptional importance of the functions carried out by the primary school, we should remember that the teacher is dealing with young people whose nervous systems are rapidly developing. We must not consider a child's brain to be a ready-made, living apparatus, presented to the teacher for the acquisition, memorisation and storage of knowledge in its memory. From the age of seven to eleven a child's brain is in a process of rapid development. If a teacher forgets that it is necessary to take care to develop a person's nervous system and to strengthen the cells of the cortex, study will dull a child's intellect.

Study should not be reduced to the constant accumulation of knowledge, to training only the memory, to stupefying, mind-numbing, unnecessary cramming, which is harmful both to a child's health and to their intellectual development. I set myself the aim of making study part of a rich spiritual life, a part that facilitated children's development and the enrichment of their minds. Not cramming, but a vigorous intellectual life flowing into a world of play, stories, beauty, music, fantasy and creativity—that is what I wanted for my pupils. I wanted the children to be travellers, explorers and creators in that world: to observe, to think, to reason, to experience the joy of work and to take pride in what they created; to create beauty and joy for other people, and to find happiness in that act of creativity; to admire the beauty in nature, music and art, and to enrich their spiritual lives with that beauty; to take to heart other people's grief and joy, and to care about what happens to them at a deeply personal level—that was my ideal of education. At the same time I must not forget those precise, strictly defined goals: what exactly the children needed to know; what words they needed to learn to write and never forget how to spell; what rules of arithmetic they needed to commit to memory forever. During the School of Joy I had already compiled a list of words from their native language that the children should commit to long term memory in grades one to four.

Children must learn how to study—this is one of the most important functions of the primary school. I considered the mastery of methods and forms of intellectual work to be an educational objective of great importance. I was disturbed by the condescending attitude of many principals and inspectors towards primary classes. When school inspectors arrive they are mainly interested in the senior and middle school classes. They seem to have the attitude that what is happening in the primary classes is not real education, but some kind of childish game. Feelings of condescending sentimentality towards this cute game only turn to concern about poor standards when students move into grade five.

No condescending sentimentality—that is the challenge I set myself as I began my work with the little children. By the end of grade two they should be able to read fluently, expressively and consciously, so as to perceive whole small sentences or the endings of large sentences as a single unit. Reading is one of the sources of thought and intellectual development. I set myself the objective of teaching the children to think while they read. For a child, reading should be a sensitive instrument for acquiring knowledge and at the same time a way to nourish their spiritual lives.

In this second part of my book I will explain how over a four year period—from the autumn of 1952 to the spring of 1956—I managed to combine two equally important functions of primary school: firstly to impart deep, sound knowledge; and secondly to avoid cramming, care for the health of the children, and give them a rich spiritual life.

# Health, health and once again health

I AM NOT AFRAID OF repeating again and again: caring for students' health is extremely important educational work. Children's spiritual lives, their outlook, their intellectual development, the soundness of their knowledge, their faith in their abilities—all of these things depend on their vitality and joy in living. If I were to measure all my cares and concerns for children during the first four years of study, a good half of them would be about health.

Caring for health is impossible without constant contact with the family. Just because a child is not complaining of any symptoms does not mean they are perfectly healthy. If you closely examine a child who is not interested in anything at school, who is indifferent to everything, in nine cases out of ten you will find that the cause is a very disturbing phenomenon: a hidden health condition of which neither the parents, nor the child are aware. I always strive to ensure that children are healthy and happy. The overwhelming majority of my conversations with parents, especially during the first two years of schooling, are about children's health.

I explained to the parents that I would not be giving their children school work to do at home. The children would memorise rules and definitions during lessons. At home the students would mainly need to do exercises aimed at facilitating deep comprehension of the material. Apart from that, the children would read, draw, observe natural phenomena, write little compositions about objects and phenomena in the surrounding world, and learn their favourite poems by heart. Intellectual work done at home should not be exhausting, but we could not completely manage without it. The argument that by perfecting work during lessons it is possible to give up homework altogether cannot be taken seriously. Such suggestions do not reflect the true aims and norms of study, if only because it is impossible to concentrate all of a child's intellectual work into three or four consecutive hours.

The parents promised to make sure the children spent most of their time outdoors, went to bed early and got up early, and slept with the ventilation window open. During summer and the warmer autumn and spring months, the children would sleep outside. The parents agreed to this as well. The mothers and fathers arranged special 'sleeping quarters', on hay under an awning, out of the rain. The children really liked that. In every family with school students a gazebo was constructed, in which, from early spring to late autumn, children could read, draw and rest. This was also agreed with the parents several years earlier, and the senior students helped to construct gazebos for little children whose mothers were not able to do it themselves.

The children had already got used to doing morning exercises during the School of Joy. Now it was important to ensure that this habit continued. I am convinced that the habit of doing morning exercises is best established during early childhood. The parents trained their children to get up at the same time every day. After exercising in the fresh air the children washed. In summer they got used to bathing in the pond. Apart from that, many parents set up showers outside in their yards and the children took showers for six months of the year (from May to September). This became such an established habit that they continued washing from the waist up during the winter months—indoors, of course.

With the help of the parent community, six outdoor showers were constructed for those students who especially needed them: Tina, Tolya, Kostya, Larisa, Nina, Sasha and Slava. I took particular care to make sure that morning showers and exercise were carried out by those girls and boys who by nature had some defect such as a stoop or disproportion of the torso or face … A person should be not only healthy, but beautiful, and beauty is inseparable from health and the harmonious development of the organism.

Diet exerts a great influence on the harmonious, proportionate development of various parts of the body, including skeletal tissue and especially the lung cage. Many years of observation have shown that if there is a lack of minerals and trace elements in the diet, some parts of the skeleton do not develop proportionately, which is reflected in our posture for the rest of our lives. To prevent that, I took care to see that the children's diets contained a balanced combination of vitamins and minerals.

Observations and research conducted previously over a number of years led to some disturbing conclusions: 25% of young children do not have breakfast before coming to school—they are not hungry in the morning; 30% eat less than half what is required for normal nutrition each morning; 23% eat half a complete breakfast; and only 22% eat a breakfast that meets normal requirements. After several hours in the classroom, children who have not had breakfast have a sinking feeling in the pit of the stomach and their heads are spinning. They come home from school, not having eaten for several hours, but still do not have a real, healthy appetite. (The parents often complain that their children do not want to eat simple healthy food—soup, porridge, milk; they want to eat 'something tasty'.)

A lack of appetite is a terrible health scourge that can lead to illnesses and poor health. The main cause is prolonged sitting in stuffy classrooms, monotony in children's intellectual work, the absence of a variety of outdoor activities, and general 'oxygen starvation'—all day the child is breathing air saturated with carbon dioxide. Many years of observation have led me to another disturbing conclusion: prolonged time in rooms saturated with carbon dioxide leads to disturbances in the function of the endocrine glands that play an important role in digestion. Moreover these disturbances become chronic and do not respond to treatment. Serious illnesses of the digestive organs also arise when parents, in an attempt to awaken appetite, give children all sorts of treats including sweets. To prevent oxygen starvation and develop adequate fresh air routines—this became one of the most important measures we took to promote health.

I advised parents to prepare tasty, healthy food for their children and to preserve lots of vitamin rich fruit for the winter. At that time we had several bee hives, and we fed the little ones honey in the school dining room over the winter.

Thanks to the fact that the children in my group spent most of the day in the fresh air, moved around a lot, did physical work, and did not sit down to textbooks straight after school, they had wonderful appetites. In the morning all the children ate a proper breakfast. Three hours after leaving home (approximately two and a half hours after the start of classes), they ate in the school dining room: a hot soup containing meat, a rissole, a glass of milk, bread and butter. After classes they ate at home (three to three and a half hours after the school dinner).

The children spent the second half of the day in the fresh air, either at home or at school. They were only indoors if it was raining or snowing.

In a child's harmonious development everything is interconnected. Children's health depends on what homework they are given, and how and when they do it. A huge role is played by the emotions that accompany the process of carrying out independent intellectual work at home. If children take to their books with reluctance, it not only saps their spiritual energy but also has a negative influence on the complex system of interactions between their internal organs. I know of many cases when a child who experienced a strong aversion to study developed serious digestive problems or gastro-intestinal illnesses.

We always spend the autumn, spring and winter holidays in the fresh air surrounded by nature—on hikes or camps, in the forest playing games ... On our first winter holiday all the children learnt to ski by going into the forest and skiing down hills. Just as we did during winter in the School of Joy, we built a town of snow and a merry-go-round on the ice. When the children became Pioneers, they had their most interesting troop meetings in the forest.

Work conducted in the fresh air during winter was very important for the children's health. When the frosts were moderate (up to ten degrees of frost) eight-year-old children worked once a week for two hours, children aged nine or ten worked for three hours and eleven-year-olds for four hours. They wrapped the trunks of trees with reeds, carted snow on little sleds to protect plants from the cold, and carried out other similar tasks. Such work is a wonderful way to condition the body and prevent colds.

The children spent the summer holidays on hikes and journeys through meadows, fields and forests. The months of direct contact with nature were very beneficial for the children's health and intellectual development. After finishing grade one, the children spent August in the collective farm orchard and the apiary. After finishing grade two, they spent a month at the melon plantation.

August is the month when we receive nature's most generous gifts and marks a peak in the flowering of her beauty. It is a time for celebrating the fruits of human labour. At this time, the air becomes particularly clear, transparent and invigorating, as if infused with the scent of cut wheat, ripening melons, grapes and apples. When summer turns to autumn the air is particularly saturated with phytoncides. If you want to strengthen the health of children who are prone to respiratory or rheumatic illnesses, get them to spend twenty-four hours a day outside in the fresh air at this time of year.

On one occasion the children spent a day on the collective farm's melon plantation. They were treated to all the watermelon and rockmelon they could eat. It was with sadness that we parted with the charming, wide open expanses of the steppe. That very evening, the chairman of the collective farm gave a directive to construct four new shelters on the melon plantation. The construction was completed in a single day. When I told the children we would holiday on the melon plantation they did not believe me: 'Do you really think they'll let us stay there?' They only believed it when they saw the shelters that had been constructed for them, covered in hay. The news that we would be sleeping in them had the children in raptures. The earth floors of the shelters were covered in sweet scented hay, sheets and blankets were brought in, wash basins were set up, and the parents erected a kitchen and supplied food for the children. Two of the shelters were for the boys and two for the girls. That month in the melon plantation remained in the children's memories for the rest of their lives, like a charming song about blue skies and bright sunshine.

We would get up at dawn and admire the unique beauty of nature as she woke from her night's slumber. We wandered through the dew-soaked fields and washed ourselves in spring water, which had been brought in a large wooden barrel and poured into the wash basins. In the pure air everything gave the children pleasure: the morning exercise, washing from the waist up in cold water, boiled potatoes with tomatoes, and watermelon. After breakfast we worked, helping the collective farm workers to harvest the melons.

We were also visited by some city children and their parents. We showed them around the melon plantation with pride, and treated them to watermelons and rockmelons. The children had learnt how to tell if a watermelon was ripe from its outward appearance. Next to the plantation, nectar rich grasses had been sown and the collective farm apiary was brought there each August. Every day we visited Grandpa Andrei and took him watermelons and hot rissoles, cooked for us by our chef Aunty Pasha. Grandpa Andrei gave our class a bee hive. 'Take it and set it up in your school grounds', he said. The children observed the life of the bees with interest.

Every day the children bathed in a pond, walked to the forest, picked wildflowers in the steppe and brought them to Grandpa Andrei and Aunty Pasha. During the hot midday hours the children lay down to have a sleep in the shelters, opening a few little 'windows' in the walls to let in fresh air, and hanging field grasses over the openings so their scent would repel flies and mosquitoes. Outside it was hot, but in the shelters it was cool. From the very first days of the School of Joy we had taught the children not to be afraid of draughts. Life has convinced me that there is no need to be afraid of draughts if you are accustomed to them from childhood. Developing intolerance for the stuffy air of unventilated rooms is just as important as developing good sanitation and hygiene.

When the temperature had gone down the children went out to work. During the hours before dusk was when most people came to the plantation for melons. After sunset, when the fields, hills and meadows were wrapped in a lilac haze and the stars appeared in the sky one after another, the children gathered around one of the shelters. In the evening hours, children like to hear stories about unusual adventures and journeys, about heroic deeds. I told them about the mythical creatures created by the imagination of our people—about mermaids and nymphs, and about Autumn Beauty who, according to folklore, distributes the gifts of fertility on quiet autumn nights.

In the stillness of the night we sometimes heard an enchanting melody. Above the fields where wheat had recently been harvested, a melodic sound rang out, similar to the resonant sound of a folk pipe. It must have been the song of some nocturnal bird unknown to us, but the children's imaginations created the image of a kindly spirit—a little boy wearing a garland of wheat stalks. He played on a pipe to give people joy. The children named him 'Solntsekolos' ['Sunear': combining the words for 'sun' and 'an ear of wheat']. In their imaginations Solntsekolos was a child of the sun and the fertile earth. Wherever the wheat forms ears of grain, there Solntsekolos is born. The wheat is harvested and he moves into a sweet scented hay stack. In the evenings he sings his bitter sweet song: the winter is coming and he must retreat into the warm earth, where life-giving fertility slumbers. But as soon as the wheat grows green in the fields, Solntsekolos will again emerge and sing his beautiful songs.

It may seem to some that the children personified nature too much, and that their fantasy may have led them to retreat from reality somewhat. A thousand times no. This is a story about life, about fertility and about humanity—a powerful source of inspiration. Inspired by the fairytale image of a creature who was an incarnation of life, beauty, fertility and abundance, the children composed a song about Solntsekolos. Here is their simple little song:

> *The sun woke the earth,*
> *An ear of wheat ripened;*
> *Who is playing on his pipe?*
> *It is Solntsekolos, Solntsekolos.*
> *This magician wears clothes,*
> *Made from ears, made from wheat;*
> *Of green beards are his eyebrows made,*
> *And his jolly eyelashes too …*[13]

---

13 Translator's note: This is a fairly literal translation of the poem, with no attempt to convey metre or rhyme.

A wonderful thing happens when children are under the influence of fairytale images. A word, heard or read at some time in the past, seems to wake up in the hidden recesses of the child's mind, shines with bright colours, and is filled with the scent of field and meadow; and the child creates, constructing poetic images.

The reader may ask: why are you talking about fairytales, fantastic images and children's creativity on pages devoted to health? Because this is the joy of childhood, and without joy the harmony of a healthy spirit in a healthy body is impossible. If children who are captivated by the beauty of the fields, the twinkling stars, the endless song of the grasshoppers and the scent of wildflowers compose a song, that means they are experiencing this harmony of body and spirit to the highest degree. Concern for human health, especially when we are dealing with children, is not just a set of rules for sanitation and hygiene, not just a list of demands concerning routines, diet, work and recreation. Above all it is a concern for a harmonious abundance of physical and spiritual energy, and the crowning glory of that harmony is the joy of creativity.

We spent the holidays at the melon plantation again at the end of grade three, but in a different location next to the grapevines. The children worked on the plantation helping adults pack bunches of grapes into baskets. In the evenings and the mornings they bathed in the pond. The children invented an interesting game. In their imaginations our three boats turned into a whaling flotilla, the little lake became an ocean, and we set out on an expedition looking for whales … Here we made reed pipes and gathered in the evenings to make music. We played folk songs and composed music about our summer evenings, about a thunderstorm, about a crimson sky, about a secret whirlpool by the dam, and about migratory birds. With each passing year, music entered more deeply into our spiritual lives. Wherever the children were spending their holidays, they listened to recordings of folk songs and the works of famous composers.

We completed our fourth year of studies and the summer of 1956 arrived. The children spent the holiday in a meadow next to an oak grove, on the banks of a lake. They built shelters out of branches and covered them with straw. The parents helped us to construct a bathing shed and a kitchen. This time the children helped the chef prepare food and travelled to the village for bread, potatoes, fish, milk and vegetables. We were responsible for the care of twenty calves and two horses. During the day the children put the calves out to pasture, and in the evening they herded them into a small enclosure by the lake. They all learnt to ride a horse and rode to the village for provisions. Everyone took their turn in strict order: each one wanted to gallop several kilometres. I was very glad that Volodya, Sanya and Tina turned out to be especially good riders. Horse riding would help these children to strengthen their health.

That year all the children became strong swimmers in the deep lake. I chose a safe place to swim and only took one child for a swim at a time.

The hay cutting days were an especially happy time. We helped the adults to dry and stack the hay, and in the evening we climbed on to a tall hay stack. Those evenings were a magic time for the children. They wanted to hear stories about the stars and distant worlds. Under the vault of stars the children felt themselves face to face with the universe and asked their teacher, 'Where does it all come from—the earth, the sun and the stars?' I became convinced that such questions arise in children's consciousness when their minds and their feelings are full of wonder and amazement at the beauty and majesty of nature.

I will never forget how, after one of my explanations about other worlds, the children asked, 'And what about further, beyond that?' Upon hearing that beyond the visible stars there were other galaxies and that there were more than it was possible to count, the children were amazed: 'So where does the world end?' The most incomprehensible idea for them was the notion of the limitlessness of the universe. I remember how the children fell silent, shocked by this fact; how they tried to imagine infinity and could not. That night the children did not go to sleep for a long time, and more than one of them dreamt of distant suns and planets. The next day from time to time the children would return to the question that disturbed them: what was infinity? Through all the years of their schooling this question never lost its stunning novelty.

From the first days of the School of Joy I had considered sport to be of major significance. With the help of the older students I had equipped a sports ground and erected swings. We always had an adequate supply of balls, and in grade two the children started to play table tennis. The children also enjoyed hurling a discus or ball, and climbing up a pole or a rope.

All summer the children went barefoot and were not afraid of rain. I considered this an especially important means of physical conditioning. During grades one and two we had only three cases of a child catching cold. In grades three and four no-one fell ill.

I considered it especially important to develop resistance to all types of head cold. For many years this problem gave me no rest. When there was a rapid change in the weather, nearly half the children were sneezing. Even if children do not have a high temperature, they cannot work normally when feeling sick. There are no radical treatments for curing a head cold. Medical science has proven that many types of head cold are not infectious diseases but the reaction of a sensitive organism to sudden changes in the environment. Many years' experience has shown that the feet are particularly sensitive. If the feet are sensitive to the slightest cold, a person is prone to non-infectious colds. The system for strengthening the organism that has developed in our educational work begins with conditioning the feet. Of course a child's general state of health is taken into consideration. For conditioning the feet there are no special exercises to be followed for a definite period of time. It is simply necessary to observe some general guidelines: not to accustom children to too much warmth, and not to overprotect a child and weaken the organism's natural defences. If a child does not walk barefoot in summer, no baths or rubbing down with a wet towel will help.

And so the children finished primary school. It was the last day of the holidays. They gathered on some green grass after bathing in the lake—strong, suntanned, beautiful. They were each eleven years old but they looked like strong children of twelve or thirteen. Even little Danko, who for a long time everyone nicknamed 'crumb', was as tall as many grade five students.

Each year the doctor checked the children's eyes, heart and lungs. In grade one, four children had weak vision, in grade two there were only two, and in grade three not a single one. Life had confirmed that weakened vision is not a disease of the eyes but due to the fact that a child's physical and spiritual development have not progressed in harmony with each other. Medical examinations during the first two years revealed that three children had symptoms of cardio-vascular weakness, two had residual symptoms from previous bouts of pleurisy, two had signs of bronchitis, and one was suspected of having latent tuberculosis. By the time they finished primary school only one child had symptoms of cardio-vascular weakness, and those symptoms were much improved when compared with observations taken during the first two years of studies.

## *Study is a part of our spiritual life*

IT IS VERY IMPORTANT THAT the wonderful world of nature, play, beauty, music, fantasy and creativity that surrounds a child before schooling commences, should not be shut out by the classroom door. During the first months and years of school life, study should not become the only form of activity. Children will only love school if teachers generously show them the same joys that they had before.

At the same time study cannot be tailored to childish joys and deliberately made easy with the sole aim of not boring the child. Gradually, indirectly, the child must be prepared for the main business of human life—serious, persistent, painstaking work—which is impossible without mental exertion.

One important educational objective was to accustom children to intense, creative, intellectual work. Children must be able to detach themselves from everything that surrounds them at a given moment, in order to focus their mental energy on the attainment of a goal set by the teacher or by themselves. I tried to ensure that the children gradually became accustomed to such a level of concentration. Only under those conditions will intellectual work enter one's spiritual life and become a favourite activity.

The primary school should aim to train children to overcome difficulties, not only in physical but also in intellectual work. Children should understand the essence of intellectual work: concentrating the mind; gaining insight into the various complexities and subtleties, details and contradictions inherent in objects, facts and phenomena. Under no circumstances should everything come easily to students; children should know what it is to face difficulty. The skills and self-discipline of intellectual work are educated during the process of acquiring knowledge. Intellectual education is one of those areas of spiritual life in which the influence of the educator organically blends with self-education. The education of the will begins with mentally setting a goal for oneself, concentrating one's mental energies, thinking things through, and exercising self-control. For me it was an important educational objective to see that children experienced what it is to face difficulty in intellectual work.

If everything comes easily to children in their studies they gradually become accustomed to laziness of thought, which corrupts them and leads them to develop a superficial attitude to life. Strange as it may seem, laziness of thought is most likely to develop in capable children, when the process of study does not expose them to tasks of appropriate difficulty. And laziness of thought develops most often in the younger classes, when a capable child easily masters work that requires a certain intellectual exertion for other children, and is essentially idle. Another of our educational objectives should be not to allow students to be idle.

Our grade one class was located in a separate building. The big, bright room we studied in had windows looking out to the east and the south, so there was always lots of sunlight in the classroom. Next to the windows were nut trees, behind them apple, pear and apricot trees, and further on was an oak grove. Not only our building, but all the school buildings were surrounded by greenery, and the leaves of the trees enriched the air with oxygen. In the school grounds it was always quiet. Our classroom opened on to a large corridor, off which a door led to another room: here we dreamt of creating a story room.

In front of the entrance to our building was a concrete slab with a device that used rainwater to clean the soles of the children's shoes. From this slab several paths fanned out, lined with peach, linden and chestnut trees. One path led to the grapevines situated in the centre of the school grounds; a second path led to our nearest neighbours, a building housing two grade five classes; a third path led to green lawns and groves; and a fourth to a gully overgrown with bushes.

Even back then it seemed advisable for first and second grade classes to be located in a separate building, especially in the first grade as they have their own special routines for study, work and rest. For children in the early school years, the shouting and the hurly-burly characteristic of a large school community are particularly unacceptable. Let the younger students enjoy peace and quiet for as long as possible, as it is indispensable for full intellectual development. Many years of observation have led me to conclude that the environment that children encounter during the first days of school overwhelms them. The children are exhausted—not so much by the intellectual work as by the constant excitement created by the shouting, running and commotion during breaks and before classes. Over a period of five years I observed first grade students after the main break. For half an hour the children are surrounded by the noise, shouting, pushing and commotion of a large school community. When the break ends and the students return to class, experienced teachers spend the first ten minutes of the lesson settling the children. It was a different picture when the first grade students rested during the break in their own small group. No more than two minutes were needed to settle the children and calm their excitement.

Unrestrained shouting and running are not good signs for a school. However full the children's river of joy is, it must have some banks restraining its impulses and desires.

At the current time, our first and second grade classes study in a cosy, separate building surrounded by greenery. The environment created for the little ones facilitates the rotation of work and rest.

During the first weeks, I gradually introduced the children to their new life. In essence, our studies did not differ much from the School of Joy, and this is what I was aiming for. In September we were in the classroom no more than forty minutes per day, and in October no more than two hours. This time was allocated for lessons in writing and arithmetic. The remaining two hours we spent in the open air. The children looked forward to their 'real lessons'—that is what they called lessons in the classroom. I was delighted by their enthusiasm and thought to myself, 'If only you knew, children, how other children your age get worn out in their stuffy classroom and cannot wait for the bell so they can go out and play.'

It is essential to take things gradually when preparing children for classroom lessons, if one hopes to achieve the best outcomes in vocational, moral, physical and intellectual education. The ultimate aim is to teach young people to work in a variety of circumstances. Classroom lessons are not some sad necessity, that, like it or not, one has to accept. They provide the most favourable conditions for intellectual work, but you have to accustom children to them gradually—this is a special requirement for lessons with young students. If you immediately force them to work for four hours a day, conditions that may be favourable for intellectual work in the future will have a detrimental effect on children's health.

In the classroom we read our alphabet book, wrote circles, sticks and letters, and composed and solved problems. All of these things gradually became part of the children's spiritual life and did not weary them with monotony. We did not need to read the same thing over and over in the alphabet book, as the children already knew their letters well and I used a variety of activities to develop their reading skills. The children made up and wrote down miniature compositions about nature, and that helped to develop their reading skills much more than reading the alphabet book over and over.

I monitored each child to make sure they were developing the necessary reading skills. You will get nowhere without practice and a certain volume of reading. It is not enough to know the letters and be able to read syllables and words. Reading is a window on the world and is the most important study tool. It must be fluent and rapid—only then is the tool ready for use. I tried to ensure that a variety of activities—including expressive reading, writing and drawing—helped to make reading become a semi-automatic process, so that by grade two multisyllabic words would be perceived as single units. And if I resorted to miniature compositions about nature, if I tried to awaken the children's lively interest in such work, it was essentially a pedagogical 'trick of the trade' necessary for the attainment of a single objective—to teach children to read well.

One such trick of the trade is to vary the types of work during lessons. Experience shows that at the beginning of the first grade there should not be 'pure' lessons in reading, writing or arithmetic. Children quickly tire from monotony. As soon as the children began to tire I tried to switch to a fresh type of work. Drawing is a powerful means of introducing variety into the work. If I noticed that the children were beginning to tire of reading, I would say, 'Open your sketch books children. Let's draw the story we are reading.' Those early signs of tiredness disappeared and sparks of joy appeared in the children's eyes. Creativity took the place of monotony … An analogous situation arose during arithmetic lessons, when I noticed that the children were having difficulty understanding the terms of a problem set for independent work. Once again I found it helpful to turn to creative work—drawing. The children read the problem again and 'drew' it. Then they understood the relationships that up to that point had seemed completely incomprehensible … Prolonged listening is also tiring. If I noticed the children's eyes glazing over, I would wind up a story and we would begin to draw.

Three weeks after the beginning of the school year, my pupils began to compile picture books about nature. The senior students made each child a hard-covered exercise book with twenty sheets of thick paper and a pencil attached to the cover. Once a week we walked to the sources of thought and words, and wrote an illustrated story about the surrounding world. Our first journey was to the orchard to see an apple tree whose fruit ripens late. The little ones composed stories that reflected each child's individual world of perceptions and concepts. 'The apples were leaning towards the earth', 'The apples are warming themselves in the sun', 'Red apples amongst green leaves', 'The sun caresses, while the branch rocks the little apple', 'White flowers in spring, golden apples in autumn', 'We came to visit the apples'—wrote the children in their picture books about nature. The children read their miniature compositions in class, which gave them great pleasure.

Study in the orchard was not an end in itself. Writing miniature compositions is a wonderful way to prepare children for persistent, strenuous intellectual work in the future. Starting in grade one, and especially in grade two, I tried to ensure that each child had their own individual assignment and saw it through to the end. This is very important for educating discipline in intellectual work.

During the first year of study all the picture books were filled with drawings and compositions. The children wrote about the bunches of red berries on the guelder-rose; about the harvest; about the sleeping lake (they probably said it was sleeping because on our journeys the water there was always as clear and still as a mirror); about how they worked in the school orchard; about the crimson sky at sunset; about the first autumn frosts; about a rainy, overcast autumn day; about the life of our village; about the first snow; about a January blizzard; about fairytale Grandpa Frost binding the rivers and lakes with ice; about the drip of melting snow in February; about blue shadows on the snow in March; about the first snowdrops; about starlings returning too early from warmer lands and being caught unawares by March blizzards; about the joyful spring flocks of migratory birds ('joyful spring flocks' in the words of the children); about bees flying one sunny day of an Indian summer to say goodbye to the camomile flowers.

These picture books about nature grew into a class anthology of poetry, reflecting the subtlest shades of colour in our natural surroundings, the music of earth and sky, the flavour of words. They provided that joy without which study cannot enter into the spiritual lives of children.

If we measure the time spent by children in class in lessons, then we had one lesson per day during the first two months of the school year; two per day during the third and fourth months; two and a half during the fifth and sixth months; and three lessons per day during the seventh and eighth months. The duration of lessons between breaks during the first two months was half an hour; after that it was forty-five minutes. If a child needed to go out before a break, they asked permission. If the child could not interrupt the teacher's explanation, they left the room without permission: the teacher saw that the child needed to leave and gave tacit approval. But some children found it difficult to adapt to routines that the vast majority easily accepted. Tolya, Katya, Kostya and Shura tired quickly. What tired them was most probably the tension they experienced sitting in a lesson, feeling that the strict routine restricted their freedom to a significantly greater extent than before. Of course we cannot indulge every desire; we must gradually accustom all students to persistent, serious work; but we should not try to break childish desires and habits too suddenly. For several weeks I allowed those children to leave the classroom in the middle of a lesson and gradually trained them to work persistently. After three or four months all the children followed school work routines.

On sunny autumn days we worked in one of the 'green classrooms', which was located on a lawn amongst some tall apple trees. Several years earlier, some of the senior students and I had constructed a frame of metal rods and wire, for a future green classroom, and planted climbing plants—wild grapes and hops. After two years a green classroom had formed—the plants had covered the ceiling as well. Several 'windows' guaranteed adequate light. On hot days it was cool in there, and in autumn it was warm and cosy. In the green classroom peace and quiet reigned. When the 'windows' were covered with grape and hop branches a green twilight descended, and unusual patterns of light and shade were created by the sun's rays finding their way between gaps in the leaves. The children called this 'shutting the window for stories'. In the classroom were little tables and stools, where the children wrote, read and solved problems.

A second green classroom consisted of a lawn surrounded on three sides by a frost-resistant variety of grape. When it was very hot—and hot days are not uncommon in our locality in spring and autumn—it was cool in there.

We have one other green classroom on some grass surrounded by green trees in a distant grove next to a ravine. We sometimes went there for the last lesson of the day, when it was not necessary to return to the school building. We spent about 40% of lessons through the year not in our regular classroom, but in one of these 'green classrooms'. Of the remaining 60% of lessons, a significant number were held in the 'green laboratory' or in the school greenhouse. The 'green laboratory' is a separate building surrounded on all sides by trees and grapevines. In it there is a classroom containing many plants and flowers.

The fact that a significant proportion of lessons were conducted in natural surroundings, in the fresh air under the open sky, was extraordinarily significant for the children. For the duration of their hours of study the children were in good spirits, bright and cheerful, and never went home with a headache.

After lessons, the children rested at home. Whatever measures are taken to ensure that lessons do not exhaust children, they still get very tired and need to rest. Many years' experience has convinced me that during the second half of the day, students should generally not engage in intellectual work as intensely as they do at school. It is even more unacceptable to overload children in the early years.

If, after three or four hours of intellectual work at school, children are forced to work just as intensively at home, they will soon reach breaking point.

We cannot manage without homework. Children need to be taught to concentrate their intellectual energies and focus their attention. But this should be done mainly during lessons, gradually teaching the habit of independent intellectual work. It is not easy for a child to learn to work with attention and concentration. Experienced teachers engage children's attention to their story, explanation or exposition with the content of the lesson, and not with any special techniques for influencing the students. Skill in organising the intellectual work in the early years consists of getting children to listen to the teacher attentively, to memorise and think without noticing that they are making an effort, without forcing themselves to listen attentively, to memorise or think.

If a teacher can do this, the pupil will remember everything that caught their interest and especially those things that inspired wonder. Why did the children remember their letters so easily and learn to read and write? Because they were never expected to do so. Because every letter was an embodiment of a vivid image that had inspired feelings of admiration and delight. If every day I had given the little preschoolers a 'portion of knowledge'—shown them a letter and demanded they memorise it—I would have gotten nowhere. That does not mean, of course, that you have to hide your goals from children. You need to teach in such a way that children are not thinking about the goals—that is what lightens intellectual work. All this is not as simple as it may first seem. We are talking about a particular stage in the intellectual development of children, about a stage that Professor VL Ryzhov calls 'the infancy of the human nervous system'.[14] During this developmental stage—during the early years, and especially during the first year of school—children simply do not have the ability to concentrate. The teacher must engage the children's attention by awakening what in psychology is called involuntary attention.

The attention of a little child is a fickle creature. To me it seems like a timid little bird that flies further away from its nest as soon as you try to get close to it. If you do manage at last to catch the little bird, you can only keep it by holding it in your hands or putting it in a cage. Do not expect any songs from the bird if it feels itself to be a prisoner. It is the same with the attention of a little child: if you hold it captive like an imprisoned bird, it will be of little help to you.

---

14 See Ryzhov, VL, 'Molekulyarnaya osnova pamyati' [The Molecular basis of memory], *Priroda* [Nature]. 1965, no. 7, p. 2.

There are some teachers who are proud of the fact that they can create an 'environment of constant intellectual exertion' during their lessons. More often than not this is achieved through external factors that act as a bridle, restraining the attention of the child: frequent reminders ('listen carefully'); rapid rotations from one form of work to another; the prospect of knowledge being checked immediately after an explanation is given (more precisely, the threat of receiving a failing grade if you do not listen to what I am saying); the requirement to carry out some form of practical work as soon as a theoretical proposition has been explained.

All these methods create an initial appearance of active intellectual work: the work activities rotate like a kaleidoscope; the children, concentrating, listen to the teacher's every word; and there is a tense silence in the classroom. But what is the cost of achieving this, and what results does it lead to? Constant straining to be attentive and not to miss anything (and students at this age cannot force themselves to be attentive) overstrains and exhausts the nervous system. Not to lose a single minute during a lesson, not to go for one moment without active intellectual work—what could be more stupid in the subtle business of educating a human being? Such a direction in a teacher's work means, in effect, to squeeze everything out of children that they can give. After such 'effective' lessons children go home tired. They are easily irritated and upset. They need to have a really good rest, but they still have homework to do and one look at that schoolbag with its textbooks and exercise books is enough to make children feel sick.

It is no accident that there are many discipline problems in schools that lead to conflicts, with students being rude to the teacher and to each other and cheekily answering back when they are reprimanded. During the lesson children's nerves are stretched to the limit, and the teachers themselves are not electronic machines. Just try holding the attention of a class for the duration of a lesson with an emphasis on 'high effectiveness' and with work activities rotating like a kaleidoscope. It is no accident that children often come home from lessons gloomy, not wanting to talk, indifferent to everything, or sometimes just the opposite—abnormally irritable.

No, we should not seek children's attentiveness, concentration and intellectual activity at such a cost. Student's intellectual strength and nervous energy, especially at a young age, is not a bottomless well from which one can draw endlessly. We must take from that well with wisdom, and very circumspectly, and most importantly we must constantly replenish the child's sources of nervous energy. The sources of this replenishment are to be found in observation of the objects and phenomena of the surrounding world, in life in the midst of nature, in reading (but in reading which is motivated by interest, by the desire to learn something, and not from a fear of being questioned), and in journeys to the source of living thought and language.

In the life of a school community there is an attribute that is hard to put your finger on, which might be called psychological equilibrium. What I mean by this term is that the children feel the fullness of life, think clearly, have confidence in their abilities, and faith in their capacity to overcome difficulties. Characteristic features of psychological equilibrium are a calm environment with purposeful work; even-tempered, friendly relationships and the absence of irritability. It is impossible to work normally without psychological equilibrium. The life of a school community becomes a living hell when this equilibrium is disturbed: the students insult and annoy each other, and nervousness and irritability reign throughout the school. How can we establish and, most importantly, maintain psychological equilibrium? The experience of the best teachers has convinced me that the most important thing in this very subtle area of education is constant thinking activity—without overtaxing, without sudden bursts of activity, without rushing or straining the mental faculties.

Psychological equilibrium is characterised by an atmosphere of goodwill, mutual support, and an alignment between each student's intellectual ability and the work assigned to them, which should be of an appropriate level of difficulty. The primary school teachers VP Novitskaya, EM Zhalenko and AA Nesterenko were true masters of psychological equilibrium, and I studied their work very closely. I tried to understand the secret behind that wisest, and at the same time most natural thing: all their children were studying to the best of their ability. There was no child who was capable of excellence but only working at a satisfactory level. Those who were just studying at a satisfactory level and being awarded a grade of three[15] did not consider themselves to be failures or cursed by fate, and their friends did not look down on them with condescending pity.

I was always very concerned about the psychosis of pursuing only excellent grades. This psychosis begins in the family and takes hold of educators, laying a heavy burden on the young souls of students and crippling them. At that time a child does not have the capacity to earn an excellent grade, but the parents demand nothing less than a five, or at the very least a four, and the poor student receiving a three feels like a criminal. This never happened in the classes of VP Novitskaya, EM Zhalenko or AA Nesterenko. The ones who received excellent grades did not feel especially fortunate and the ones who received satisfactory grades were not afflicted with feelings of inadequacy. I tried to learn the art of intelligent, concentrated intellectual work from these master teachers.

I noticed what seemed to me to be a very subtle characteristic of their educational artistry: the ability to kindle a feeling of joy in learning in children's hearts and minds. For each and every child,

---

15 Translator's note: In the Soviet education system students were awarded grades on a scale of one to five. 'Five' stood for 'excellent', 'four' for 'good', 'three' for 'satisfactory' and 'two' for unsatisfactory. In practice 'one' was almost never awarded, but could be awarded for not answering at all, or for showing disrespect.

every little success in learning was accompanied by joyful enthusiasm, associated with the uncovering of some truth, with research and discovery. Generalising from the precious experience of these master teachers, I tried to ensure that children did not work in order to receive a grade, but from an urge to experience intellectual excitement. I was very glad that there was no unhealthy pursuit of excellent grades in our class, nor the equally harmful unhealthy reaction to satisfactory grades.

Each week we devoted several lessons to journeys to the sources of thought and language—to observation. This involved direct contact with nature, without which the well of a child's intellectual strength and nervous energy will quickly run dry. When the weather was warm in autumn, spring and summer, we would set out on a journey long before dawn: country children are able to get up early. Talking about nature, about the objects and phenomena of the surrounding world, awakened the children's curiosity and I had to answer many questions. Here are some of those questions: Why is the sun red early in the morning and fiery at midday? Where do clouds come from? Why does a dandelion flower open in the morning and close at midday? What causes lightning and thunder? Why does a wind from the west bring rain, but a wind from the east bring drought? Why does a sunflower turn its head to the sun—surely it cannot see like a person? Why does iron rust? Why do doves never land on a tree? Why shouldn't you transplant a tree in summer when it has leaves? Why are snowflakes so beautiful, as if someone has carved them? How do birds know the way when they have to fly so far? Where does the white ring around the moon come from? Why is the sky red at sunset before rain? Why does a bee 'dance' before flying off to look for nectar? Why do they burn straw in orchards when the trees are in flower? Why do you hear an echo in the forest? What is a rainbow? Why is there no thunder and lightning in winter? Why does salt water only freeze in a very strong frost? Why does a rabbit dig a burrow when a hare doesn't? Why is it that if you wrap a jug of milk in a wet towel in summer the milk does not heat up, even if the weather is very hot? Why do swallows fly close to the ground before it rains? Why do larks make their nests in crops, and starlings and tomtits make their nests in trees? Why do ducks swim and hens not swim? Why does an aeroplane leave a fine trail of mist in the sky today when it did not leave a trail yesterday? Why do stars fall from the sky, and where do they fall? Why does the wind raise a column of dust like a whirlpool? Why does the willow 'weep'? Why do snowdrops flower only in early spring? Why do they sow winter wheat in autumn but spring wheat in spring? Why do glow-worms glow? Why does a cow only have one calf when a pig has several piglets? Why is the sun high in the sky in summer but low in winter? Why do beautiful patterns form on frozen window panes? Why do the leaves on the trees turn yellow in autumn?[16]

I have listed only a small proportion of the hundreds of questions that the children asked me. Not a single question should be left unanswered—a child wants to know everything. I tried to answer each question in such a way that I not only revealed to children the essence of natural phenomena, but also kindled the fire of their curiosity even more. Answering children's questions and chatting about the surrounding world—I would call this the first school of thought and will write about these lessons in thought in more detail below—is one of the most important elements in the multifaceted spiritual life of a child.

If our journeys into nature took place during the last lesson of the day, we would play afterwards. The children themselves invented a collective game. In their game the world of natural phenomena was interwoven with the world of fairytales. The game that the children enjoyed so much was called 'In search of the secret island'. We all

---

16 These are questions the children asked on walks during 1952 and 1953.

divided into two groups. One group positioned itself in some remote corner of the forest. We surrounded the chosen area with a chain of markers known only to us, indicating the shore of the island, with cliffs and many wild animals. The children who remained on the secret island were travellers who had been shipwrecked. In several places they placed well-disguised markers, showing a narrow path by which it was possible to gain access to the island (markers were agreed on by both groups beforehand). The goal was to save the shipwrecked travellers. The children spread out over the forest, exploring the shore of the island step by step, seeking those places where it was possible to gain access. In this game you not only needed a keen eye and courage, but also the ability to recognise many natural phenomena and to think logically. The game also fostered honesty and truthfulness. The children found the secret passages onto the island and helped the travellers. The sick ones were sent to hospital, and pilots and doctors appeared in the game. The game ended with the shipwrecked travellers and their rescuers making porridge. We would sit by the campfire and I would tell a story. During the story many children would draw, giving their own interpretation of the story's fairytale images.

A lot of attention was given to observing the animal and bird life on our journeys into nature. We discovered an amazing new world. During a period of quiet autumn weather, we spied a whole litter of baby hedgehogs on their way from their nest to get a drink of water, while the old mother hedgehog protected her little babies. During the spring we observed some hares. The children observed how a mother hare leaves her new born baby, never to return to it, and how the baby hare waits for some other mother hare to chance upon it and feed it. In July we observed tree frogs. Once, in a remote place, we managed to find a fox's lair. The children saw how the mother fox took her little children for a walk, taught them how to run, and played with them. In another remote corner of the forest we observed beavers.

Our journeys and observations enriched our thinking, developing imagination and speech. The more questions the children had on our walks and excursions, the more brightly their curiosity and thirst for knowledge manifested themselves in class when we talked about natural phenomena, work and distant countries. Observing the children's emotional state after our journeys into nature, I became more convinced each time of the truth in that ancient saying: 'thought begins with wonder'.

I strove to ensure that wonder at the secrets of nature and the experience of joy in learning provided stimulus and motivation for the children. In our class there were students who needed a lot of time to make sense of even a simple problem (Valya, Petrik and Nina). In each case there were different causes but the result was one and the same: for these children the cells of the cerebral cortex experienced a depressed level of activity. The children were indifferent to what was being explained in class.

Observation revealed that the thinking processes of these children suffered from a defect that could be described as a lethargy and inertia of the cells of the cerebral cortex. This defect manifested as follows: the children found it hard to establish, and especially to retain in their memories, the connections between a number of objects or phenomena. For example, they were presented with a problem about apples, baskets and children. While they thought about the apples and baskets, they forgot about the children. When they were reminded of the children, they forgot about the apples and baskets. But when we thought about the cause and effect relationships between objects and phenomena present in the surrounding world, when we made our little discoveries and experienced feelings of wonder at discovering the truth—these experiences caused Valya, Petrik and Nina to feel an elemental joy. They experienced significant psychological arousal. Their eyes shone with joyful excitement. Their indifference disappeared and they became interested in what we were studying.

Once we are able to awaken a question in a child's consciousness, a question with strong emotional associations, it is as if dormant forces are aroused in the child's mind, and thought processes proceed with great energy. I observed with joy that those children whose intellectual development was most problematic were becoming more and more alert. They listened to stories and explanations with interest, and made more sense of the problems. Of course a great deal of painstaking educational work still lay ahead. I shared my observations with other experienced teachers of early childhood classes and we referred to this work as the 'emotional arousal of the intellect'.

I tried to understand what was happening with children like Valya, Petrik and Nina when the teacher succeeded in awakening their interest in an object of cognition. I read works by biologists, psychologists, educators and neuropathologists. I came across some interesting thoughts about the interaction between the cells of the cerebral cortex and the subcortical centres in the works of Sigmund Freud. Freud attributes a decisive role in thinking to the subcortical centres, which, as has been shown by many investigations, govern the emotional processes of the human psyche. Freud compares the feelings and the intellect to a horse and rider. In his opinion, it is the horse who determines the rider's direction (that is, the feelings—the subcortical centres). The horse carries the rider wherever it wishes, but does this so cunningly that the rider thinks they are directing the horse. So according to Freud, the sub-cortex is more important than the cortex.

While he took issue with Freud's categorical assertion, the Russian physiologist Ivan Pavlov also credited the sub-cortex with a very significant role. 'The main impulse for the activity of the cortex proceeds from the sub-cortex', he wrote. 'In the absence of those emotions, the cortex loses its main source of energy.' But Pavlov considered the cerebral cortex to be the main regulator of human thought and behaviour (the rider has the power to both stop the horse and turn it in a different direction).

Observation of the children's intellectual work convinced me more and more that the emotional impulses flowing from the sub-cortex to the cortex (feelings of joyful excitement, wonder and amazement) have the effect of arousing the sleeping cells of the cortex and triggering their activity. Experience showed that a central focus for the intellectual education of little children must be the development of a thirst for knowledge—curiosity, inquisitiveness.

Journeys into nature became a tradition in our junior classes. The children always looked forward to going to the forest, the fields or the pond, and thought up games in advance. The children's favourite games were ones in which they overcame difficulties, games in which they pretended to be imaginary or real heroes. In grade two I told the little ones about Robinson Crusoe, which led to an interesting game that lasted for several months. After hearing about Spartacus, the children constructed an imaginary camp of rebellious slaves, on a big hill next to a cliff and a deep ravine. The children were so interested to hear about the Scythian herdsmen, hunters and fisherman who lived in our parts in ancient times that they created a game in which they reconstructed the way of life of those ancient workers.

Study must be closely connected with the multi-faceted play of a child's mental and physical energy, so that this play of energy will give rise to bright, exciting feelings, and the surrounding world will stand before the child like an interesting book that they want to read. Apart from journeys into nature and games, there is great scope for developing a child's intellectual and physical abilities in physical work. It is impossible to imagine a full and happy childhood without the joyful, excited feelings inspired by work activities. Experience has convinced me that, for a small child, physical work is not only a way of acquiring certain skills and habits, not only a form of moral education, but also a boundless, amazingly rich environment for thought. This environment awakens moral, intellectual and aesthetic feelings, without which it is impossible to explore the world or to study. I view physical work, alternating with study, as a child's fascinating journey into a world of dream and creativity. It was in the process of carrying out physical work that my pupil's most important intellectual attributes took shape: curiosity, inquisitiveness, resourcefulness in thought, and clarity of imagination.

When physical work inspired by thought is a part of children's lives, intellectual work during lessons becomes desirable and attractive to children, developing their abilities and enriching their experience. In grade two we had one hour a week for our favourite work, and the children were involved in projects that fully engaged their thoughts and feelings. In grades three and four there were two hours per week of our favourite work.

Favourite work … That does not mean that the teacher should wait passively until a child develops an interest. In work education, as in all educational work, nothing should be left to happen of its own accord. The children should be surrounded by an atmosphere of enthusiasm. My pupils were surrounded by adolescent and senior students who were busy working. All the students were involved in dozens of interesting activities. They were cultivating trees and grain crops, constructing model engines and machines, creating blends of soil, looking after animals, building a new greenhouse or workshop, or installing a water supply.

A spirit of inquiry, inquisitiveness and curiosity—that is what an interest in work awakens in children. My motto was always: work is not an end in itself, but a means for attaining a whole series of multi-facetted educational goals—social, ideological, moral, intellectual, creative, aesthetic and emotional.

Study can become an interesting, attractive enterprise for children if it is illuminated by the bright light of thought, feeling, creativity, beauty and play. My concern for success in study began with concern for how children eat and sleep, how they are feeling, how they play, and how many hours per day they are out in the fresh air. What books are they reading, what stories are they listening to, what are they drawing, and how do they express their thoughts and feelings in their drawings? What feelings are awakened in their souls by the music of nature and the musical melodies created by our folk musicians and composers, what favourite work do they have, and how sensitive are they to the joys and sorrows of other people? What have they created for other people, and what feelings did they experience as a consequence?

Study becomes a part of children's spiritual life when knowledge is inseparable from active work. It is very difficult for a child to get enthusiastic about the multiplication tables for their own sake, or about the rule for calculating the area of a triangle. Knowledge becomes desirable for a little person when it is a means for achieving creative or work-oriented goals. I tried to ensure that even at an early age children were excited by physical work, and saw in it a way to demonstrate their quick-wittedness and inventiveness. One of the most important aims of study is to teach students how to use knowledge. The danger of knowledge becoming 'dead weight' first appears in the junior classes, when intellectual work of necessity involves learning more and more new skills and habits. If these skills and habits are only acquired and never applied in practical activities, study gradually becomes disengaged from the spiritual life of children; it becomes something separate from their interests and passions. In order to prevent this from happening, the teacher must take care to see that all children find a creative application for their new skills.

## *Three hundred pages of the 'book of nature'*

THE GERMAN MATHEMATICIAN FELIX KLEIN compared a school student to a cannon that is primed with knowledge for ten years and then fired, after which nothing remains. I remembered this sad joke when I observed the work of children who were forced to memorise material they did not understand—material that did not awaken vivid ideas, images and associations in their minds. The substitution of memorisation for thought, the replacement of direct perception and observation of the essence of phenomena with rote learning, is a major vice that blunts a child's wits and, in the end, destroys the will to study.

Which one of us has not been amazed at the sharp, retentive memories of little preschool children? Consider a five-year-old child who has just returned from a walk with his mother and father in the forest or fields. He is bursting with impressions of vivid images, pictures and phenomena. A month passes, and then a year, and the mother and father are planning another walk. Their son is looking forward to the quiet sunny morning and remembers how, an unimaginable time ago, he went with his mum and dad to the forest. The mother and father are struck by the vivid, living details that sparkle in the child's recollections: the child remembers a wonderful flower with petals of two different colours. The father is amazed to hear him repeat the beautiful legend of the brother and sister who turned into this flower; the father had recounted that legend to the mother on the edge of the forest. At the time the child had not appeared to be listening to what his father was saying; he had been chasing a butterfly. How had his memory retained these apparently minute details from the surrounding world?

The point is that children are amazingly sensitive to bright images, vibrant with many shades of colour and sound, and retain them deep in their memories. A little child will surprise older people with the most unexpected questions that arise in the process of perceiving images from the surrounding world. In this case, remembering the wonderful flower, the child asks his father, 'Can the brother and sister see each other or not? You said that plants are alive—does that mean they can hear and see? And talk to each other? And can we hear them talking?' This torrent of thought amazes the father: why did his son not ask about this a year ago? How could he retain not only the vivid image of the flower but the emotions of those unforgettable moments for so long? The father is convinced that the little child can still see the edge of the forest with its many-coloured carpet of flowers, and hear the distant sound of an aeroplane.

Reflecting on this, I asked myself: why is it that after two or three years studying in school, a child with a lively, vivid imagination and a keen memory, with such a sensitive emotional reaction to the surrounding world, cannot remember a grammatical rule and has difficulty remembering how to spell the word 'steppe' or what six times nine equals? I came to a conclusion no less sorrowful than that of the German mathematician: the process of acquiring knowledge at school is often disconnected from the spiritual life of students. The reason a child's memory is so keen and retentive is that it is fed by a clear stream of vivid images, pictures, perceptions and ideas. The reason a child's thought strikes us with its keen, unexpected, 'philosophical' questions is that it is fed by the living source of this stream. How important it is not to allow the school door to shut out the surrounding world from a child's consciousness. I tried to ensure that all through the years of childhood the surrounding world of nature constantly fed the minds of the students with vivid images, pictures, perceptions and ideas; that children came to apprehend the laws of thought as a well-ordered structure, whose architecture was dictated by an even more well-ordered structure—that of nature. So as not to turn children into mere receptacles for knowledge and their minds into storerooms cluttered with truths, rules and formulas, we have to teach them to think. By their very nature, a child's consciousness and a child's memory require that the bright surrounding world, with its natural laws, should not be shut out for a single minute. If the environment in which the child is learning to think, memorise and reason can become the surrounding world, I am convinced that the keenness of children's memories and the clarity of their thought will not only not fade when they start school, but will become stronger.

At the same time we should not exaggerate the role of nature in intellectual development. Teachers are deeply mistaken if they think that being surrounded by nature will in itself provide children with a powerful stimulus for intellectual development. Nature does not have some magic power, directly influencing the intellect, feelings and will. Nature will only become a powerful stimulus for education when people attempt to understand it, and gain insight into its cause and effect relationships. I am not exaggerating the role of visual images in the intellectual development of a child. To overvalue the use of visual aids is to have too limited a view of children's thought processes, to limit cognitive activities to the sphere of the senses. We should not make a fetish of particular characteristics of a child's thought, including the characteristic that children think in images, colours and sounds. This characteristic is an objective fact, whose importance has been convincingly demonstrated by Konstantin Ushinsky. But just because children think in images, colours and sounds does not mean that we should not teach them to think abstractly. In emphasising the importance of visual images and the major role of nature in intellectual development, I see in these factors a means for developing abstract thinking and purposeful study: to help children master the logic of thought.

I carefully thought about what should stimulate my pupils' thinking and defined what the children would observe, day by day over four years; that is, which phenomena from the surrounding world would become the wellsprings of their thought. That is how the 300 pages of the 'Book of Nature' came together. It is composed of 300 observations, 300 vivid pictures, each of which made an impression on the children's minds. Twice a week we went to visit nature to learn to think. Not just to observe, but to learn to think. These were, in essence, lessons in thought. Not just enjoyable walks, but lessons. But the fact that a lesson is very enjoyable and very interesting enriches a child's spiritual world even more.

I set myself the goal of impressing the children's minds with vivid pictures of reality so that their thought processes would develop on the basis of living, graphic representations; so that while observing the surrounding world, the children would be able to establish the causes and effects of phenomena, and would be able to compare the qualities and characteristics of objects. My observations confirmed a very important principle regarding the intellectual education of children: the more abstract truths and generalisations that have to be mastered during a lesson and the more intense that intellectual work is, the more frequently students need to turn to nature—to the original source of knowledge—and the more vividly the images and pictures from the surrounding world need to be impressed on their minds. But vivid images are not just recorded in a child's brain as if on a roll of film. However vivid they are, representations are not an aim in themselves and not the goal of study. Intellectual education begins with theoretical thought, where living contemplation is not the end goal but a means to an end. A vivid image from the surrounding world is, for the teacher, a stimulus whose various forms, colours and sounds give rise to a thousand questions. In raising these questions the teacher is, so to speak, turning the pages of the Book of Nature.

I am looking at the first page of our 300 page Book of Nature. It is called 'Living and non-living'. At noon, on a warm, sunny day in early autumn, we walk to the bank of the river and stop in a grassy clearing. In front of us is a meadow, sprinkled with autumn flowers. In the transparent depths of the river fish are swimming. Butterflies are flitting in the air, and swallows are flying in the blue sky. We walk over to a tall cliff face, on which over many years a cross-section of soil has been exposed. With interest the children examine the many-coloured layers of clay and sand—yellow, red, orange and white.

We notice a thin layer of white clay, under it some golden sand, and below that some beautiful cube-shaped crystals. The children compare the top layer of soil—black earth—with the deeper layers.

'What can we see in the top layer of soil, children?'

'Plant roots', answer the children. 'Down deep there aren't any roots.'

'Look, children, at the green clump of grass growing on the very edge of the cliff, and at that layer of golden sand. What is the difference between the grass and the sand?'

'The grass grows in summer, fades in autumn, and comes to life again in spring', say the children. 'The grass has little seeds that scatter on the earth and new shoots grow from them …'

'And the sand?' I want all the children—especially the slow thinkers: Petrik, Valya and Nina—to compare objects in the surrounding world. There are still children in the class whose stream of thought can be compared to a slow, full river: Misha and Sashko. And there is one little girl, Lyuda, whose thinking processes are still a complete mystery to me. At first I thought that her intellectual development was delayed and that it was difficult for her to understand things that the other children grasped easily. But in the girl's lively, impressionable eyes I sensed thoughts that were restrained by some inner effort; it was as if the child was in no hurry to say what she knew very well …

'Look children, here is some golden sand, and here is some green grass. Or even better, here is some green sand, and here is some green grass. In what way are they unlike each other; what makes them different?'

The children think, looking at the green meadow and the bare cliff. Lyuda's eyes are thoughtful; Petrik is frowning; Valya is pouring sand from one hand to the other.

'Sand does not have any flowers, but grass does', says Lyuda.

'Cows graze on grass, but just try grazing cows on sand!' exclaims Petrik.

'Grass grows when it rains', reflects Misha, 'but have you ever heard of sand growing from rain?'

'Sand is deep in the earth, but grass is on the surface of the earth', suggests Yura.

But Seryozha objects: 'Don't you get sand on the river bank? Grass reaches for the sun, but sand only warms itself in the sun …'

Then we compare a little pebble that someone has picked up with the small green leaf of a maple tree, a shard of red glass with a camomile flower, a fish swimming in a pond with a goose feather, the iron railings of a bridge with the stalk of a hop plant entwining a tree. The children's thoughts are bubbling over. The boys and girls notice obvious connections between the objects and phenomena of the surrounding world, and also discover connections that are not so obvious. Gradually in the children's minds their first notions of living and non-living take shape. Some things are alive and some are not alive—the children can see this from many observations—but they cannot answer when I ask them, 'What distinguishes the living from the non-living?' Gradually working towards a conclusion, their thinking constantly comes back to what their eyes can see. Along with correct characteristics, the children make some mistakes, which are corrected in the process of real life observations made on the spot. When Kostya says: 'Living things move, but non-living things do not move', nearly everyone agrees with him, but then there is a silence while the children look around them, and objections are heard:

'That stick is moving, floating on the river, but does that make it alive?'

'A tractor moves, but it's not alive.'

'The moss on an old roof doesn't move, but it's alive, isn't it? Or is moss non-living?'

'And sand also moves. When we were at the quarry we saw the sand flowing in streams.'

No, it turns out that movement is not what matters. How is the living distinguished from the non-living? The children compare objects from the surrounding world over and over. Shura exclaims joyfully,

'Living things grow, but non-living things do not grow!'

The children consider these words, and again their gazes are directed to the surrounding objects. They reason aloud: grass is alive, grass grows; a tree is alive, it grows; the dogrose bush is alive, the dogrose grows; a stone is not alive, it does not grow; sand is not alive, because it does not grow. It is true: everything that is alive grows; everything that is not alive does not grow … Misha is thinking about something and looking off into the distance. Is he hearing the words of his friends? When the children have listed all the living and non-living things surrounding them, the boy says,

'Living things cannot live without the sun', and he points at the forest, the meadow and the field.

These words convince me yet again, that slow thinkers are often distinguished by their keen perception, attentiveness and observation. Misha's words light up the children's minds. 'Why didn't I think of that before?' the girls and boys are asking themselves. Their tenacious thoughts again reach out to explore the objects of the surrounding world, and the children again think aloud: 'Neither grass, nor flowers, nor trees, nor wheat can live without the sun. People also cannot live without the sun … Or could a human being live without the sun? No, is it possible to imagine people living deep underground? We know very well that grass dies in the shade of a spreading tree. And father says, "If the sun warms the soil after the rain the winter crops will send up green shoots, but if the sun does not shine things will be bad …" But a stone is the same, whether it is in the sun or in a cellar. No, not quite the same, in a cellar it will be covered with mould … And what about mould? Is that alive or not? The sun is not always helpful; it can burn the crops if there is no rain for a long time. So all living things love not only sunshine, but water.'

In such streams the children's thoughts flow in all directions, and then come together into a single current as it becomes more and more clear to the children that there are processes going on in all living things that we do not yet understand, but that depend on the sun, on water, and on everything that surrounds us in nature ... The children are reading the first lines on the first of 300 pages of the Book of Nature. They have understood that the whole world consists of two elements—living and non-living. Their first notions of living and non-living give rise to a multiplicity of questions. On the way home, the children examine phenomena that had previously seemed commonplace, noticing things they had not noticed before, and the more they notice the more questions arise: why does the little shoot from an acorn turn into a mighty oak tree? Where do the leaves, branches and the thick trunk come from? Why do leaves fall from the trees in autumn? Do trees grow in winter or not? It is not possible to answer all these questions at once and we should not set ourselves such a goal. It is good that the children have all these questions. It is good that in thinking, the children are turning to the primary source of knowledge and thought: to the surrounding world. It is good that they find precise, appropriate words to convey their thoughts. Clarity of thought—that most important attribute of thinking—is acquired in the process of direct communion with the surrounding world.

Children think in images, colours and sounds, but that does not mean that they should remain at the stage of concrete thinking. Thinking in images is a necessary stage for the transition to thinking in concepts. I tried to ensure that the children were gradually able to operate with concepts such as phenomenon, cause, effect, event, conditionality, dependency, difference, similarity, commonality, compatibility, incompatibility, possibility, impossibility and others. The experience of many years had convinced me that such concepts play a major role in the development of abstract thinking. It is impossible to master such concepts without investigating living facts and phenomena, without reflection on what children can see with their own eyes, without a gradual transition from concrete objects, facts and phenomena to abstract generalisation. The questions that arise in children's minds as they study nature facilitate this transition. I taught my pupils to observe the concrete phenomena of nature, and to seek cause and effect relationships. Thanks to this close connection between thought and concrete images, the children gradually acquired the ability to operate with abstract concepts. Of course this was a lengthy process that took years.

Reading the Book of Nature was of great interest to the children, but that interest is not an end in itself. Soviet pedagogy does not believe in relying too heavily on what children's immediate interests are or in making children's activities the ultimate objective of the process of instruction. Even in the nineteenth century, Konstantin Ushinsky wrote: 'Teach a child to do not only what is entertaining, but also what is not entertaining—to do it for the sake of fulfilling his duty. You will prepare a child for life, for in life not all duties are entertaining.'[17]

\* \* \*

In Soviet pedagogy the personal interests of the child are seen as a means of achieving the school's instructional and educational goals—the acquisition of a range of scientific knowledge, the formation of personal scientific-materialist convictions. I did not see reading the pages of the Book of Nature as an entertaining pastime or an amusing game, but as a pathway into the world of scientific knowledge. The children were reflecting on phenomena in the surrounding world in which the laws of nature were revealed. The teacher

---

17 Ushinsky, KD, *Sochineniya*, vol. 6, Moscow: Russian Academy of Pedagogical Sciences Press, 1949, p. 252.

had chosen the content of the Book of Nature not on the basis of the personal interests of each child, but on the basis of the dialectic of scientific knowledge of the world. This is the main difference between the aims of student activities in Soviet pedagogical theory and the well-known position of the pragmatists: that activity of itself gives knowledge.

Activities in Soviet pedagogy are not a substitute for systematic scientific education, but a means of achieving instructional and educational goals. At the same time, activities facilitating the acquisition of knowledge are meaningless without the personal interest of the child. In Soviet pedagogy, interest is considered to be the active involvement of the student's creative spiritual energies in the process of interpreting and investigating. Interest in what is studied and learnt deepens as the truths that the student assimilates become personal convictions.

We read the pages of the Book of Nature one after another and learn to think. The second page with which the children become acquainted is called 'The non-living is connected to the living'. We go to the greenhouse to see how the older students are growing cucumbers, tomatoes, barley and oats in that very same golden sand that is taken from deep underground, and in small fragments of crushed rock. The little ones see how they pour sand and crushed rock into metal and wooden boxes, and irrigate that mixture with a solution of chemicals. The roots of the cucumbers and tomatoes derive nourishment from that medium so they can grow and bear fruit. Dead fragments of rock and a white powder dissolved in water—that seems to be all that is needed for life. And in some flat containers, green stalks of barley are growing even without the sand and rock: the roots are absorbing nutrients from the solution of white powder. But when the children carefully examine the process of flowering and fruit bearing, they see that the non-living becomes a medium for the living only in the presence of sunlight and water. Life is impossible without light, warmth and water. Today is overcast and electric lamps are burning in the greenhouse. Outside it is a cool morning, but in the greenhouse central heating pipes are warming the air.

The teacher says, 'Look very carefully at everything you can see, and consider whether the living can exist without the non-living. Here is a big chest with lots of little drawers containing various chemical fertilisers. Look at how your older schoolmates are taking white, yellow and grey powder from different drawers, mixing it, and dissolving it in water. And over here they are making a fertile soil, mixing course sand with humus. Can you see the juicy tomatoes that are growing in this mixture? Where does a plant get the building material for its leaves, stems and fruit? From the non-living. The non-living provides an environment for the living.' These truths awaken in the children's souls a feeling of wonder at the secrets of nature.

Again I am reminded of an ancient saying attributed to Aristotle: thinking begins with wonder. Sincere feelings of wonder as one discovers the secrets of nature provide a powerful stimulus for burgeoning thought. Yes, I have been convinced of the deep meaning of these words a thousand times. Wonder and amazement give rise to questions. When the children see how so many different plants—tomatoes, cucumbers, barley—are growing in a solution of chemicals, they bombard me with questions: 'How does that transparent solution turn into thick stems, bright flowers with bees flitting about them, and juicy fruit?', 'Where does the life come from? The sun does not carry bits of green to the plant; it only gives light and warmth', 'Why do green cucumbers and red tomatoes grow from the same solution?', 'Why is the cucumber green and the tomato red when they are growing next to each other?', 'What is in those different coloured powders?', 'Why do plants get greener from humus in the soil?'

Those first visual demonstrations of the link between the living and the non-living are so important for children's ongoing intellectual development! As they reflect on the questions 'Where does living substance come from?' and 'How does the sun "make" the living out of the non-living?', children are preparing to read the great book of life, to learn the secrets of complex processes.

I saw reading the Book of Nature as a means of promoting independent intellectual activity. Concepts, pictures, images—these are just the beginning of active thought. 'Any method is bad', wrote Diesterweg, 'if it teaches students only perception and passivity, and is good to the extent that it awakens independence.'[18] I tried to ensure that reading the pages of the Book of Nature did not take the form of just perceiving the pictures and images of nature, but provided a basis for active thought, for theorising about the world, for systematic scientific knowledge.

'The best content', writes the Soviet psychologist G Kostyuk, 'reaches the consciousness of students when it is part of their own activity.'[19] Not activity for activity's sake, or for satisfying personal interests, but activity that reveals the content of scientific knowledge: therein lies the true link between activity and scientific efficacy in Soviet pedagogy.

'Everything in nature changes'—that is the name of the next page in our Book of Nature. We return to this page several times. On a clear midday in autumn the class goes to the orchard. The branches of the apple and pear trees are weighed down with fruit. 'Do you remember, children, what the orchard was like in winter?' asks the teacher. 'Bare branches covered in frost, trunks covered in snow ... And now the branches are covered in thick foliage, and the apples and pears are swelling with the sap of the earth.'

---

18 Diesterweg, A, *Izbrannye pedagogicheskie sochineniya* [Selected pedagogical works], Moscow: Uchpedgiz, 1956, p. 128.

19 Kostyuk, G, 'Psikhologichni pitannya polipshennya yakosti uroku' [Psychological issues in improving the quality of lessons], in *Psikhologichni pitannya polipshennya yakosti uroku: zbirnik*, Kyiv: Radianska shkola, 1959, p. 5.

Two months later we return to the orchard. What is it like now? Yellow leaves form a soft carpet on the earth and the branches are half bare. Standing next to each other are an old, hollow apple tree and a little self-sown tree. The old apple tree was planted by our grandparents. Half its branches have withered. Only a few branches have leaves, but they bear large, juicy fruit. The old apple tree will stand in the sunshine for another year or two, and then we will have to cut it down. But on the slender trunk of the self-sown tree is a tender green shoot where students have grafted a bud from the old tree. The years will pass, and the shoot will turn into a flowering apple tree, and golden fruit will ripen.

'Look around you children. Is there even a single plant that always stays the same?'

The children do not have much life experience, but from infancy they have lived in the world of work and of nature, and they know that plants are born, flower and bear fruit … They talk about how a tender green shoot appears from the earth, how it turns into the thick stalk of the plant, how buds open on trees and leaves appear … The children are amazed at the rapid changes that happen in the world of the living, sometimes occurring in leaps and bounds. Yesterday we were in the peach orchard and saw black buds on bare branches. Today we come early in the morning and a new picture greets us: the branches are covered in little pink flowers … Why did the buds open so quickly, in a single night? Why did the whole tree flower at once? Does the tree sleep at night or not? In general, do trees sleep or not? Does it hurt the tree when they prune branches? Why does a tree get old and die? I had to think for a long time to find answers to these questions. But the answers led to a new barrage of questions.

We read this page of the Book of Nature on the bank of a pond, in a gulley, in a thicket and in a field. In shallow water some little tadpoles are swimming—the children know they turn into frogs, but how does that happen? Why is it that a little fish in an aquarium already looks like a fish, but a tadpole looks nothing like a frog? We observe how the collective farm workers rear silkworms. From a little egg, as small as a poppy seed, appears a voracious baby worm. It eats only mulberry leaves—why? The baby worm grows into a big worm that sheds its skin several times, leaving the old skin behind—why? Then it wraps a silken web around itself and hides in a little golden house, its cocoon. What is happening to it inside? We take several cocoons, put them on the window sill, and after some time we see some beautiful, big butterflies emerge. The butterflies lay eggs and the same cycle repeats itself all over again. How does the worm make the fine silk thread? Why does it eat so many mulberry leaves before it is time to spin its cocoon?

The more their activity is connected with the active exploration of nature, the deeper and more meaningful the children's perception of the surrounding world becomes. With every month they notice more and more phenomena that they had not previously paid attention to. For instance they observe forms of life unlike anything they had seen before. In a dark, damp cellar, white threads appear on potato tubers. What are they, roots or future shoots? On the dark, northern side of tree trunks, green moss grows—why is it hiding from the sun? Why doesn't moss have seeds? How does it reproduce? All plants flower, but moss doesn't flower. What sort of plant is that?

Some lines in the Book of Nature convince the children that it is not only living things that change. We go to a cliff on the river bank. The children examine the grey stones and notice that they have fine cracks in them. On one stone a thin layer peels off, and crumbles in our hands. Does that mean a stone does not always remain a stone? The children remember how several months earlier, they had said, 'A stone is the same, whether it is in the sun or in a cellar.' During the day stones heat up, and at night they cool down. Cracks appear, and water seeps into the cracks. It turns out that a stone does not last forever.

Analysing the lessons in thought devoted to the page 'Everything in nature changes', I became convinced that as children learn more and discover previously unnoticed natural laws in everyday life, their desire to learn deepens, their sense organs become more sensitive to the phenomena of the surrounding world, and connections between sense organs and thought processes become more subtle. In the works of the Soviet anthropologist Professor MF Nesturkh there are some words that, in my opinion, provide a key to understanding the process of a child's intellectual development: 'Subjected, during the childhood years, to a constant flow of more and more new information, it is at this age in particular that a human being develops a growing urge to learn.'

The flow of information: that is the most important precondition for full intellectual development. But what happens if, for one reason or another, that flow of information weakens and is not augmented? What a child sees by himself is not a flow of information. Human education consists of elders passing their knowledge of the surrounding world on to children, constantly feeding the flow of information with the energy of their thought, bringing their influence to bear upon the child.

I began to study the family environment of each child, from the time of their birth up to their enrolment at school. I discovered some interesting correlations. If children are left to themselves during the preschool years and their elders do not create the flow of information essential to a normal human environment, a child's brain remains in a state of inertia. Curiosity and the thirst for knowledge fade, and indifference develops. Is it not true that a growing urge to learn provides the driving force behind thinking, and determines to a huge extent the intellectual development of a child? This does appear to be true.

Petrik was left to himself as a child. His mother and grandfather left for work in the morning, and he was left at home alone. He was left inside a play pen under the eaves of the barn or on some grass. From time to time a neighbour looked in to make sure he was all right. That is how Petrik was 'brought up' from the age of two to the age of five. It was a vegetative kind of upbringing. The child was well fed, clothed and shod, but deprived of the most important thing: human company. From the age of five Petrik played outside with other children, mainly his own age. When he came to school he did not know the meaning of some very simple words in his native language. His indifferent eyes skimmed over the things that surrounded him and seemed like the eyes of a little old man. I concluded that the living material supporting thought—the cells of the cerebral cortex—were inert in this child, because during the most important period in the development of the nervous system, during the infancy of the brain, the boy was deprived of the natural flow of information from the surrounding world. That is why reading the Book of Nature should play a major role in this child's education.

We turn to the next page: 'The seeds of life'. In autumn the children collect the seeds of pears, apples, peaches and plums to sow in our fruit tree nursery bed. The children know from experience that plants grow from seeds. In spring and summer, when life blooms in the steppe, forests and woods, seeds ripen on the plants and the life of the species continues. We go on an excursion. The spring breeze plucks white balls of fluff from the poplars and the dandelions. The children find little seeds in the middle of these light fluffy balls. They are amazed at the care nature has taken to look after these seeds. They do not grip the surface of dry soil, but as soon as they come in contact with damp soil they stick, 'anchoring themselves', and the seeds send forth shoots. The children read each line of this page of the Book of Nature with interest. They see how many plants 'shoot' out little grains so that little seeds of life fly in all directions. They see how, when a poppy head is tossed in the wind, the first poppy seeds to ripen fly out of little 'windows'. With a magnifying glass we examine the 'cunning' hooks, pads and 'crampons' by which many seeds grip on to people's clothes or the fur of animals. We make a collection of seeds from grain crops. The children think about how a big plant grows from a little seed. Is a seed living or non-living? The children read some interesting lines from this page in winter: some plants cast their seeds in the snow. The seed have to lie in the snow for several weeks before they will germinate.

The stronger the urge to acquire knowledge, the greater the interest with which children work and the more deeply they explore the experimental nature of work. The flow of information from the surrounding world becomes a particularly strong stimulus for learning when the hands assist thinking, when through their work children are trying to find the answers to exciting questions, to solve a puzzle, to prove the truth of something that is still only a hypothesis. Children who have become hard workers, not because they are forced to but because they really want to, will become true thinkers. Children's desire to work hard comes mainly from the desire to find out something new. If that desire is developed, children's interest in work will be strengthened. The love for work that we speak of in educational practice is in fact a fusion of curiosity, the thirst for knowledge and a child's feeling of self-worth.

A deep impression is made on the minds and the emotional memories of the children by journeys devoted to one of the most exciting pages of the Book of Nature: 'The sun is the source of life'. On a hot and sultry day in summer we visit a field, an orchard and a grape plantation. We can see a field of wheat and sunflowers, bunches of grapes, pears turning yellow, and ripening tomatoes. In these gifts of fertility the children see the light and warmth of the sun. Thanks to the sun, the earth gives people everything they need. This conclusion was arrived at after numerous observations and comparisons, and the establishment of cause and effect relationships, awakening the little ones' sense of wonder and providing a fresh stimulus for their flights of thought. The children examine the surrounding world, thinking about the origins of each object, and their sense of wonder deepens even more when they become convinced that the sun is the sole source of life.

Grain, potatoes, sunflowers—nothing could exist without the sun. Meat, milk and butter would also not exist, because animals feed on what grows in the earth thanks to the sun's light and warmth. The astounded children ask: 'And what is the sun? Where does the warmth of the sun come from? Why does the sun warm the earth so little in winter? It won't go out will it? What will happen if it is put out?'

The questions that arise while reading the Book of Nature mark the beginning of a headlong flight of thought towards that high point in learning, from which, in several years' time, the complexity of life's secrets will become apparent. I took care to see that my pupils were inquisitive researchers and explorers of the world; that truth was not presented to them by the teacher on a platter as a ready-made conclusion, but as a vivid picture of the surrounding world experienced with a quickened heartbeat. If a discovery excited children, the truth would become a personal conviction, treasured for life. Intellectual feelings, experiencing the joy of discovery, awe at nature's grandeur and at the beauty and harmony of her laws—these give rise to a strong memory.

I saw in such intellectual feelings the main means for developing and strengthening the memories of certain children. Valya had a very poor memory. Everything seemed to go in one ear and out the other. I had to ensure that the girl's heart beat faster from a feeling of wonder at the images of the surrounding world. For several days we went to the fields, the forest, the river bank, the orchard and the apiary, to study the page of the Book of Nature entitled 'Every living creature adapts to its environment'. I directed the children's attention to the fact that some flowers close their petals in hot weather and open them when the cool of evening comes. I showed them how the slender stem of a snowdrop pierces a thick layer of dead leaves like an arrow, how bees build hives and fill the honeycomb with honey, how the roots of a grapevine penetrate the soil to a depth of three metres to obtain moisture, how the branch of a weeping willow sends down roots when it drops into silt so a new tree can grow … These discoveries filled the girl's heart with joyful excitement. The expression of indifference in the child's eyes was replaced with lively interest. Silent Valya started talking, and asked: 'And how does a bee know which way to fly home? How does it find its hive? Aren't the snowdrops cold? There is still snow under the trees.' Wherever there is a question, there is thought; and wherever there is thought, the memory retains pictures of the surrounding world and of the laws of nature.

Here are the names of some pages of the Book of Nature that we read one after another: 'The plant and animal kingdoms', 'The journey of a drop of water', 'People use the forces of nature', 'Nature wakes up in spring', 'The longest days of summer', 'Spring flowers in the forests, fields and meadows', 'Summer flowers', 'Lilies and violets', 'Chrysanthemums—the children of autumn', 'Life in a pond', 'The last days of an Indian summer', 'Nature waits for winter', 'The first winter morning', 'The life of birds in a winter forest', 'Ears of wheat', 'The life of a bee colony', 'A swallow builds its nest', 'A thunderstorm approaches', 'Gloomy autumn weather', 'The world of flowers in the middle of winter', 'A forest stores moisture', 'The storks have arrived', 'Birds prepare to migrate to warmer lands', 'The sun after a summer shower', 'A rainbow over the river', 'Winter and spring crops', 'The sunflowers have bloomed', 'Stars in the sky', 'The life of the soil', 'A green leaf is the sun's pantry', 'Mushrooms and moss', 'How an oak tree grows from an acorn' and many others.

'A bad teacher presents the truth, a good one teaches how to discover it', wrote Diesterweg.[20] Nowadays an investigative approach to the phenomena of the surrounding world takes on a special significance. It is very important that children's thinking is based on investigation and research, that the realisation of a scientific truth should be preceded by the accumulation, analysis, juxtaposition and comparison of facts. Observing the phenomena and pictures of nature, a child learns to master the forms and processes of thought and acquires concepts, each of which embodies real cause and effect relationships, detected by the sharp eyes of the inquisitive observer. Experience confirmed that the thought processes of children reading the Book of Nature were distinguished by a remarkable characteristic: when operating with abstract concepts, the children mentally referred to those ideas, images and pictures that had formed a basis for the development of those concepts.

When my pupils who had read the Book of Nature in childhood became adolescents and then young men and women, I was especially interested to see how their active exploration of the surrounding world influenced their general intellectual development, the character and style of their intellectual work, and the variety of their intellectual interests. I became convinced that the intellectual life of those students was distinguished by a thirst for knowledge. They were interested in everything. Everything that surrounded them touched their feelings and thoughts. One of the features of the intellectual life of my pupils in adolescence and youth was the ability to see the interconnections between various phenomena and objects. Anything that was not clear, that they did not understand, they looked up in books. For them books became a source of knowledge and a spiritual imperative.

---

20 Diesterweg, A, *Izbrannye pedagogicheskie sochineniya* [Selected pedagogical works], Moscow: Uchpedgiz, 1956, p. 158.

# *What comes from where?*[21]

NATURE IS AN ABUNDANT RESOURCE for educating people. But knowledge of nature is just a starting point for the development of the intellect, emotions, attitudes and convictions. People live in society, and in essence a person's whole life is made up of the relationships entered into with other people. I tried to ensure that during the four years the children were studying in primary school, they gradually came to an understanding of an important truth. People owe their lives to the fact that their material and spiritual needs are met by hundreds and thousands of other people. It is impossible to live in society without providing material and spiritual benefits to hundreds and thousands of other people. In work, through the process of interrelating with society, people's moral characters are formed: their spiritual culture, attitudes to life, and world outlook. One of a teacher's main educational objectives is to ensure that children understand and feel with their hearts that, in our society, one person's relationship to another and their social identity as a citizen, is expressed through the creation of material and spiritual wealth.

Experience has convinced me that children come to an understanding of social relationships via an understanding of things, in part from thinking about the question of what comes from where.

We are dining in the school cafeteria and washing the dishes. Wait a moment children, do not leave the cafeteria. Let us sit here at the tables for half an hour. Let us think about where all the things we

---

21 Translator's note: This short chapter was not in the original 1966 manuscript, but was written for the first edition in response to editorial advice. The translator has included it in the belief that it will be of interest to educators in English-speaking countries.

have made use of today have come from. Where have all the things that we enjoy here in the cafeteria come from?

The children list everything they have eaten: bread, meat, potatoes, milk, butter, eggs ... The food was cooked in an oven built not long ago with new bricks by stove-setters. The oven is fired by coal, and the coal has been brought from a mine. We are sitting at a table on chairs. The table and chairs are made from metal tubes and plastic ...

'Is that everything?' I ask.

'That's everything', the children reply.

'Look a bit harder. There are some things you have not noticed ...'

In the corner is a refrigerator. It could not work without electricity. On the walls are light fittings in which electric light globes are shining. Will the little ones notice these things?

They notice them. They are full of wonder at the thought that without electricity it would be so difficult to live at home or study at school.

Where did all these things without which we could not live come from?

With this question we began our journeys into the world of economic activity, into the complex world of work relationships. Every step we took brought new discoveries. The children experienced feelings of deep respect for working people when they realised that the work of nearly all their parents was essential in order to put bread on the table. But that was not all. The work of all the workers who built tractors, ploughs and combine harvesters was also essential. Without these machines you could not grow grain. The work of miners was essential. Without coal you could not smelt the metal required to make machines.

Equally striking discoveries were made when we familiarised ourselves with other things. Hundreds of people in many different trades in near and distant cities and villages of our homeland had to work hard to bring the coal from the mines to our school kitchen. Hundreds of people had to work to smelt metal, and to make our tables from it, to make bricks for us from sand and clay.

Then in the same way we took further steps in the study of economic activity and the world of work relationships, learning where our clothes came from, where paper comes from, who made our books and films, and who composed our music. Week after week, month after month, we discovered the complex web of social relationships. We came to know people through the world of things. Things—our material and spiritual wealth—helped us to see, understand and feel humanity. In the children's eyes the baker, Stepan Maksimovich, who we met at his workplace, was not just a person earning money through his simple work so he could buy bread, clothes and many other things, but a creator of life. Without him hundreds, even thousands of people could not live. Each week we met with workers who produced material and spiritual benefits for hundreds and thousands of other people: combine operators, tractor drivers, metalworkers and lathe operators. One spring day after the completion of studies in grade three, we travelled to the Kremenchuk hydroelectric power station to see how electricity is produced and met with the power engineers.

For the formation of children's moral character it is very important what attitude the people they meet have towards their work. The fact that these people, who produced such ordinary and apparently unremarkable material goods as bread, meat, milk and sugar, took pride in their work and saw it as a service to society, made a profound impact on the children's hearts. The truth that work elevates people and brings them great happiness was not some abstraction for the children, but the very essence of life. Even in childhood, these young people were convinced that the most important field of endeavour in which they could develop their strength and their creative abilities was honest work in the service of society.

# A thousand problems from the maths book of life

ONE OF A SCHOOL'S MAIN objectives is to educate people with inquisitive, creative minds. I see the childhood years as a school in thought and the teacher as someone who nurtures the spiritual world of his pupils during the formative years. To care for the development and strengthening of a child's brain, to ensure that this mirror reflecting the world always remains sensitive and receptive, is one of the main responsibilities of an educator. Just as the muscles develop and strengthen from physical exercise in the process of overcoming difficulty, so work and exercise are essential for the formation and development of the brain.

A child's brain develops and strengthens as a result of a complex internal process of excitement of the cells, which occurs simultaneously with the establishment of multiple connections between various objects and phenomena in the surrounding world—cause and effect, temporal and functional connections. When students ponder, seek understanding, and try to make sense of connections that are not yet understood, it is as if microscopic muscles in the cells of the cortex are exerting themselves, developing the strength which will become the intellect. I considered it my role to help the children understand the connections between the phenomena of the surrounding world so that those 'microscopic muscles' gained new energy each time they were exercised. This complex phenomenon is what happens during the formation, strengthening and development of the brain and of its most important quality—an inquisitive, sharp, observant mind.

The functioning of the human brain is discrete (discontinuous, interrupted). The excitement stimulated by the flow of information from the surrounding world occurs now in one group of cells of the cerebral cortex, now in another. Thought instantly switches between the objects of cognition, and this switching back and forth is an important characteristic of the process of thought. The ability to quickly switch thought—and this switching corresponds to the transmission of an impulse from one group of cells to another—is the main precondition for good intellectual ability. A child can think—this means that in the course of a given interval of time (for example a second) thought switches from one object to another many times—so quickly that the person thinking is not aware of the switching. It seems to them that they are simultaneously thinking of the area of a swimming pool and of two taps from which water is flowing at different rates into the pool. In other words, the student is simultaneously holding in their mind various objects and phenomena, analysing and comparing them. Our task is to see that this crucial ability of the brain is developed in every child.

Problems whose solutions require quick-wittedness are a form of exercise that arouses the internal energies of the brain, stimulating the play of the 'intellectual muscles'. Such problems are to be found in the objects and phenomena of the surrounding world. I would direct children's attention to some phenomenon or other and try to get them to see hidden connections that they had not yet grasped, so as to awaken an urge to understand the essence of those connections, to understand the truth. The key to understanding a problem is always found in activity and work. Making an intellectual effort, striving to establish connections between objects and phenomena, the children carry out certain work. In the surrounding world there are thousands of problems. They are part of our folk culture and take the form of interesting stories and riddles. Here is one of the first problems that the children solved during their leisure time:

'You have to transport a wolf, a goat and a cabbage from one side of a river to the other. You must not leave together or take at the same time the wolf and the goat, or the goat and the cabbage. You can only take the wolf with the cabbage or each "passenger" by itself. You can make as many trips as you like. How is it possible to take the wolf, the goat and the cabbage across the river, without any mishaps?'

Folk pedagogy knows hundreds of such riddles. Little children show a lot of interest in these problems. So all the boys and girls started thinking about how to take the 'passengers' across in such a way that the wolf does not eat the goat and the goat does not eat the cabbage. We were sitting on the bank of a pond. The children drew the river in the sand, and found little pebbles. Perhaps not all the children would be able to solve the problem, but the fact that the children were thinking intensely meant they were developing their mental powers.

Solving such riddles is similar to the intellectual effort involved in playing chess. In both activities you have to remember several planned moves. I gave this problem to the children when they were seven years old, soon after they started their first year at school. In ten minutes three of the children had solved it: Shura, Seryozha and Yura. With these children a rapid chain of thoughts, racing ahead, was combined with a keen, retentive memory. After fifteen minutes nearly all the children had solved the riddle, but again Valya, Nina, Petrik and Slava got nowhere. I saw that their train of thought seemed to break midstream. The little ones understood the meaning of the problem and had a clear conception of the objects and phenomena, but as soon as they made their first assumptions the concepts that had been so clear in their minds began to fade; in other words, the children forgot what they had remembered only a moment earlier.

From the rich treasure house of our folk pedagogy I chose more and more problems, mostly in the hope that my slow thinkers would develop interest in the content and storylines of these riddles. A few days later I set the following folk riddle:

'A small detachment of soldiers came to a river that they had to cross. The bridge was broken and the river was deep. What could they do? Suddenly the officer noticed two boys playing in a boat near the river bank. But the boat was so small that it would hold only one soldier or the two boys, and no more. However, all the soldiers crossed in that boat. How?'

Again I observed the children thinking. Again they drew in the sand, trying to hold several 'chess moves' in their memory. Again I noticed that Nina, Slava and Petrik looked despondent. Valya's eyes were shining with joy: she had solved the problem.

I began to work separately with the slow thinkers. I gave them simpler folk riddles aimed at developing understanding of a sequence of natural numbers, and at establishing the interrelationships between numbers. Here are five such riddles:

1. Falcons and Oaks. Some falcons flew down and settled in some oak trees. If one falcon sits in each oak tree, there will be a falcon left over. If two falcons sit in each oak tree, there will be an oak tree left over. How many falcons are there and how many oak trees?

2. In the Pasture. Two boys were grazing some sheep. If the first boy gave the second boy one sheep, they would have the same number. If the second boy gave the first boy one sheep, the first boy would have twice as many sheep as the second boy. How many sheep did each shepherd have?

3. How many Geese? A flock of geese is flying and a lone goose flies to meet them. 'Hello a hundred geese', says the lone goose. 'No, there are not a hundred of us', say the geese. 'If there were as many as there are, and as many again, and half as many again, and a quarter as many again, plus you goose, only then would there be a hundred.' How many geese were flying altogether?

4. Heads and feet. In the yard hens are strutting and rabbits are hopping: ten heads and twenty-four feet altogether. How many rabbits and how many hens?

5. How many balls? In a bag are ten yellow balls, ten red balls, five green balls and five black balls. With your eyes closed, how many

balls do you need to take before you can be sure you have seven balls the same colour?

These riddles are an indispensable means for training the mind. To solve each of them you need to remember between two and four previous and subsequent 'chess moves'. Half a year after beginning this work Valya and Slava were able to solve riddles like these. Petrik and Nina still could not. They could not hold in their memories the information they needed to make the next 'chess move'.

How can we explain this phenomenon? It would appear that some children have not yet mastered the ability to switch their thought from one object to another, which is experienced subjectively as the ability to hold in one's memory all the component elements of a problem, to mentally grasp several 'chess moves'. Why this capacity of the cells of the cerebral cortex has not been developed is another question. It is certainly not always the case that this is determined by some inherited characteristics of the grey matter, but we should not ignore this as a possible cause. Observations confirm: if the train of thought is suddenly broken, if a child cannot simultaneously pay attention to things they are picturing now and things pictured several moments ago, they do not have the ability to think and it is difficult for them to establish connections between various objects and phenomena.

I studied children's thought, especially that of the slow thinkers like Valya, Petrik and Nina, not for theoretical purposes, but in order to lighten their intellectual load and teach them how to study. My observations confirmed that first of all we need to teach children to picture a series of objects, phenomena or events and work out the connections between them. A child must gradually progress from a deepened awareness of the essence and internal properties of a single object to an awareness of a series of objects, as if seeing them from a distance. Studying the thought processes of the slow thinkers, I became more and more convinced that the inability to comprehend a problem, for example, is the result of an inability to think abstractly, to abstract oneself from the concrete. We have to teach children to think using abstract concepts. It would be better if Valya was not constructing a concrete image of the wolf in her imagination, if her thought was not distracted by the image of the goat reaching for the cabbage. For her these images should be abstract concepts. But the way to the abstract is through a deep understanding of the concrete. We have to imagine what is going on in children's heads when they are thinking. We have to educate the ability to think; otherwise children will strain their memories and cram, which will blunt their thinking even more.

I tried to imagine what was occurring in my pupils' heads. Perhaps my conception of it is over-simplified, but I am convinced that to some extent it gives a true reflection of the picture of thought. When a child mentally transfers attention from one object to another, a new group of brain cells are excited. The train of thought will continue its onward surge as long as the threads linking the new centre of excitement and the centre that was excited under the influence of the previous picture (image, perception) are not broken, and impulses or signals continue to be sent back and forth between them. It is as if the new mental image announces its presence to the earlier, already established image, and the earlier mental image reminds the new one of its existence. This extremely rapid exchange occurs many times in an instant, and this process is what we are talking about when we say a child is thinking or considering. The stronger the threads linking the centres of excitement, the deeper a thought is, and the wider the circle of objects and phenomena that children can encompass with their intellects.

The strength of these threads apparently depends upon the very nature of the living material of the brain, upon the individual characteristics of the grey matter and the subtle biochemical processes taking place in the brain. But it also depends upon characteristics of the environment (such as the flow of information discussed earlier), which determine, to a large extent, the formation of intellectual capabilities during the infancy of the nervous system. There was no doubt that in the brain cells of Valya, Nina and Petrik, there was inadequate development of the nervous energy that determines the strength of the threads connecting the living islands of thought. The threads were weak, the connections between centres of excitement quickly faded, and the children were not able to simultaneously grasp several mental images. When Petrik tried to remember what was clear to him just a moment earlier and could not, it was as if I was witnessing the breaking of the thread of thought.

The reasons for this characteristic of some children's thought appear to vary. The main reason seems to be that during early childhood, when the flow of sensory input is particularly mixed and varied, the child does not think about the connections between the objects and phenomena of the surrounding world; the little living islands of thought in the child's brain are not connected by a two-way flow of information. This in turn is a result of the inattentiveness and indifference of adults to the development of the child's thinking. The child asks an adult 'Why?' once and does not get an answer; he asks a second time and the question remains unanswered. The indifference of adults (and sometimes the verbal abuse: 'Leave me alone, don't bother me!') weakens the fine threads that especially need strengthening at this age.

Another reason for this weakness in a child's thinking is a lack of emotional response to the phenomena of the surrounding world. In consequence the emotional impulses from the sub-cortex are weakened.

With each month of lessons I became more convinced of how important it was to give educational training to the parents of preschool children. It is necessary to have lots of discussions with mothers and fathers about education before children begin studying at school. Our concern for future generations of school children led us to create a school for parents, to which we invited the mothers and fathers of children aged from two to six. We compiled a program of lessons covering such issues as the physical, psychological, intellectual, moral and aesthetic development of children, and the role of parents in educating the thinking processes of future school students. This school for parents still continues to operate.

Parents' educational knowledge is especially important during the period when the mother and father are their child's only educators—during the preschool years. From age two to six the intellectual development and the spiritual life of children depends to a great extent on that elementary educational skill, which finds expression in a mother's or father's ability to understand the complex psychological motivation of a developing human being. We tried to equip parents with definite knowledge and skills. At the sessions of our school for parents we devoted considerable attention to the question of how to teach children to think, how to develop their intellectual capabilities. On the basis of many years' experience, we suggested 1000 questions about the surrounding world. These are questions most frequently put to parents by children and we explained how to respond when questioned by little ones, how to develop the children's curiosity and thirst for knowledge. Together with the parents we worked out a program of nature walks for preschool children and noted suitable objects for observation. Particular attention was given to promoting an atmosphere of respect for books in any family with preschool children.

Many years of observation have shown that there are also hereditary factors that can cause problems in intellectual development. Alcoholism in parents is a terrible enemy of the whole of a child's organism, but is especially harmful to the delicate grey matter of the brain.

Every time there were favourable conditions for solving problems that provided good exercise for the brain, I gathered around me those children who thought slowly and had trouble remembering things. I had to invent various riddles and problems, until eventually the first threads awoke between Nina's little living islands of thought, connecting ideas and images from the surrounding world.

I can remember a winter's day when we were sitting by the aquarium. The children were counting the fish; some counted more and some less. I set them the following problem: 'A little brother saw two big fish and four little fish in the aquarium. A little sister saw two big fish and three little fish. Mum saw three big fish and five little fish. Mum saw all the fish that were in the aquarium. How many fish were there in the aquarium?' For many of the children this problem did not present any difficulty, but Nina thought for a long time. Finally she clapped her hands joyfully: 'Of course, the little brother and sister did not see all the fish, but the mum saw all of them. In the aquarium there were three big fish and five little fish. They were hiding in the plants and you couldn't see them, but the mum saw them.' Valya and Petrik also started to solve problems like these, and some that were perhaps a little more difficult.

I gradually began to give these children more difficult problems, consolidating the success we had achieved. In the third year of school, when we were harvesting apples in the collective farm orchard, Nina solved the following riddle: 'Three brothers were cutting hay in a meadow. At midday they lay down to rest under an oak tree and fell asleep. Their sister brought them lunch: soup, bread and a few apples each. She did not wake them up, but left the lunch wrapped in a bundle and went home. The eldest brother woke up and saw the apples. He divided them into three equal shares, but he left one of his apples for the youngest brother, his favourite. Then he lay down and went back to sleep. The middle brother woke up, but he did not know that the eldest brother had already eaten some apples. He divided the apples into three equal shares, but he also left one of his apples for the youngest brother, who had a sweet tooth

… He lay down and went back to sleep. At last the youngest brother woke up. He saw seven apples in the bundle. He thought: how can I divide them into three equal shares? He thought and thought but could not work it out, until finally the other brothers woke up and explained everything. How many apples did the sister bring for her brothers?'

In our book of problems there were many problems about work that was familiar to the children. When solving these problems the children were able to draw on the experience of having observed again and again, how their elders tilled the soil and cleaned seeds, planted trees and applied fertiliser, harvested and stored food, built homes and repaired roads. The connections between ideas were strengthened by the prior establishment of corresponding connections in real life. Thought and memory were developed together. For the solution of the overwhelming majority of problems, the children resorted to a drawing or constructed a simple model of the objects under discussion. Riddles, problems and puzzles were published in a wall newspaper that the children produced from the second semester of the third year of school. Problem solving became something of a contest in persistence, determination and hard work. We conducted our first class maths Olympiad in grade three. The children were given problems of varying difficulty, to allow every child to achieve success. Gradually the maths Olympiads attracted the attention of other primary classes and were adopted across the school.

Solving problems from the maths book of the surrounding world during the childhood years awakens thought and teaches a child to think. There is no point talking about good knowledge of mathematics, or any other subject, if children have not learnt to think, if the process of thinking does not strengthen the brain.

The great Russian writer and educator Leo Tolstoy advised: 'Avoid all arithmetical definitions and rules, and instead get your students to complete as many operations as possible, and correct them not because they have not followed a rule, but because what they have done does not make sense.'[22] This is not at all to deny the role of theoretical generalisation, definitions and rules, as it may appear at first glance to a reader who has a preconceived notion regarding Tolstoy's 'free education'. On the contrary, this advice is aimed at ensuring that students have a deep understanding of the essence of definitions and rules, and that they see in a rule not some incomprehensible truth transported from somewhere external, but a principle flowing from the very nature of things. When a teacher approaches the truth in this way, children are able to discover definitions themselves. The joy of this discovery provides a powerful emotional stimulus that plays a major role in the development of thought. One should also not forget that Tolstoy's advice relates only to small children.

Solving problems from the maths book of the surrounding world is not the only means of improving learning outcomes in arithmetic. While it assisted the development of thought, it still played a supporting role and was subordinated to the requirements of the instructional and educational process during lessons. This approach can only be effective as part of a general system of methods and techniques applicable to intellectual, moral, aesthetic and vocational education. Figuratively speaking, I saw it as a bridge to the achievement of the main aim of the primary school—to give children a clearly defined range of sound knowledge and practical skills. When studying mathematics, it is particularly important to have precisely defined expectations and goals. For each year of study I defined exactly what students should have mastered and should retain firmly in their memories. The foundation of mathematical knowledge, upon which the soundness of further mathematical education depends, is knowledge of the principle of formation of the natural sequence of numbers [the

---

22 Tolstoy, LN, *Pedagogicheskie sochineniya* [Pedagogical works], Moscow: Uchpedgiz, 1953, p. 339.

positive integers]. I tried to ensure that even in grade one, every student could automatically answer any question involving addition or subtraction up to one hundred. To achieve this goal a system of exercises was compiled, incorporating an analysis of the composition of numbers. I could not imagine the creative work of students in the primary classes, or later, without a sound knowledge of the multiplication tables. The retention in the memory of a range of essential knowledge is an important precondition for creative thinking.

A child with a poor memory finds it difficult to think and to grasp new ideas. I had long been troubled by the question of how to strengthen and develop children's memories, how to equip them with concepts, truths and generalisations that would always be available as tools of thought. One means for developing memory was provided by our arithmetic box. This was a visual aid, the use of which helped children to check their knowledge of arithmetic. This checking was carried out in an entertaining way by constructing mathematical squares. The sides of the squares were made from wooden cubes and the numbers written on each cube added up to the same number on each side of the square. In the mathematics box there were special tasks aimed at repeating the multiplication tables.

Another wonderful means for developing and strengthening the memory was the electrical arithmetic board—a device that used electrical circuitry. Each student used this device to check their multiplication tables and the composition of the natural sequence of numbers. By grade three, we had begun to construct our own electrical arithmetic boards, and by the end of grade four we had four such devices. During this work I was convinced yet again of how important it is for students' intellectual development to combine thought with hands-on work. Children with poor memory strengthened it thanks to their participation in the preparation of visual aids. (Of course this yielded results in combination with other means of influencing the thought processes.)

In the education of thinking skills we reserved a special place for chess. Even during the School of Joy, Shura, Galya, Seryozha, Yura, Vanya, Misha and some other children learnt to play chess. The boys and girls often sat down to a chess board. Playing chess disciplined their thought and taught concentration. But the most important benefit was the development of memory. Observing the young chess players, I saw how the children mentally recreated past positions and imagined future positions. I really wanted Valya, Nina and Petrik to sit down to a chess board. I taught them how to play and the children pondered their next moves. The chess board helped me discover Lyuba's and Pavel's mathematical thinking. Until they played chess (these children began to play in grade three) I had not noticed the sharpness and retentiveness of their thought.

Without chess I cannot imagine the complete education of intellectual capabilities and memory. Playing chess should enter the life of primary schools as one of the elements of intellectual culture. I am talking especially of the primary school, where intellectual education occupies a special place and requires special forms and methods of working.

## *Our journeys around the globe*

A PRIMARY SCHOOL TEACHER SHOULD strive to ensure that children's horizons gradually widen to encompass not only their local fields and forests, but the natural landscapes and life of their homeland, and of the whole earth.

In grade one the children already knew that Earth is a huge sphere that turns to face the sun, now with one side, now with the other; and that at one and the same time, in different corners of the earth, it can be a sultry summer or severe winter, day or night. In grade two we began to complete journeys around the globe. The children sat in a green classroom with a large globe in front of them, lit up by an artificial 'sun'. 'Earth' rotated around the 'sun', the 'moon' around 'Earth'. 'Here children', I said to the little ones, 'are the expanses of our homeland. We live not far from its western border. Let's go on a distant journey to the east, to visit cities and villages. Let's see how other people live.' Then I told the children about the fields, rivers and population centres that we met on the way. My words were accompanied by pictures and slides.

Evening came, the two hours of our journey had passed imperceptibly and we had only travelled one hundred kilometres from home. The children looked forward to the day when they could continue their journey.

When we continued our journey, we again visited cities and villages, forests and rivers, construction sites and historic landmarks, but the journey never seemed monotonous because the children found something new and unique in every corner of our homeland. We continued our journey for several days and approached the Volga, where we saw hydroelectric stations and met shepherds on the wide Volga steppe. Holding their breath, the children listened to the story of the great battle of Stalingrad, on which the fate of humanity depended. If tens of thousands of heroes had not fought here to the death, and had not repelled the onslaught of a cruel and powerful enemy—if they had not broken its back—we would not be sitting today in this cosy classroom. From an early age children need to be led into a greater world of human lives, concerns and troubles. Let children feel that even now there are forces on the earth prepared to unleash a new and bloody war. Let a deep feeling of hatred for the enemies of peace live and grow in a little child's heart. From the heroic feats of their grandfathers and great grandfathers, let children draw confidence that people are not specks of dust in the whirlwind of fate, but a mighty force.

The children travelled further and further into the depths of their native land, and discovered new landscapes: the rich Urals with their inexhaustible mineral reserves; the mysterious taiga; the mighty Siberian rivers ... We devoted several days to the beautiful gem stone country of the Urals, travelling with geologists prospecting for natural resources. We boarded a steamship and sailed on Lake Baikal, admiring the mountains and forests, and spending a night by a campfire ... We travelled further, where the children discovered the riches of the Far East and then the ocean. We boarded an ocean ship and set off for Sakhalin and then the Kuril Islands—this is where the sun rises each day on our homeland. Our journey took about three months. Each day we covered an average of one hundred kilometres. We met representatives of more than forty nationalities and made the acquaintance of remarkable people: grain growers, builders, miners, fishermen, geologists. All of them worked so that we could have a good life.

We made several more journeys through our homeland. We went to the north, where we discovered the harsh but beautiful tundra, and the majestic Arctic Ocean. We met courageous polar explorers, deer herders and lumberjacks. In the west we got to know the life of our brother Hutsuls and admired the beauty of the mountain valley pastures. To the south we travelled through the Caucasus Mountains and the plains of Central Asia.

We travelled for a whole year. In the children's minds the idea of the homeland became filled with vivid pictures that awakened feelings of pride in the heroic work of Soviet people. Following our example, the teachers of other primary classes began to undertake journeys through our native land. We tried to ensure that children incorporated in their concept of 'homeland' all that has been won at such great cost, all that the Soviet people hold dear.

Then we began journeys beyond the borders of our country. I aimed to show the diversity and beauty of nature in various corners of the earth, to tell the students about all the good things in the life and work of the world's peoples, to kindle interest in the culture and art, the past and the present of peoples speaking different languages, to show the battle between good and evil being conducted all over the planet. On these journeys visual aids played an even greater role than on our journeys through our native land. We had to create mental pictures of distant lands, of natural environments that are not to be seen in our country.

First we spent time in lands where it is always summer. Day by day the children got to know the natural environments, the way of life, work, and culture of the peoples of Egypt, India, Ceylon and Indonesia. They listened to stories and watched films devoted to these countries. It was as if they were transported under slender palms, as if they felt the burning heat of the tropical sun and the cooling downpours, and were able to observe the life of working people. The journey to Egypt, the land of the pyramids, was fascinating. The children watched slides showing the work of the people who built the pyramids and sphinxes.

Then we set off on journeys to neighbouring countries, spending time in the Baltic states and Scandinavia, in the countries of central Europe, in Turkey, Iran and Afghanistan, and in Japan. We spent several days travelling through the fields, mountains and jungles of our great neighbour China. In the same way, we made journeys to Africa and South America, to Canada and the United States, to Australia and Antarctica. I conducted all these journeys not only with the aim of acquiring knowledge, but in order to educate the children in a spirit of peace.

A deep impression was made on the children by the images of people working in various corners of the globe. Wherever people live, whatever the colour of their skin, whatever language they speak, everywhere they work, educate their children and dream of their children's happiness. I tried to show as vividly as possible the work of our brothers—the people of other socialist countries, and to awaken feelings of friendship towards the workers of the first socialist state of workers and farmers on German land—the German Democratic Republic. Many of our students' fathers had died at the front, so it seemed to me to be particularly important to give a true picture of the life of the country whose army had brought so much grief and suffering to our people during the war. Striking examples convinced the children that fascism and the German people were not the same thing, that during the dark years under Hitler the best sons and daughters of Germany's working class gave their lives fighting against Nazism, the same enemy against which the Soviet people had fought.

Travelling around the globe, the children saw that not all people live happily; that there are countries where some people oppress others and where poverty and hunger reign. The children began to have some conception of the cause of this evil—an unjust social order.

Gradually the children became convinced that there is a fierce struggle going on in the world between the exploiters and the exploited. I wanted the suffering of working people still subject to exploitation, and the suffering of whole nations still under the yoke of colonialism, to enter my pupils' hearts.

When we travelled to the Arab countries, I showed a film containing images that staggered my pupils. Young children their own age, boys and girls, were sold into slavery and taken in shackles to perform hard labour in some countries such as Saudi Arabia. Next to the slave market stood the magnificent palaces of the country's rulers. The children's hearts ached. They began to view the free labour of citizens in their homeland in a new light, feeling that to work for the good of the homeland, for one's family and one's people, is a great source of happiness.

The children began to form their first ideas about the fierce battle going on in the world between the forces of good and evil. I wanted the children's hearts to be open to the joys and suffering of all of humanity. Everything that happens in the world should touch a child's heart. Let children from an early age choose their position in the battle between good and evil—that is one of the important principles of our system of moral education.

As long as the exploitation of one person by another exists in the world, we cannot educate love for the whole of humanity because there is no abstract humanity. There are our brothers by class who are being exploited, and their implacable opponents, the exploiters. It is very important that every child at a young age understands, and feels with their heart, the meaning of the revolutionary idea of communism. Using examples from our homeland's recent past and talking about the bloody battles of its people for freedom and independence, giving vivid examples of how the workers of colonial and capitalist countries defend their rights in our times, I gradually led the children to the conviction that people are prepared to die for the sake of an idea—and that the uncompromising battle between the classes is expressed most clearly in a battle between ideas. It is very important that people who have given their lives for the sake of noble ideas should serve as ideals for our pupils. And the reverse is also true, that people who submit to oppression without protest should inspire feelings of contempt. That is why it is necessary to reveal the world to children from the point of view of life, work and the struggle for a happy future.

Travelling to Japan, the children learnt about thousands of peaceful people who developed radiation sickness after the atomic bomb was dropped on Hiroshima, and about the little girl Sadako Sasaki who was bedridden with that serious illness. The children took to heart the grief of this distant child their own age. They wanted to help the sick little girl, but how? A few weeks after our journey to Japan, I read the children a newspaper article describing how Sadako Sasaki had set herself the goal of making 1000 paper cranes (according to a Japanese tradition, people who have made 1000 paper cranes with their own hands will always be happy). Our people have a similar belief: a loving mother will make silver paper larks for a sick child to bring good health. So our boys and girls made paper cranes and sent them to the distant land of the rising sun ... As time passed, the children took to heart any news about Sadako's health. The sorrowful news of the death of their distant friend was experienced by them as a deeply personal loss.

The world, whose horizons gradually open up before a child, is not only seas and oceans, continents and islands, exotic plants and animals, the northern lights of the Arctic and the eternal summer of the tropics. Above all it is people, their work and struggle for a happy future, and the eternal human dream of happiness and justice, which is realised in countries where human oppression is eliminated. Children should enter this world not as mere dispassionate observers, knowing what happens where and being able to talk about it, but as people who are concerned for the fate of humanity.

In making journeys through our homeland and beyond its boundaries, we should beware of one danger—the danger of overloading children with knowledge and impressions. Tolstoy advised the teachers of young children to 'avoid that common practice (especially in foreign school books) of communicating the extraordinary achievements of science, such as how much the earth and the sun weigh, how both trees and people are made of cells, and what amazing machines people have invented'.[23] According to the great writer and educator, bare facts are harmful to a student and teach them to believe anything they hear. Many decades have passed and the world has become unrecognisable. Science has achieved amazing success and young children have a different outlook. But Tolstoy's advice has not lost its relevance even today. We should not overburden our explanations to children with information that overwhelms them.

---

23 Tolstoy, LN, *Pedagogicheskie sochineniya* [Pedagogical works]. Moscow: Uchpedgiz, 1953. pp. 339–340.

# Give children the joy of success in study

STUDENTS' INTELLECTUAL WORK, THEIR SUCCESSES and failures in study, are part of their spiritual lives, their inner worlds, and to ignore this fact may lead to sad results. Children not only learn new things and master material, they experience their work emotionally and express deeply personal attitudes to their successes and failures.

For a small child, the teacher is a living embodiment of fairness. Look into the eyes of a first grade student who has received an unsatisfactory grade … The child not only feels unfortunate, he experiences a feeling of antagonism and quite often hostility towards the teacher. A teacher who gives a student a failing grade, in essence because a child has not understood something, is seen by children as an unjust person.

In one school the following incident took place. A student could not for the life of him understand how a plant breathes and absorbs nutrients, how a leaf develops from a bud, how a fruit develops from a flower. The teacher often called on the boy to answer questions and each time repeated, 'Can't you understand these simple things? What can you understand?' At one lesson he said: 'In a few days the buds will open on the chestnut trees. We will go as a class to our chestnut alley, and if Alyosha cannot tell us there what is obvious to everyone, we might as well give up.' The teacher loved his brainchild: an alley of young chestnut trees grown from seed. On the eve of his lesson he went with several students to inspect his alley and to admire the buds adorning the top of each tree.

When the class came for its lesson to the chestnut alley the next day, the teacher was shocked: all the buds on the trees were snapped off. The children were disappointed and the teacher noticed a gleam of malicious delight in Alyosha's eyes.

Behind this act was an explosion, an outburst of the child's spiritual energy, a deep heartache. The boy was protesting against the lack of faith in his ability. But in educational practice it often happens that children who receive one failing grade after another become reconciled to their lot and do not care. Sometimes a child's indifference to their grades becomes an object of teasing by their classmates. Gradually all the children come to accept that Vanya or Petya will always get failing grades. This is the most terrible thing that could be imagined for the spiritual life of a developing personality. What can be expected of someone who has already lost any feelings of self-respect in childhood? The desire to study … How many tricks of the trade are used by teachers to enlist the help of this desire? Teachers try to maintain the desire to study using all sorts of external methods to strengthen interest in what is being studied. And they are surprised when, despite all their tricks, the desire to study is not there. When and why did it disappear? The desire to study lives in children's souls as long as the desire to be a human being is alive, and as long as they have faith that they can be human beings.

One of our most important educational objectives is to make sure that in the process of acquiring knowledge, every child experiences feelings of self-worth and pride. The teacher should not only reveal the world to students, but also establish children's place in the world as active agents and creators who experience pride in their achievements. The process of instruction takes place collectively, but children take each step on the road to knowledge independently. Intellectual work is a deeply individual process, depending not only on a child's ability but on their character, and on many other factors that often go unnoticed.

Children begin school with an open heart, with a sincere desire to study well. Small children are frightened at even the thought that they might be considered lazy or as failures. The desire to study well—that beautiful human desire—seems to me like a bright flame, illuminating the whole meaning of a child's life, the world of a child's joys. This flame, weak and defenceless, is brought by the child to you, the teacher, with limitless trust and if you do not notice the child's desire, it means you have not comprehended your responsibility for the present and future of your pupils. It is very easy to snuff this flame out through careless contact with a child's heart—a sharp word that gives rise to offence or indifference. Life-giving air for this weak flame, the thirst for knowledge, comes only from a child's success in study and the proud consciousness that 'I' am taking a step forward, climbing up the steep path to knowledge.

Even for an adult, work which is done in vain with no positive result becomes irksome, dull and meaningless; but we are dealing with children. If children have no success in work, the flame kindling their thirst for knowledge dies and an icicle forms in their hearts, which you cannot melt with any amount of effort until the flame is lit again (and to light it a second time is so very difficult). Children then lose faith in their abilities, shut everyone out and become wary of any attention, bristling at the slightest hint of criticism and responding rudely to a teacher's advice or comments. Or even worse: their feelings of self-worth fade and they get used to the idea that they are not good at anything. The heart is overcome with rage and indignation when you come across such indifferent, passive children, who will patiently listen to a teacher's edifying advice for an hour and are completely indifferent to their classmates' words, telling them 'You're behind, you'll have to repeat the year …' What could be more immoral than to crush a person's feeling of self-worth?

Students' moral outlook depends to a huge extent on how they regard themselves during childhood and adolescence; how they see themselves in the world of work. Ushinsky wrote that children are not lazy by nature, that they love independent activity and like to do everything themselves. We have to teach children how to work in an intellectual way, to think and to observe, to understand what intellectual work is, what it means to work well, and only then award a grade for achievement. A child who has never known the joy of intellectual work, who has not experienced pride from overcoming difficulty, is an unhappy person. An unhappy person is a great misfortune for our society, and an unhappy child is a hundred times worse. I am not sentimental about childhood. I am disturbed by the thought that in childhood it is not uncommon for young people to become idlers who hate work and feel scorn at even the thought of working as hard as they can. But why do children become idlers? Because, dear fellow teachers, they have not known the happiness of work. Give them that happiness and teach them to value it, and they will respect themselves and will love work.

To give children the joy of work, the joy of success in study, to awaken in their hearts feelings of pride and self-worth—this is the first commandment of education. In our schools there should not be any unhappy children—children whose souls are consumed by the thought that they are not capable of anything. Success in study is the only source of a child's inner strength, giving them the energy to overcome difficulties and the desire to study.

All our ideas, research and frameworks will turn to dust like lifeless mummies if we lack the beating heart, the living flesh and blood of the desire to study. This desire comes only with success in study. It seems paradoxical: for children to succeed, they must not fall behind. But this is not a paradox, rather the dialectical oneness of the process of intellectual work. Interest in study comes only with the inspiration born of success in acquiring knowledge. Without inspiration, study becomes onerous for children. Perseverance in study comes from inspiration multiplied by children's confidence that they will achieve success.

Evaluating a student's knowledge may seem to be a simple matter at first glance, but in this activity we find an expression of a teacher's ability to find the correct approach to each child, the ability to nurture the flame in the soul that gives rise to the thirst for knowledge. During the four years of instruction in the primary classes I did not give a single failing grade for either written or oral responses. The children learnt to read, write and solve problems. Some children had already achieved positive results in their intellectual work, while others still had some way to go. Some had already mastered what the teacher wanted to teach, and others had not, but that did not mean they did not want to study. I only evaluated intellectual work when it brought a child positive results. If children had not yet achieved the results they were striving for, I did not give any grade. The children had to think, gather their thoughts, and do the work again.

In grade one I gave my first grades four months into the school year. The most important thing here is that children understand what persistent, conscientious work is. Little children perform a task poorly, not because they do not want to do it properly, but because they do not understand what is good and what is bad. So what is the point of giving them a grade? I worked in such a way that children, carrying out the same task several times, learnt from their own experience that they could do it significantly better than on the first attempt. This has great educational significance: students discover their own creative ability. They rejoice in their success. They strive to improve all the time. Comparing their more perfect work with their less perfect work, children are inspired.

Observing work in grade one, I saw that the children did not all think the same way and evaluated their work differently. Once they were writing the word 'wasp'. Lida, Seryozha, Katya, Sanya and Pavel produced beautiful, even letters. Yura's letters were lop-sided and extended beyond the lines. Kolya and Tolya drew the letters rather than wrote them, just as they had in their early picture books when they compiled their first miniature compositions about nature. In Petrik's exercise book there were some marks like hooks. I did not go on to the next exercise. The children wrote the same word again several times. Each new repetition of the same exercise was like a new step that the child was climbing, both for those whose first attempt was poor, and for those who had managed well. Each child was happy that their writing was better than it was at the beginning.

Such feelings of happiness give rise to feelings of pride and self-worth. A child who has experienced these feelings many times does not look for an easy way out, and does not copy someone else's work. Only when children have learnt to repeat their work, and have in consequence experienced feelings of joy and self-worth, do I give them grades—of course only for positive results. Some children began to receive grades after four months and some after six months. Petrik and Misha received their first grades only at the beginning of the second school year. I did extra work with them, making sure that these children worked a little bit better each day than they had the day before, and did not lose faith in their abilities.

Study is not a mechanical transfer of knowledge from teacher to child, but above all is a matter of human relationships. Children's attitudes to knowledge and study depend to a huge extent on their attitudes toward their teacher. If children feel injustice, they are shaken. And little children always consider a failing grade to be unjust and take it to heart, because it is almost never the case that they do not want to learn. They want to learn, but they do not know how. They do not yet have the capacity to concentrate and make themselves work.

If children experience injustice today, and tomorrow, and for the rest of the year, their nervous systems at first become stimulated and then inhibition sets in—depression, weakness and apathy. Sudden swings between stimulation and inhibition lead to children becoming ill. At first glance these seem like strange illnesses—school neuroses or didactogenic illnesses. The paradox of didactogenic illnesses is that they occur only in schools, in that sacred place where humanity should be the dominant characteristic governing relations between children and teacher.

Didactogenic illnesses result from injustice. Unjust relationships between parents or teacher and child come in many shades. The most common is indifference. There is nothing more inimical to the development of children's moral capacity and will power than a teacher's indifference to their success. Then there is shouting, threats, irritability and, with some people who lack proper educational training, even malicious delight: since you don't know the answer, give me your diary and I will give you a poor grade so your parents can see what a clever child they have …

I have been studying school neuroses for several years. The unhealthy reaction of the nervous system to a teacher's injustice can take a variety of forms in different children: hyperactivity, a persecution complex, bitter animosity, a feigned attitude of carelessness, indifference, depression, a fear of being punished by the teacher or the school, affectation and clowning around, and hostility which sometimes (very rarely, but it cannot be ignored) takes pathological forms. The prevention of didactogenic illnesses depends on the educational skill of the parents and the teacher. The most important aspect of this educational skill must be the ability to sense each child's inner world, and to devote enough attention and spiritual energy to each child to ensure that they feel they are not forgotten, and that their grief, hurt and suffering are shared.

From the point of view of children, the greatest injustice that a teacher can inflict on them is if, after awarding them a grade they deeply believe to be unjust, the teacher also seeks to have the parents punish them for that grade. If children see that a teacher is determined to tell parents about a failing grade, they become hostile to the teacher and the school. They develop a hatred for intellectual work. This coarsening of their feelings is transferred firstly to their relationships with their parents, and then to relationships with others.

It is hard to imagine something that would cripple a child's soul more than the emotional insensitivity born of injustice. Experiencing attitudes of indifference, children can lose sensitivity to good and evil. They cannot distinguish good and evil in the people around them. They become suspicious and lose faith in people, and this is the main reason for their bitterness. Suspecting every person around them of wishing them ill, children may behave badly without provocation and without any design or intent. They consider that all people are bad; that there is no such thing as goodness and that a teacher's explanations of goodness are hypocrisy. Children do not believe a single word from educators who unjustly award them unsatisfactory grades. The more nice words such educators say, the more children distrust them.

Amongst educators now you often hear conversations about incentives and punishment. Attractive theories are born and die like one day moths … But the main incentive and the most powerful (though not always effective) punishment in our educational work is the grade. This is the sharpest instrument and its use requires great skill and training.

To have the right to use this instrument, you first need to love children. And not tell them about your love, but express it in your care for them. Tolstoy wrote: 'If a teacher just loves his work, he will be a good teacher. If a teacher only loves the student, like a mother or father, he will be better than a teacher who has read all the books, but loves neither his work, nor the students. If a teacher combines love of his work and love for his students, he will be a complete teacher.'[24]

Heartfelt sensitivity is a quality that you cannot acquire just through study. Teachers' human sensitivity is based on their intellectual, moral, aesthetic and emotional culture, expressed as an organic unity, and this unity is attained by being highly educated and through the social experience of moral relations in a collective setting. Teachers must

---

24 Tolstoy, LN, *Polnoe sobranie sochinenii* [Complete works], vol. 4, Moscow: GIKhL, p. 26.

know and feel that they have the fate of each child on their conscience, and that their students' intellect, health and happiness depend on their spiritual culture and the wealth of their ideas.

… A grammar lesson in grade two. After studying a rule and analysing some exercises the children complete some independent work, the aim of which is both to deepen and to assess knowledge. Grades are awarded for the work. Having checked the exercise books, I see that Misha and Petrik have carried out the task poorly. If I give an unsatisfactory grade the children, who with all their hearts want to study well, will see it as a verdict: 'Your classmates have taken a step forward, but you have not progressed'. Correcting mistakes and providing samples of good handwriting, I do not give Misha or Petrik any grade. Handing back the exercise books I say to the children:

'Misha and Petrik have not earned their grades yet. You two boys need to work hard. I would like you to do another independent exercise. Try to earn your grade.'

The children are already accustomed to the fact that no grade is given for unsatisfactory work. In their minds the conviction has gradually grown that completing a task does not mark a stage of work that will end with the teacher's final verdict. The path to success is not blocked. That which a child could not do this time, they will be able to do in the future, perhaps even today or tomorrow. Misha and Petrik do not experience the doomed feeling of a child who receives a failing grade and remains a step behind his classmates. At that very lesson the boys ask, 'Give us another exercise, please'. I give it to them. During the course of the school day they find time to complete it. (Our working day is organised in such a way that every child has half an hour at their disposal to complete whatever work they consider to be of the highest priority.) The boys try with all their might to earn a grade and prove they are no worse than the others. I check the work, and as is nearly always the case in such instances it deserves a positive grade.

It is especially important to use grades prudently as a stimulus for work when the study task requires creative intellectual effort, reflection and research. One child's thought processes flow rapidly and race ahead, while another's flow slowly, but that does not mean that one child is more intelligent than another or works harder. Lessons in arithmetic in the primary school, solving problems, these activities provide a touchstone for the first commandment of education: to give children the joy of success in intellectual work, to awaken their feelings of pride and self-worth. And we have to make sure that the first difficulties do not become a stumbling block for any child. I did not give grades for solving problems until children learnt to think independently, to analyse the terms of the problem and to find a way to solve it—in other words, until they experienced the joy of success in this work. In this case a uniform approach is especially unacceptable. One child may be awarded three grades during a month and another child none, but that does not mean the second child is doing nothing and making no progress. Each one is learning to understand the problem, and the first relatively complex problem that a student solves independently is an important step in that child's development.

For many years I have been studying students who are unsuccessful in mathematics, and I am convinced that in the primary and middle school classes, those students who fall behind never solve a single problem independently. It is as if they are carried along by the current, putting their feet in their classmates' footsteps. They copy work from the board or from the student sitting next to them, but in essence they have no idea what it means to solve a problem independently. Look carefully at your students in the middle and upper classes and you will find that some of them, during all the years of their school studies, have never solved a single problem independently. And the root of this problem does not lie in the way the subject is taught.

You cannot get rid of this problem by finding some improved way of presenting the material. Intellectual work in mathematics lessons is a touchstone for thinking. The problem is that the child has not learnt to think. The surrounding world, with its objects, phenomena, dependencies and interrelationships, has not become a source of thought for the child. Experience confirms that there will not be a single child in the class who fails at mathematics if journeys into nature provide a true school of intellectual work in early childhood. Objects must teach children to think. This is an exceptionally important requirement if all normal children are to become intelligent, quick-witted, inquisitive and curious. I advised teachers: if your student does not understand something, if their thought beats helplessly like a bird in a cage, look carefully at your work. Has the consciousness of your little child become like a dried up pond, cut off from the eternal life-giving source of thought—the world of natural objects and phenomena? Connect that little pond with the ocean of nature, of objects, of the surrounding world, and you will see how a spring of living thought will begin to flow.

But it would be a mistake to assume that the surrounding world alone will teach a child to think. Without theoretical thought, objects will remain hidden from children's eyes by an impenetrable wall. Nature will only become a school for intellectual work when children generalise from the surrounding objects and engage in abstract thinking. The vivid images of reality are necessary so that a child can learn to discover interactions as an important feature of the surrounding world. Affirming the truth of Hegel's idea that interaction is the *causa finalis* (ultimate cause) of everything that exists, Engels wrote, 'We cannot go beyond the knowledge of this interaction for the simple reason that there is nothing beyond it to discover.'[25] The discovery of interaction as a precursor to abstract thinking is an important

---

25  Marx, K and Engels, F, *Sochineniya* [Works], vol. 20, p. 546.

precondition for the development of mathematical thinking. The ability to solve problems successfully depends on whether children have learnt to see the interactions between objects and phenomena.

Independent intellectual work to solve problems also bears fruit when children have thoroughly memorised those generalisations without which thought is impossible (the multiplication tables, the composition of the sequence of natural numbers).

For a long time Petrik could not understand the meaning (the terms) of mathematical problems. I did not rush to explain things. The most important thing was that the child should understand the interactions between objects and phenomena through his own intellectual effort. But living thought will not flow if you do not prepare children for theoretical thought, if they cannot compare and analyse what they are seeing. I took the children to natural settings and taught them again and again to observe, to compare objects, qualities and phenomena, and to discern interactions. I directed Petrik's attention to those phenomena of the surrounding world that help a child to form notions of size and number as important qualities of objects. I managed to reach a point where the child understood number relationships and was convinced that someone had not just dreamt them up, but that they really existed. What is really important here is not that children immediately learn to count and to operate with numbers, but that they understand the essence of number relationships.

Once we were sitting in a shelter at the melon plantation observing how a combine harvester was harvesting wheat. From time to time a truck loaded with grain drove away from the harvester. How many minutes would it take to fill a truck? The children watched the clock with interest. It turned out that it took seventeen minutes. How had the workers timed their operation so the harvester would not have to stop working? Only five minutes remained until the truck would be full again … four minutes, three minutes. The children became worried: it looked like the harvester would have to stop. With only two minutes remaining a truck drove out from the forest. But it had to drive for a whole hour to get there from the storage depot, so people must have calculated the relationship between the distance and the travelling time. They had allocated just the right number of trucks to allow the combine harvester to work without stopping.

And what if the truck had to drive not for one hour but for two hours to get to the storage depot? Would they need more or fewer trucks to deliver the grain?

'Of course they would need more', said Petrik, and his eyes shone joyfully. 'At the moment there are three trucks on their way here, while one truck is being loaded and one is being unloaded at the depot. If the road was longer, there would be more trucks on their way here.'

The child was making a big mental effort. I could see that he was already trying to work out how many trucks would be needed if the road was twice as long. But that was not the most important thing. The most important thing was that he had realised that maths problems are not just the invention of people with nothing better to do. Problems exist in the surrounding world because of movement, life and human work.

Petrik was already in grade three, but he still did not understand how to solve problems. He had still not solved a single problem independently (without assistance from his friends or the teacher) and that worried me. But I still believed the boy would learn to think. Mentally analysing the phenomena that provide the foundation for an arithmetical problem was not the only way I prepared the boy for abstract thought. A thinker who cannot count cannot learn. It was very important for Petrik to gradually memorise those facts without which thought is impossible. The boy sat down at the mathematics box and trained, checking his knowledge. I carefully monitored that the child did not need to think about what 12−8, 19+13 or 41−19 equalled. (If grade three students have to think about such number facts they will not be able to focus on the problem.)

Life has convinced me that students are often unable to master algebra for the simple reason that they have not fully comprehended the composition of natural numbers, have not comprehended them to the extent that, without thinking about elementary number facts, they can concentrate all their mental energy on abstract thinking. Just as reading cannot become a semi-automatic process unless children have read the syllables that make up words thousands of times, so abstract mathematical thinking will remain a closed book unless students have memorised hundreds of number facts, which people do not think about in their daily practice because they have permanently memorised them. I tried to ensure that the slow thinkers, especially Petrik, mastered as many as possible of the simple building blocks of mathematical thought: addition, subtraction, multiplication and division number facts.

We went on nature walks and I directed the boy's attention to the multitude of problems that people solve in the process of doing their work. At last the day arrived that I had long believed in: Petrik solved a problem completely independently. The boy's eyes lit up, and he began to explain what the problem was about. His explanation was not very coherent but I could see that the boy had uncovered what previously had been shrouded in darkness. Petrik was happy. I also breathed a sigh of relief: at last! The boy could not wait for lessons to end and ran home to share his joy with his mother. His mother was not at home. 'I solved a problem by myself!' he told his grandfather joyfully. Petrik was proud of his achievement, and such pure, moral pride is a source of human dignity. Without pride in one's work one cannot be fully human.

This example gave our teaching staff food for thought. We began to see those children who struggle with studies in a different light. We should never rush to make a categorical judgement: those children will never succeed—that is their fate. Perhaps for one, two, or three years success will elude them, but in time they will taste success.

Thought is like a flower that gradually absorbs life-giving moisture. If we keep providing moisture to the roots and keep exposing the flower to the sun, eventually it will bloom. Let us teach children to think and expose them to the source of all thought: the surrounding world. Let us give them the greatest human joy: the joy of knowledge and discovery.

We should not allow grades to become shackles fettering children's thought. I always gave the weakest students, even ones who seemed to be hopelessly slow-witted, the opportunity to think about what they did not yet understand. The children never lost interest in study. Awakening their feelings of pride, honour and self-worth, I managed to ensure that the children wanted to work independently.

To give children the opportunity to think … This is not as simple a matter as it first seems. Look hard at the intellectual work of your students in grades one, two, three and four, and you will see that in the overwhelming majority of cases (sometimes nearly always), children are unable to answer your question (or to complete a task) for the simple reason that they did not have time to gather their thoughts and to concentrate. (And sometimes a child is caught unawares by the question and is in a state of shock.) The teachers of our primary classes met to discuss how we could give children the opportunity to think. We came to the conclusion that we should never rush to conclude whether or not a child knows something. It often happens that a teacher asks a child to sit down because they do not know the answer. The child sits down and at that very moment their head clears, and it turns out that they know the answer very well … They feel deeply offended at the teacher. Why does this happen? We could not immediately find an answer to this question. We had to observe, observe and observe again, and to study a multitude of facts.

A child who has achieved a goal through the strenuous exercise of thought and will has an aversion to prompting, cheating and copying. The children and I always had relations of mutual trust and good will.

Students were never afraid to tell me that they were struggling with a problem. The children brought all their doubts, joys and sorrows to their teacher. I was never a bearer of grievous news to a child—and for a child a failing grade is a grievous matter. How a child's soul is damaged when the teacher tells them nearly every day, 'You have failed'. How little grief it takes for children to feel unhappy. The tragedy is made worse by the fact that little children, growing accustomed to their grief, become indifferent to everything around them. Their hearts harden, and a hardened heart is fertile soil for cruelty. If there are unhappy children in your class and their classmates do not try to lighten their lot, you will never have a good, friendly class.

But neither should grades spoil students, as is unfortunately often the case in schools. A student says a word and is immediately given 'excellent'. It is not uncommon for several students to be given the same question and for each one to be awarded a grade. This results in students developing a frivolous attitude to study. Students must always see grades as being the result of intellectual effort.

Learning how to achieve success in intellectual work from their own experience, children learn self-control. The habit of working with determination and striving for better results than those already achieved, teaches children intolerance for carelessly completed work, idleness or negligence.

When the joy of work and success in study is the main stimulus motivating students to study, there will not be any idlers in the class. Genuine masters of the art of education very rarely resort to battling with individual idlers; they battle with the laziness that comes from sleeping minds.

A system based on awarding grades only for the positive results of intellectual work gradually became adopted by all teachers in the primary, middle and senior classes. The reader may wonder: what happened at the end of the term or end of the academic year if a student had not received a grade for some subject. The point is that the absence of a grade is a much greater misfortune for a child than a failing grade. The child is convinced: if I have not received a grade, that means I have not worked as hard as I needed to. For this reason it almost never happens that a child gets to the end of an academic year without receiving a grade. Over a period of four years there were only six occasions when I did not give a grade at the end of a term. The parents knew: if their son or daughter had not received a grade in their diary, something was not right. They also knew that this was not the child's fault, but a misfortune; and you need to help someone in misfortune. And together we helped the student. I convinced the parents that they should never demand that their child receive the highest grades or see an unsatisfactory grade as a sign of laziness, negligence or insufficient effort.

Some teachers use grades—that most subtle of educational tools—thoughtlessly. In many schools a satisfactory grade, a 'three', is seen as something reprehensible. 'We will study without threes!' Such slogans ring out not only at Pioneer meetings but even in children's newspapers. In encouraging such an attitude to satisfactory success in studies, teachers are essentially cutting the branch they are sitting on. They are teaching children to be superficial and frivolous.

In grade two, a few weeks after the start of the school year, the children began to keep diaries in which the grades they received during lessons were recorded. There was not a single case where children tried to hide grades from their parents. It cannot be any other way if a grade reflects the joy of success. Children cannot hide a source of joy from their parents. It is not necessary for the teacher to sign the diary. That is a relic of the old school, with its atmosphere of mutual distrust and suspicion between teacher and student. If there is no mutual trust in a class, if children try to deceive the teacher, if the grade turns into a whip used by adults to spur children on, the very foundation of good education will be destroyed.

Unjustly awarded failing grades give rise to one of the greatest evils in schools: children's dishonesty; the attempt to deceive teacher and parents. The lengths that children will go to in order to hide their failure at school from their mother and father, and to hide their negligence from their teacher! The greater the level of distrust shown to students, the more inventive they become in their deception and the more fertile conditions are for laziness and negligence. Laziness is a child of mistrust. The young people I am teaching are first and foremost living human beings, children, and only secondarily students. The grades that I give them are not only an assessment of their knowledge but, even more importantly, an expression of my attitude to them as human beings.

I advise all teachers: nurture children's spark of inquisitiveness, their curiosity, their thirst for knowledge. The only fuel that can keep that spark alive is the joy of success in work, the feelings of pride experienced by the toiler. Reward every success, every triumph over difficulty, with the deserved grade, but do not misuse grades. Do not forget that the soil on which you are constructing your educational edifice is in each child, in their attitude to knowledge and to you, the teacher. Everything is built on the desire to study, on inspiration, on a preparedness to overcome difficulties. Take care to make this soil fertile, for no school can stand without it.

# *The story room*

STORIES, PLAY AND FANTASY PROVIDE a life-giving stimulus for children's thought, for noble feelings and aspirations. Many years' experience has convinced me that the aesthetic, moral and intellectual feelings that arise in the soul of a child under the influence of fairytale images activate streams of thought, which arouse the activity of the brain, connecting little islands of thought with vital living threads. Through fairytale images words enter a child's consciousness, with all their subtle shades. Words become a part of a child's spiritual life, a means for expressing thoughts and feelings, the living reality of thought. Under the influence of the feelings inspired by fairytale images, a child learns to think in words. Without lively, vivid stories that engage children's hearts and minds, it is impossible to imagine children's thought or speech as a particular stage in the development of human thought and speech.

Children experience deep satisfaction when their thoughts inhabit the world of fairytale images. A child can retell the same story five times, ten times, and still find something new in it each time. Fairytale images provide the first stepping stones from the vivid, living and concrete to the abstract. My pupils would not have mastered abstract thinking if fairytales had not constituted a whole stage in their spiritual lives. Children know very well that there is no such thing as the Frog Princess, the witch Baba-Yaga, or the wizard Kashchei the Immortal, but for them these images are an embodiment of good and evil, and each time they retell the same story they are expressing a personal attitude to good and evil.

A fairytale is inseparable from beauty and aids the development of aesthetic feelings, without which nobility of soul is unthinkable, as is heartfelt sensitivity to another's misfortune, grief and suffering. Thanks to fairytales, children apprehend the world not only with their minds but with their hearts. And they not only apprehend, they respond to events in the surrounding world and express their attitudes to good and evil. From fairytales they draw their first notions of justice and injustice. Without aesthetic education, a child's moral and ideological education would be unthinkable. Children understand an idea only when it is embodied in vivid images.

Three months after we had begun our work in the School of Joy we set up the Story Room. With the help of the senior students, we created an environment in which children felt as if they were in a world of fairytale images. We had to work hard so that everything that surrounded the children took them back to memories of the stories their mothers had told them in early childhood, to memories of evening twilight and a fire crackling merrily in the fireplace. There was Baba-Yaga's home—a fairytale hut on a giant chicken's leg—surrounded by tall trees and stumps. Next to the hut were the figures of fairytale characters: the cunning fox, the grey wolf, and the wise owl. In another corner was a hut where the grandfather and grandmother lived; in the sky were geese and swans carrying a little boy—the hero of the Ukrainian folk tale about Ivasik-Telesik—on their wings. In a third corner was the dark blue ocean. On the shore stood the dilapidated dwelling of the kind old man and his mean wife, with their old trough by the door. The old man and his wife were sitting on an earthen dyke while a golden fish swam in the sea. In the fourth corner was a winter forest with snow-drifts, through which a little girl was struggling. Her stepmother had sent her out in the freezing weather to look for berries ... A baby goat was looking out from a window of the hut. And over there was a large mitten in which a mouse was living, with all her unexpected guests approaching. Puppets sat on a large stump made from plywood: a little girl, a grey hare, sister fox, a bear, a wolf, a goat, a straw bull-calf and Little Red Riding Hood.

We made all of this gradually. I cut out the pieces, painted them and stuck them together, with the children helping me. I attached great significance to the aesthetic character of the environment in which children listened to stories. Each picture, each visual image, heightened the children's receptivity to literary language and revealed the ideas behind the story more deeply. Even the lighting in the story room played an important role. When we listened to the story of the Frog Princess, some little lights came on in a forest thicket and the room was bathed in a green haze, which corresponded well to the setting of the story.

I did not take the children into the story room very often—every week or two. Aesthetic needs should not be satisfied to excess. Overindulgence makes children hard to please and leads to disillusionment, boredom, and the search for ways to 'kill' free time … We would go there at dusk in autumn or winter. At such times the story sounded special and was listened to quite differently than on a bright summer's day. It would be getting dark outside but we did not turn on the light; we enjoyed the half-light. Suddenly a light would come on in the windows of a fairytale cottage, the stars would light up in the sky, and the moon would rise over the forest. The room was dimly lit and in the corners it became even darker. I told the children the folk tale about Baba-Yaga with the bony leg. It would seem that there could be nothing new for the children in my words, but their eyes shone with delight. The children lived through every minute of the characters' experiences, hating evil and feeling the warmest sympathy for good. The figures of the wicked woman, the trusting daughter Alyonka, and the kind geese and swans came alive in the children's imaginations, and took on the quality of living creatures endowed with reason and emotions. For little children, a fairytale is not just a story about fantastic events; it is a whole world in which the children live and fight, pitting their good will against evil. The words in a fairytale provide a real form of expression for a child's spiritual energy, just as movement does in a game or a melody in music. Children do not just want to listen to a story; they want to tell it; just as they do not just want to just listen to a song, but to sing it; or to watch a game, but to take part in it.

After a few days the children would ask, 'When are we going to the Story Room?' They were excited at the prospect of more happy moments. Again we would gather at dusk and again I would tell the story first, followed by the children. Even the shyest children became bold and decisive when they told the story. Their speech, at other times broken and incoherent, became fluent, expressive and resonant.

Stories were retold by Nina, Petrik, Lyuda, Slava and Valya, children in whom I had observed some difficulties in the development of their speech and thought.

Each time we went to the Story Room the children wanted to play. All of them, boys and girls, found a favourite puppet or toy. The games became creative: the little ones became the fairytale heroes and the puppets in their hands helped them to communicate their thoughts and feelings. One child took a toy—the straw bull-calf (the hero of a well-known Ukrainian folk tale)—a second child selected a grandmother puppet, and a third a grandfather puppet. And straight away they began living in a fairytale world. They did not just repeat the words of the characters, but innovated, introducing the play of their imaginations into the story. Some girls just wanted to play dolls. One would sit a doll on a little sofa and speak gently and comfortingly to it in a singing voice. Another girl had a sick baby doll and was treating it.

It did not bother me that boys and girls played with dolls or puppets for several years. This is not some sort of 'childishness' as some teachers think but the same fairytale make-believe, the same process of bringing creatures to life, which permeates the process of composing or listening to a fairytale. Dolls or puppets provide an animated image of that which, in the words of the French writer Saint-Exupéry, children are seeking to 'tame'.[26] Every child wants to have something that is infinitely dear to them. I carefully observed what sort of psychological relationships children were developing with their favourite dolls. I was glad that boys were forming long-term friendships with dolls. Kostya had an unremarkable doll—an old fisherman with a fishing rod. One of the doll's legs broke off several times, and in the end Kostya made him a wooden leg and carved a knotty walking stick for him, so the doll

---

26 Translator's note: Saint-Exupery uses the word 'tame' in *The little prince*, to refer to the process of establishing ties with another being.

could walk to the river bank. The boy liked to talk with his old friend, telling him the best places to catch crucian carp and bream ... Larisa's favourite dolls were a grandmother and granddaughter. The little girl made glasses for the grandmother and put a warm rug under her legs, covering her shoulders with a shawl. Valya also had two dolls—a cat and a mouse. The little girl changed the bow on the cat's neck every week, and for some reason brought a green rug for the mouse.

In the Story Room, children's imaginations knew no bounds. As soon as they saw a new object they linked it with other objects, and their childish imaginations went to work. A new idea would be born, their thoughts raced, their eyes shone, and their speech flowed smoothly and rhythmically. Taking this into consideration, I made sure that there were always a variety of objects in different corners of the Story Room, between which it would be possible to make real or imaginary connections. I wanted the children to exercise their imaginations and create new stories. A frightened little kitten was sitting next to a heron standing on one leg and the children's imaginations created several interesting stories around those two characters. There was a little boat with an oar and next to it a frog: these just begged to have a story told about them. A cave with a baby bear peeping out, a mosquito and a fly, unnaturally large compared with the baby bear (such things are permissible in a story), a baby pig with a wash basin and soap—all of these things not only made the children smile, they stimulated their imaginations.

If I managed to get a child who was experiencing serious difficulties in developing their thinking processes to make up a story that linked several objects from the surrounding world, it meant that I could confidently say the child had learnt to think. I have already described the difficulty I had awakening Valya's thought processes and strengthening her memory. One means for awakening her thinking was through the feelings of wonder she experienced when discovering unexpected links between objects and phenomena of the surrounding world. A second, no less important means was stories. For a long time Valya was unable to make up a single story and that worried me. At last, when she was in grade three, the girl made up a story about a frog, a boat and a fish. Here is the content of that story:

'A frog saw a boat by the bank of a river. An old fisherman had left the boat there while he went to the village for bread. The frog wanted to have a ride. It crawled out of its puddle, jumped into the boat, and grabbed the oar. Just then a fish swam up and said, "What are you thinking. You only swim in puddles, but a boat likes deep water." The frog did not listen to the fish's advice, and set off for its puddle. It was getting close when the boat said, "Frog, frog, where are you taking me?" The frog answered, "To my home puddle. I want all my relatives to see how I can row a boat." The boat smiled and thought, "Soon grandpa will come. He'll teach you how to row a boat." The frog just managed to get the boat to his puddle. The boat got bogged in the mud and would move no further. The frog wheezed and grunted, but it could not move the boat. All the other frogs had crawled out of the puddle to watch because the frog had called out, "Come and see how well I am rowing the boat!" The frog was ashamed and jumped into the puddle, making mud fly in all directions, and all the frogs laughed and laughed. Then the old fisherman came and dragged the boat out of the puddle. He frightened the frogs and they all hid in the green slime. In the evening they got their courage back, crawled out, and laughed and laughed. Since then, they laugh every night. From dusk till dawn their cries resound all over the swamp. That is them laughing at the boastful frog.'

For children, making up stories is one of the most interesting forms of poetic creativity. It is also an important means of intellectual development. If you want children to create artistic images you must be prepared to kindle their creativity with your own. If you do not know how to create, or if descending to the world of children's interests seems to you to be a waste of time, you will not get anywhere.

I have recorded the tales that the children created during our twilight evenings. Those tales are dear to me. They represent bright flames of thought that I managed to kindle in the children. If not for this creativity, this telling of tales, the speech of many of the children would have been incoherent and confused, and their thought chaotic. I became convinced that there is a direct correlation between aesthetic feelings and the richness of children's oral vocabulary. Aesthetic feelings clothe words with emotions. The more interesting a tale is and the more unusual the setting that children find themselves in, the more powerful the play of children's imaginations, and the more unexpected the images that the little ones create. During our twilight evenings my pupils composed dozens of stories that have been brought together in a handwritten collection entitled 'Evening Twilight Tales'.

Amongst the Evening Twilight Tales are interesting stories about animals and birds, trees and flowers. The composition of stories about flowers brought me and the children particular joy. I told the boys and girls about the emotional life of human beings and about the embodiment of those feelings in songs and legends about flowers. I would suggest the beginning for a story and the children's imaginations created striking images.

Every two or three months we renewed the props in each corner of the Story Room, cutting figures, trees and bushes from plywood, building towers, palaces, fishing shacks and shelters. The children learnt how to make fairytale characters from papier-mâché to enrich our fairytale world. Each new setting in one of the corners was devoted to a new tale. In this way we 'illustrated' many tales: 'Ivasik-Telesik' (a Ukrainian folk tale), 'The sleeping princess' (Vasily Zhukovsky), 'The scarlet flower' (Sergei Aksakov), 'The sharp-toothed mouse and the rich sparrow' (Vladimir Dal'), 'The frog-traveller' (Vsevolod Garshin), 'The snow queen' (Hans Christian Andersen), 'The musicians of Bremen' (Brothers Grimm), 'Sleeping beauty' (Charles

Perrault), 'Maria the beauty with the long plait and Vanyushka' (a Russian folk tale), 'A nail from my native home' (a Swedish folk tale), 'The hunchback sparrow' (a Japanese folk tale). These tales entered the children's spiritual lives in the same way that the image of a much-loved person who has brought us happiness enters our consciousness for ever. The children remembered what they had heard, word for word, for the rest of their lives, though nobody had expected that of them. When words excite a child with their unique beauty, with their subtle shades of colour and meaning, they are memorised for life. Such memorisation does not overload the memory; it just makes it sharper.

The first telling of a new tale was a major event in the children's lives. I will never forget the excitement when we created the setting for Hans Christian Andersen's 'The snow queen'. It was in grade two. The early twilight of winter had arrived and the children gathered in the Story Room. The setting for the action includes homes with steep rooves, a fairytale palace surrounded by tall cliffs, swift-footed deer and snow drifts, all of which the children created with their own hands. But not everyone had heard the fairytale yet. Lights came on in the windows of the homes, snowflakes fell from the sky, and the evening darkness surrounded us. The children listened to the teacher with bated breath … When the tale was finished, the children wanted to hear it again. That ability to be charmed by words was very dear to me. I repeated the tale as many times as the children asked for it. And the children wanted to hear about the Snow Queen again and again, not because they wanted to memorise the words, but because the words sounded like wonderful music.

A teacher constantly thinks: what do I have to do so children will have a deep knowledge of their native language, so it will become part of their spiritual life, a sharp, incisive tool, a colourful palette, and a subtle means for discovering truth? Language is the material expression of thought, and children will only fully know their language when, along with meaning, they take in the emotional colouring and thrilling music of each word. Without experiencing the beauty of a word, the hidden facets of its meaning will remain inaccessible to children's minds. And the experience of beauty is inconceivable without fantasy, without children's personal participation in the creativity associated with stories. Stories provide an opportunity for active aesthetic creativity, embracing all aspects of a child's spiritual life: intellect, feelings, imagination and will. Such creativity begins with retelling a story and its highest stage is dramatic performance.

In the Story Room we started a puppet theatre and a drama group. Here we first staged a dramatic performance of the folk tale about the Mitten, which somehow accommodates so many brave animals. Then, with great interest, we prepared performances of the tale of the Frog Princess and the Japanese tale about the Hunchback Sparrow. In grade four the children collectively wrote a tale about a grasshopper musician and acted out all the roles.

In the Story Room I first read the children *Robinson Crusoe*, *The adventures of Baron Munchausen*, *Gulliver's travels*, 'The tale of the Tsar Sultan', and *Janko the Musician*. For the rest of their lives the children would remember the charm of those winter evenings, when a blizzard whirled outside the windows and they clambered up the shore of an uninhabited island together with the shipwrecked Robinson Crusoe, and experienced the hardships of his battle with nature. In the Story Room we read all the tales of Hans Christian Andersen, Leo Tolstoy, Konstantin Ushinsky and the Brothers Grimm.

One aspect of our reading was a little unusual. I knew all the tales and stories I have mentioned by heart and only used books to show the little ones the illustrations. Just like telling fairytales, reading stories was a powerful means for educating the intellect and developing kindly, humane feelings.

It is possible to say without exaggeration that reading in childhood is mostly about the education of the heart: human nobility touching the hidden recesses of a child's soul. The words that expose children to noble ideas leave in their hearts the seeds of humanity and support the development of a conscience.

## *The story continues—our Island of Wonders*

CHILDREN ARE ATTRACTED BY ANYTHING unusual, by the romance of travel and adventure or a battle with the elemental forces of nature. When I first told the children the tale of Robinson Crusoe they wanted to pretend to be travellers, to hear the sound of the ocean waves and the thunder of a waterfall. The children decided to make their own 'Island of Wonders'—a secret place where they could live in a world of make-believe. We created this 'island' in a thicket of blackthorn and acacia. We built Crusoe's dwelling surrounded by a picket fence to keep out wild animals and with the same sort of hearth as the hero of the story had. We made a little window through which we could look out at the boundless expanse of 'ocean'. We dug a vegetable bed and sowed a few dozen seeds of wheat and barley. Kolya even brought a baby goat from home—after all Crusoe had goats. We brought an old barrel, some rope and bricks. We made knives from the hoops on the barrel and fish nets from the rope. Like prehistoric hunters, we made fire by rubbing two pieces of dry wood together. After all, it might well have happened that Crusoe had no other means of obtaining fire.

During some rain, a hollow from which we had dug earth for our dwelling filled with water and made a small pond. The children splashed in the water, imagining they were bathing in the limitless ocean. And where there is ocean there must be ships. The children found a piece of willow and began to fashion a boat from it. It was not easy work, but their efforts were crowned with success. They added sails to the boat and it set off on a voyage.

Behind a small hill—in the children's imaginations it was a high mountain—we created the land of Lilliput. From plywood and reeds we built a city—the capital of Lilliput. From clay we moulded the figures of horses, cattle and sheep, and of the legendary hero Ilya Muromets and his enemy Nightingale the Robber. We put the figures amongst some bushes. This was the dense forest of Ancient Russia. We came here on quiet summer evenings and everyone wanted to tell stories about the bold, courageous warrior, Ilya Muromets.

Forcing our way through the dense bushes, we found a small hole on the side of the gulley. This was the cave of the wicked wizard Kashchei the Immortal. Somewhere in its hidden depths a beautiful princess was languishing.

In warm weather when we could not manage a longer journey, we spent our rest days on the Island of Wonders. Near Crusoe's dwelling we built a shelter of branches and straw. This was a favourite spot, from which the wings of fantasy carried us into a fairytale world. The fairytale heroes were nearby, and as night descended on the earth we seemed to hear the whistle of Nightingale the Robber, the scratchy wheezing of Kashchei the Immortal, and the cautious footsteps of Puss in Boots. The flames of children's imaginations blazed especially brightly here. Yura, Galya, Tina and Vitya created wonderful stories in this magic place. The setting itself stimulated the play of their imaginations. Their thoughts flowed freely and irrepressibly, and the children found vivid language to express their feelings. Here is a tale about a golden rainbow composed by Seryozha:

'One day the giant blacksmiths came to the sun and said, "Oh Sun, our iron hammers are worn out; soon we will not be able to forge the silver threads. Our anvil is also old. Let us go down to Earth to get some iron." The sun let the blacksmiths go. The giant blacksmiths set off for the world of people, but dark clouds blocked their way. The blacksmiths looked down at Earth through the clouds, from way up high. How could they get down? They returned to the sun and said, "Oh Sun, how are we to get down to Earth? Please make us a bridge." The sun threw its rays through the clouds and a sun bridge shone in the sky. From the earth people saw a golden rainbow. The blacksmiths climbed down to the earth, got iron from the people, and returned to the sun over the sun bridge. As soon as the sun saw their white beards, he took away the golden rays and the rainbow disappeared. Since that time, whenever dark clouds appear in the sky the sun sends the giant blacksmiths to the earth for iron. But in winter there are no rainbows, because the days are short and the giant blacksmiths do not use their hammers much.'

I was very glad that every child made up a story here. I will never forget one quiet summer evening when after sunset the sky took on an ash-grey hue. Such evenings only happen a few times a year when summer is at its zenith. It is as if the sky itself is radiating a weak luminescence; dusk lasts longer than usual on such evenings and the stars take a long time to come out … The children were silent, enchanted by the beauty of nature. At such moments the fire of imagination burns especially brightly. And then Nina began to tell a story she had thought up:

'The sun went away to rest in his magic garden. He lay down to rest but forgot to close his eyes, and the giant blacksmiths thought that it was still day. They kept hammering and hammering at the silver threads. The threads fell apart and turned to dust. The silver dust spread all over the sky, burning and shining …'

My heart beat more quickly when I heard this wonderful story. How could I not feel joy, when wonder at the beauty of nature and fantastic fairytale characters had unlocked the wellsprings of thought in a child's mind? I am not sure why, but on those longest of June evenings, when the ash-grey firmament appears like a mysterious veil, children's imaginations were particularly active.

After finishing grade three, the children wanted to create 'the headquarters of a detachment of partisans' on our Island of Wonders. As you would expect, the 'headquarters' were located in an underground bunker, which the senior students helped us to dig and fit out. Thus began an entertaining game that lasted several months. The children wanted to play at night and it was difficult to stop them. They went on reconnaissance missions and learnt to use a compass. They made wooden 'automatic weapons' and 'machine guns', and issued orders before each military operation.

During their last year of primary school, the students were very taken with *The malachite casket*, a collection of fairytales by the Russian writer Pavel Bazhov. The children's eyes shone with joy when I read about the wonderful semi-precious stones of the Urals, and the amazing beauty of the caves where malachite deposits are to be found—the untold riches of the good Mistress of Copper Mountain. The children wanted to make something beautiful, mysterious and romantic. Someone had the idea of creating an underground emerald kingdom. We began to collect fragments of glass of many colours: green, blue, orange, red and violet, and embedded them in the wall of our cave. It is hard to describe in words the feelings of wonder and delight when a little electric lamp came on in our cave, and the walls lit up with a rainbow coloured glow. New stories were born here, and I was convinced yet again of the enormous power of aesthetic feelings in educating, developing and strengthening the intellect. Before my eyes the thinking of Valya, Petrik and Nina took another leap forward, as those children composed stories that impressed me with the richness of their imaginations. Lyuda also made up a story here. I became convinced that the reason for her silence was not a delay in her intellectual development, but dreaminess and thoughtfulness.

# *Song reveals to children the beauty of the world*

IN THE PRIMARY CLASSES, AS in the School of Joy, we listened to the music of nature, which is an important source of rich emotional associations for language and a key to understanding and appreciating the beauty of melodies.

Listening to the music of nature, children prepared themselves emotionally for choral singing. I tried to give the children opportunities to discern music in nature that was in harmony with the song we were about to sing.

Not far from our school there is a beautiful spot. The evening sky is reflected in the mirror-like surface of a pond, the songs of birds carry from a nearby meadow, and the resonant song of the grasshoppers greets the cool of the evening. Here, on several occasions, we listened to the music of nature, before learning 'Evening sunset', a song by the Ukrainian composer Yakiv Stepovyi. This song gives a beautiful portrayal of the wonder of the evening sky. In its melody the children recognised the music that had charmed them on quiet summer evenings. We learnt the song at that beautiful spot. The children wanted to sing. Then a few weeks later the children performed the song in our music room. The song reminded the children of the beauty of the evening sunset and their faces shone with joy.

One sunny day we listened to the music of the forest at noon. The leaves were quietly rustling on the tall trees, a woodpecker was tapping, a wild turtle-dove was cooing in the distance, and the song of a cuckoo could be heard.

The feelings inspired by this natural music opened the children's ears to the beauty of Anton Arensky's song 'The cuckoo'.

The children loved their choral singing of Mozart's 'Lullaby', a Czech folk song called 'The magpie', Tchaikovsky's 'Children's song', Speier's 'A goat with horns comes tramping', Vasiliev-Bulgai's 'Autumn song', the Polish 'Bird song', Lysenko's 'Song of the fox', and Iordansky's 'Song about a lapwing'. As a rule, our choir sang unaccompanied. I was very glad that everyone loved to sing. The children began to have their favourite compositions: Dunaevsky's 'Fly, doves, fly', Mozart's 'Lullaby', Sandler's 'A song about Mum', the Ukrainian folk songs 'Flood waters', 'On the mountain the reapers are reaping', 'The girl from Podolia', 'Blow, wind, to Ukraine', the Russian folk songs 'A girl was walking through the forest', 'Oh, street so wide', 'The orchard', the Belarussian folk song 'Two doves flew by', and the Czech folk song 'The shepherd boy'.

The children were always keen to get together and sing. Song became a part of their spiritual lives, imparting vivid emotional associations to their thoughts, and awakening feelings of love for their native land and the beauty of the surrounding world.

The Ukrainian folk song 'On the mountain the reapers are reaping' made a particularly strong impression on the children. It gave rise to vivid images of our people's distant past and heroic struggle against invaders. The melody of the song transported the children to a difficult time when the homeland was fighting for independence, and they saw the world through the eyes of our distant ancestors several centuries ago. They saw reapers harvesting wheat in the fields. From time to time the men and women looked anxiously to the horizon, from whence at any moment the enemy could appear. Then it would be necessary to put down their scythes and take up swords, to defend their homes and their little children, who were sleeping in the shade of the sheaves of wheat. Only a song, with its bewitching melodies, could impress such images on a child's heart and mind. Only song can reveal the beauty of a nation's soul. The melody and words of a national song have great educational power, capable of revealing to a child a nation's ideals and aspirations.

After singing that wonderful song the children wanted to dream of those places in which the beauty of our natural surroundings is most strikingly revealed. Places that were apparently unremarkable came to mind: a willow leaning over a pond, a tall and slender poplar at a crossroad, a little stream flowing into the Dnieper, a ripening wheat field, a meadow lit up by bright sunlight. The children spoke with enthusiasm of the things they loved most about our native village. After each such evening the conviction grew in me that song provides, figuratively speaking, a magic window through which the soul views the world, our homeland, the past and present of our nation, and the beauty of nature. Song opens that magic window. Song awakens feelings of wonder at everything that humanises our perception of the world. If that window remains closed, people remain deaf and blind. Nothing connects them to their native land; they do not have a homeland; they do not feel the beauty of their native tongue.

There is a human quality that we might call sensitivity or emotional responsiveness. It is expressed in the fact that the surrounding world heightens our ability to experience emotion. People with a sensitive, emotionally responsive nature cannot turn a blind eye to another person's grief, suffering or misfortune. Their conscience compels them to lend a hand. This quality is educated by music and song.

The emotional character of a morally and aesthetically educated person is also expressed in their responsiveness to kind words, advice or good wishes. If you want your words to teach people how to live, if you want your pupils to strive to be good, educate emotional sensitivity in their young hearts. Music plays an important role in influencing young hearts. Music and morality: this is a topic that is yet to be thoroughly studied and researched.

Song instils a poetic vision of the world. I remember how once, after singing a song into which our nation had poured deep feeling, we went into the steppe. Before us stretched an endless sea of wheat, beyond which the dark blue shapes of ancient burial mounds could be seen on the horizon. A road wound in a narrow ribbon between the yellow fields, and a lark sang in the blue sky. The children stood, as if seeing this part of their native land for the first time. 'It is like the song about the reapers', said sensitive, impressionable Varya. I felt then that in each child's soul the words of their favourite song were playing. Song opens our eyes to the beauty of our native land, and that beauty becomes even dearer to us.

Our native songs revealed to the children the priceless spiritual richness of their native language. Thanks to song, the children were more sensitive to the sound of words.

At first we did not have many recordings of those instrumental musical works that I considered just as essential as the stories of Tolstoy and Chekhov, Gorky and Korolenko, Gaidar and Chukovsky, Sienkiewicz and Jack London, the poetry of Pushkin and Shevchenko, the fairytales of Hans Christian Andersen and the Brothers Grimm. I could not imagine education without listening to music, without young people having their favourite melodies during the childhood years. At the beginning of our work in the School of Joy our staff collected several recordings of musical works on tapes and records. We considered this a great treasure, but the fact that it did not adequately represent the spiritual treasures of humanity concerned us. By the end of our work in grade one, we had recordings of twenty-seven works, of which seven were songs and twenty were instrumental works. We went to the music room to listen to music twice a week. Some of the songs and melodies were already familiar to the children from the School of Joy. Many times the children listened to Tchaikovsky's 'The song of the lark' and 'The snowdrop', Mozart's 'Lullaby', Schumann's 'The wild rider', Grieg's 'In the hall of the mountain king', Lysenko's 'Song of the fox', 'Song of the goat' and 'Song of the baby wolf' from his children's opera, and the Ukrainian folk songs 'I wonder at the sky', 'Rage and groan, Dnieper so wide' and 'The sun is setting, the mountains grow dark'.

During four years of work with the children our music collection roughly doubled in size. That was not a lot, but I was less concerned with the quantity than with ensuring the children got to hear musical treasures (especially of Ukrainian and Russian music). I wanted them to receive aesthetic pleasure from listening to the same works several times, and for this to leave its mark on their thought and their emotional life.

It did not matter that the children heard only one new melody in a month if that melody became a source of spiritual pleasure for the rest of their lives. I avoided exposing them to too many new works, which would only have entertained them without leaving any trace in their hearts.

Apart from the works already mentioned, the children listened to the following works over a period of four years: 'Chernomor's march' from Glinka's opera *Ruslan and Lyudmila*, the march from Gounod's opera *Faust*, Grieg's 'Norwegian dance' and 'Kobold', and numerous works by Tchaikovsky: 'The grass grows green', the dance of the shepherds from the ballet *The nutcracker*, 'March of the wooden soldiers', 'An old French song', 'The sick doll', 'Italian song', 'A children's song', 'Kamarinskaya', 'Dance of the little swans' from *Swan Lake* and 'Dance of the sugar plum fairy'. We also listened to 'The flight of the bumblebee' and 'Three miracles' from Rimsky-Korsakov's opera *Tale of the Tsar Sultan*, Schumann's 'The happy farmer', Grieg's 'Dance of the elves', Schubert's 'Ecossaise', Dunaevsky's 'The starlings have returned', a passage from Stetsenko's opera *The fox, the cat and the rooster*, a passage from Lysenko's opera *Winter and spring*, Beethoven's 'Marmotte', the Swiss song 'The cuckoo', the Polish song 'Birdsong', the Ukrainian folk songs 'The neighbour', 'There is flax on the mountain', 'The mountain stands high' and 'Blow, wind, to Ukraine', the Hungarian folk song 'The nightingale' and the Russian folk song 'In the field a birch tree stood'.

Before listening to music I would explain the real or fantastic images that were reflected in the music. I gave considerable significance to this introduction, which put the children into the mood for listening to the musical work. For example, before listening to 'The dance of the sugar plum fairy' from *The nutcracker*, I told the children the original story by ETA Hoffmann upon which Tchaikovsky's ballet was based. Using vivid, expressive language, I tried to create an image of the good fairy in the children's minds: light, ethereal and gracious. 'You will hear the tinkling of little crystal bells', I told the children. 'This wonderful music paints a picture of the beautiful fairy's surroundings. When I listen to it, I imagine the light, slender columns of a wonderful palace, brightly lit.' The children listened to the music and then talked about how they imagined the fairy's palace. Their imaginations drew ponds, fountains, shady groves and secret caves. These fantastic images prompted a desire to listen to the music again.

The interpretation of a musical work, especially one that is new to children, requires considerable tact and educational skill. We must never forget that music is the language of feeling. Even a folk song, with its unsophisticated and at times elementary words, is perceived as a work of art because of its melody. In order to clarify the essence of the artistic images of a musical work, the teacher must understand the composer's descriptive devices. The explanation should be a complete artistic narrative heard by the child from the lips of the teacher. This narrative should itself stimulate feelings and emotions, creating vivid pictures in the child's imagination.

I am deeply convinced that the beauty of music is a powerful stimulus for thought. The vivid images that arise in a child's mind under the influence of musical melodies invigorate thought, as if directing its many currents into a single stream. The children strive to describe in words that which their imagination has created and that which they feel. For those children with delayed intellectual development, listening to music was a truly powerful stimulus for thought. After listening to music, I encouraged the children to convey their impressions in a relaxed way.

In the music room we played on folk pipes and learnt our favourite tunes. In grade two our amateur group for playing folk pipes included nine of my pupils and four students from other classes. The children made their own instruments. Seryozha, Yura, Tina and Lida were highly skilled at making folk pipes. They would go to a grove and choose suitable material, store the cut branches in the shade, and test the sound of each instrument until they achieved a pure, melodious sound. In grade three we obtained two bayans[27] and three violins. Yura, Seryozha, Fedya, Lida, Kolya, Tina, Larisa, Sanya, and Shura learnt to play the bayan and the violin. By the time they completed primary school nineteen children had musical instruments at home: bayans and violins. But the children did not forget their folk pipes. Some of the children discovered a gift for music, but my main aim was not so much to nurture individual talent as to ensure that all students loved music and that it became a spiritual requirement for all of them.

That which is neglected in childhood will never be made up for in young adulthood, and especially at a mature age. This rule applies to all areas of a child's spiritual life and especially to aesthetic education. Sensitivity and responsiveness to beauty is much deeper during the childhood years than during later periods of personality development. One of the main tasks facing primary teachers is the education of a thirst for beauty, which determines to a considerable extent the tenor of children's spiritual lives and their relationships in groups. A thirst for beauty helps to establish moral beauty, giving rise to intolerance for anything vulgar or ugly.

'People with violins in their hands are not capable of doing evil', says an old Ukrainian saying attributed to the remarkable thinker

---

[27] Translator's note: A bayan is a type of chromatic button accordion.

Grigory Skovoroda. Evil is incompatible with true beauty. One of an educator's most important tasks is, figuratively speaking, to give each child a violin so they can feel how music is born. In our times, when the technology for recording and distributing music has become so universal, this educational task takes on a special significance.

Not to allow the younger generation to become merely consumers of beauty: this is an issue not only for aesthetic, but for moral education.

## Books in the spiritual life of a child

BOOKS PLAY A MAJOR ROLE in the spiritual lives of children, but only when children are able to read well. What does it mean 'to read well'? Above all it means to have mastered the elementary skills of reading. I tried to ensure that children had a real thirst for individual reading. In grades one and two I tried to make sure that every child borrowed a book from the library every week or two and read it aloud. Without this it is impossible to develop sound skills and the ability to read fluently with good comprehension.

In grade two every child began keeping a notebook: a 'word casket'. In it each child recorded words that seemed interesting or that were not understood. (I explained to the children the meaning or the emotional colouring of the recorded words.) In grades three and four, as well as recording individual words in their 'word caskets', the students recorded turns of speech, phrases and sentences that appealed to them.

Reading as a source of spiritual enrichment is not limited to the ability to read; it just begins with that ability. It often happens that a student can read fluently and without errors, but books have not yet become a path leading to heightened intellectual, moral and aesthetic development. To be able to read also means to be sensitive to the meaning and beauty of words, to their subtle nuances. A student is only really 'reading' when the words on the page play and palpitate, overflowing with the colours and melodies of the surrounding world. Reading is a window through which children see and discover the world and themselves. That window opens for children only when along with reading (beginning at the same time or even before a book is opened), painstaking work is conducted around language. This work should encompass all spheres of children's activity and spiritual lives: work, play, communion with nature, music and creativity. Without working to create beauty, without stories and fantasy, without play and music, it is impossible to imagine reading as a significant area of a child's spiritual life. The foundational experiences required for the development of speech and thought are several. They include journeys to the living source of thought, imparting emotional and aesthetic colouring to words through the beauty of speech, and reading literary treasures.

Before reading their first words, children should hear the reading of their teacher, mother and father, and feel the beauty of literary images. Journeys to the world of nature should not be seen as something divorced from books. Children will not appreciate the beauty of the surrounding world if they have not felt the beauty of words read in books. The heart and mind of a child may be approached from two directions, which at first glance may appear to be contradictory: from books, from the written word to oral language; and from living words that have already entered the spiritual world of a child to books, reading and writing. Emotional and aesthetic preparation for reading and writing is an important precondition for children to actually learn to read and write; not in order to receive a grade, but because reading and writing are essential for their spiritual lives, because the inability to read and write will deprive them of many joys.

The fact that the children had already learnt in the School of Joy to convey their feelings and thoughts about the beauty of the surrounding world in pictures and expressive captions, was the result of emotional and aesthetic preparation for reading and writing. In our system of education, journeys to nature are not an end in themselves but a means of facilitating a child's intellectual development via language. The children might have been indifferent to nature, to the play of colours and sounds, to the limitless variety of life, if not for words, if not for intellectual development, if not for efforts directed at that most important educational goal—to teach children to think, to notice the interactions between objects and phenomena, to generalise, and to make abstractions from nature, visual images and representations.

I ensured that even in grade one, children felt a need to read, and that reading was not limited to exercises developing the skills of fluent perception and pronunciation of words. To become a part of students' spiritual lives, reading must correspond to their level of development—intellectual, emotional and aesthetic—and at the same time facilitate further development. The correct choice of reading material is an extremely important matter for an educator. Books designed to teach reading unfortunately lack many literary attributes accessible to a child's understanding. Three months after the beginning of grade one we began to read interesting fairytales and stories that were not in the reading text book.

I handed out to the children the book *Ukrainian and Russian tales*. I prepared them to read the Ukrainian folk tale 'The straw bullock' by outlining its content and illustrating my account with pictures. The children opened the book. One child read the story, then a second and a third. However many times we read the same thing—of course it had to be interesting for the children—they did not get sick of it, because for each child reading was a deeply personal experience rather than just the repetition of an exercise. Each child invested the words with their own individual interpretation. The children listened to the reading just as attentively as if each one of them—one after another—had sung the same song, one whose words and melody moved them. Each one would sing in their own way, the words taking on their own colouration and communicating subtle variations in experience, perceptions and ideas. During such reading, words sound like music, like a melody.

When preparing for emotionally expressive, individual reading it is particularly important that children should have frequently visited the source of thought and experienced the beauty of words. A student reads the sentence: 'The bullock went into a dark forest, and a grey wolf met him there.' In the children's minds there are unforgettable pictures associated with the words 'dark forest': evening twilight in the forest, mysterious rustling at night, and the disturbing sound of leaves before a storm. All of these associations are already a part of their spiritual life, and come to life with all the vivid colours and beautiful sounds of nature when they hear the words 'dark forest'. No explanations from the teacher—how to read, how to pronounce, what intonation to use—can teach children to read with deep emotion if they do not know the way to the source of living words and thought.

From the very first days of our work at the school I was concerned that not a single bad book should find its way into the children's hands; that the children should live in a world of interesting works that were part of the golden treasury of national and world culture. This is an exceptionally important matter. During a whole lifetime a person can only read around 2000 books. Consequently in childhood and early youth we should choose reading material very thoughtfully. Children may not read many books, but let each book leave a deep impression on their hearts and minds so that they return to it many times, each time discovering new riches in it. It is very important that children should experience satisfaction and pleasure from expressive reading. The power and beauty of words is revealed in the way they are spoken, so it is very important that the experience of a word's emotional colouring should come from hearing the word spoken aloud during expressive reading.

We already had a class library in grade one. It consisted of three sections. The first section contained stories that were, in my view, of the greatest value for the moral, intellectual and aesthetic education of children. (We bought fifteen copies of each of these books so that during reading lessons there would be a copy for each desk.) This section was intended to be read during the four years of primary schooling. It included stories selected for their deeply humane ideas, presented in a form accessible to children and embodied in vivid literary images. They included Leo Tolstoy's 'Shark', 'The Leap' and 'A prisoner of the Caucasus'; Pyotr Yershov's *The little humpbacked horse*; Mykhailo Kotsiubynsky's 'The fir tree'; Vasily Zhukovsky's 'Sleeping princess' and *Odysseus in the cave of the cyclops*; Dmitry Mamin-Sibiryak's 'Emelya the hunter', 'Wintering station on the Studenaya River', 'The rich man and Yeremka', 'The adopted child' and *Grey neck*; Hans Christian Andersen's 'Thumbelina', 'The ugly duckling' and 'The emperor's new clothes'; Victor Hugo's 'Cosette' and 'Gavroche' (from *Les Miserables*); the Brothers Grimm's 'Hansel and Gretel', 'Lazy Hans' and 'The three children of fortune'; Alexander Pushkin's 'Tale of the Tsar Sultan', 'Tale of the dead princess', 'The stationmaster', 'Anchar', 'The prisoner', 'Nanny', 'The little bird' and 'Winter Evening'; Janusz Korczak's 'When I am little again'; Vladimir Korolenko's 'Children of the underground', Nikolai Nekrasov's 'Peasant children', 'Uncle Yakov' and 'Grandpa Mazai and the hares'; Ivan Turgenev's 'The quail'; Dmitry Grigorovich's 'The gutta-percha boy'; Vsevolod Garshin's 'Signal'; Konstantin Stanyukovich's 'Maksimka', 'Nanny' and 'The escape'; Anton Chekhov's 'Kashtanka', 'Whitebrow', 'Vanka', 'The runaway', 'Boys' and 'The chameleon'; Henryk Sienkiewicz's *Janko the musician*; Jack London's 'The story of Keesh'; Mark Twain's *The adventures of Tom*

*Sawyer*; Maksim Gorky's 'Pepe', 'Children of Parma', 'The incident with Yevseika', 'Ilya's childhood' and 'Morning'; Arkady Gaidar's 'Chuk and Gek', 'Distant lands' and 'Timur and his team'; Vladimir Bonch-Bruyevich's 'Lenin and children'; Arkhip Teslenko's 'The school student'; Panas Mirny's 'Morozenko'; and Ivan Franko's 'Gryts' school lesson'.

A common feature of these books is the vivid, artistic portrayal of humane ideals—above all respect for the human personality. For the children, reading these stories was not just a way of coming to know the world, not just an exercise facilitating the acquisition of sound reading habits and skills, but a school in emotional and moral education. Each book left a deep impression on the children's souls. Mamin-Sibiryak's wonderful story 'Wintering station on the Studenaya River' left an enormous impression. It tells of a lonely old man, forgotten by everyone, whiling away his days deep in the taiga. I noticed that after reading such stories the children became more acutely aware of their surroundings.

We read these stories both during lessons and as an extracurricular activity. This section of our library could be compared to a collection of musical works intended for collective listening.

The second section was made up of fairytales, poems and fables. These books were for independent reading outside lesson time. Each child chose a work that interested them (and such interest could be prompted by a good illustration or by a teacher's or friend's description of what they had read).

The third section of our class library contained stories from ancient Greek mythology. This collection contained books that had been found with great difficulty, in which the myths of Hellas were retold in a form accessible to children. My pupils remembered for the rest of their lives those evenings when I told them about the adventures of Odysseus, about the Titans, Poseidon and Zeus, about Antaeus and the feats of Hercules. Ancient mythology not only introduces children to a wonderful page in humanity's history; it awakens the imagination, develops the intellect, and fosters an interest in the distant past.

From the middle of grade one, we began to conduct collective readings. I issued all the children with copies of the same book so they could read it at home as preparation for our collective reading. The reader may question going to the Story Room to read a story whose content everyone already knew well. How could children want to do that, and would it not be better to read something new? Yes, you also need to read new, unfamiliar books, and we did read new books. But a work will enter the spiritual world of children only when they want to read to their friends something that they have taken to heart, when they want to convey their feelings in words. We read each book from the first section of our library at least ten times, and that repetition did not cause the children's interest to wane. The book may have been read two or three weeks ago, but the children had not forgotten it; they wanted to read it again, and came to school especially for that purpose. Three or four months passed and again the children wanted to read a book that they loved, and again we devoted a collective reading session to it.

But the beauty and power of a work will touch the heart and excite the mind only if children have felt the subtle nuances of words before they learn to read. Those who have not discovered the enchanting beauty of words during journeys to the living source of thought, will never want to listen two, three or ten times to something they already know.

We also devoted lessons to our favourite stories. The children excitedly prepared for reading. Each one read the passage they liked best and that moved them the most.

We set aside special time for reading poetry. I recited by heart the finest models of poetry from the treasure house of human culture: poems by Pushkin, Lermontov, Zhukovsky, Fet, Shevchenko,

Lesya Ukrainka, Schiller, Mickiewicz, Heine, Béranger and other poets. The children developed a desire to learn their own favourite poems by heart. During four years of study the students learnt many poems, but only after they had experienced the magic sound of poetic verse.

Good poetry combines the beauty of words, images and melody. I wanted the children to experience at an early age the oneness of these aesthetic attributes, and I recited poems by Ukrainian and Russian poets to them. We read Pushkin's 'The song of wise Oleg' and Shevchenko's 'The maidservant' many times. Nearly all the children knew these poems by heart (without any special work to memorise them). The children also learnt many short, lyrical poems describing the beauty of nature. The children especially loved serial reading of long works in instalments. In the Nook of Dreams we read *The adventures of Tom Sawyer* over a period of several weeks. The setting in which we read the book strengthened its impact. We also read Maksim Gorky's *Childhood*, Valentin Kataev's *A white sail gleams* and Pavel Bazhov's *The malachite casket* in instalments.

With the passage of time we began to hold evening and morning performances of expressive reading. Each student who wanted to participate prepared their favourite short story or poem for public performance. These evenings and mornings were attended by many children from other classes, and eventually such readings were conducted as whole-school activities.

Twice a year, at the end of each semester, we held celebrations of our native language. Certain rituals became traditional at these celebrations. The children invited the oldest people in the village, who chose the best reader of a poem or story. It was a sort of performing arts competition and the winners received books as prizes. The prizes were presented to the children by senior collective farm workers who respected and valued our native language. They also told stories and recited poems. Sometimes a student and an old collective farm worker recited the same work. At the end of our fourth year of studies the spring celebration of our native language lasted for two days, because there were so many people wanting to recite a story, poem or fable.

Constant contact with elders—mothers, fathers, grandmothers and grandfathers—led to the formation of another interesting tradition. Our best readers began to read at home to their parents, and adults began to come to the school to hear children read. Several clubs sprang up for admirers and devotees of our native language, and these clubs were made up of highly respected adults. The fact that the children appeared to be the organisers of these clubs strengthened interest in books and reading.

The celebration of books became a school-wide tradition. The children came to school with their parents on 31 August, the eve of the first day of the school year. On this day everyone gave books as presents: the children to each other, and the parents to the children. Gradually it became the custom on this day for the collective farm management to give books to the leaders of our clubs for admirers and devotees of our native language.

I tried to make sure that each child gradually compiled their own personal library and that reading became an important spiritual requirement for each child. During the first two years of study in the primary classes, I made sure that a library was set up in each family. In some families the library contained over 500 books, in some less, but in every home the book collection grew each month. I became concerned if a whole month passed without a family adding a single book to their collection.

Self-education and an individual's spiritual life begin with books. There comes a point in the education process when mentors who have carefully led their pupils by the hand for so long are able to release the hand and say, 'Go on by yourself, and learn how to live'.

To be able to decide on such a step takes great educational insight. To prepare people spiritually for an independent life you have to lead them into the world of books. For each pupil, books have to become a friend, a mentor and a wise teacher. One of my main educational goals was to ensure that by the time each boy or girl completed primary school they sought solitude with a book, for thought and reflection. Solitude does not mean loneliness. Seeking solitude marks the beginning of self-directed training of a person's thoughts, feelings, convictions and attitudes. This is only possible if books have become a spiritual requirement in the life of a young person. In individual conversations I learnt which books interested each boy or girl, and what questions they were seeking answers to in books. I needed to know these things in order to be able to give judicious advice and help children find the books that were important to them.

A school only becomes a true centre for culture when four great loves rule in it: love for one's homeland, love for people, love for books and love for our native language.

Before beginning work with my pupils I had heard a lot about the difficulty of educational work with adolescents. I was told: 'It is easier to work with small children. As soon as little children become adolescents they change, and you will not recognise them. Their kindness, sensitivity and shyness will disappear, and in their place rudeness, harshness and indifference will appear.' Later on I became convinced how mistaken these words are. All the goodness 'disappears' in an adolescent only if it has never been created, if the educator thought that goodness is given to a child by nature. If you do not educate a love for books from childhood, if it has not become a spiritual imperative for life, upon reaching the adolescent years a young person's soul will be empty and evil will appear as if from nowhere.

# *Love for our native language*

FOR UKRAINIANS, OUR NATIVE LANGUAGE is Ukrainian. More than 36 million people speak that language today. But because of the historical path our nation has taken, the Russian language is very near and dear to us as well. These two related languages are interwoven by many threads. This makes mastery of the two languages both easier and more difficult. Hundreds of words that sound the same in both languages have different meanings. In hundreds of instances a word that has certain emotional connotations in Ukrainian, has different connotations in Russian. A word that sounds quite solemn in one language takes on ironic connotations in the other. For teachers in Ukrainian schools, these differing shades of meaning, these subtle differences in emotional and aesthetic connotations that are found in the two languages, are a source of cultural richness that we need to pass on to the next generation.

A language is a national treasure. 'However many languages I know, that many times I am a human being', a folk saying tells us. But the wealth enshrined in the languages of other nations will remain inaccessible if people have not mastered their native tongue and felt its beauty. The more deeply people appreciate the subtleties of their native language and the more sensitive they are to its nuances, the better prepared their minds are to master the languages of other nations, and the more actively their hearts apprehend the beauty of words.

I tried to make sure that this life-giving source—the richness of our native language—was accessible to children from the very first steps of their school lives. Journeying to the living source of thought and words, my pupils simultaneously discovered the emotional, aesthetic and semantic nuances of words from their native language and from the Russian language. I wanted the children to feel the beauty of language, to use words carefully, and to preserve their purity.

The way people speak is a mirror of their spiritual culture. The beauty, strength and expressiveness of our native language provides an important means for educating children, ennobling their feelings, their soul, their thoughts and emotions. It is difficult to place too high a value on this in the primary school when every encounter with new phenomena in the surrounding world arouses feelings of wonder in the hearts of children.

We went into nature—to the forest, the orchard, the fields, the meadows and the river bank—and I used words as a tool for opening the children's eyes to the richness of the surrounding world. Feeling and experiencing the beauty of everything they saw and heard, the children were receptive to the subtlest nuances of words, and it was through words that beauty entered their souls. Journeys to nature provided an initial stimulus for creativity. The children felt an urge to communicate their feelings and experiences, to talk about beauty. The children made up little compositions about nature. These compositions were an important way of developing language and thought. Each child first made up their composition and then wrote it down in class. I will provide some examples of these miniature compositions, composed orally during the first year of school and then written down in the 'Our native language' album, or in individual notebooks.[28]

## *The song of the lark (Larisa)*

A grey ball shimmers in the blue sky. It is a lark. I listen to its wonderful song, and cannot hear enough of it. It is as if it is playing on the finest of silver strings. It stretches strings from the golden wheat to the sun. The ears of wheat listen to its song.

---

28 All compositions are given in Russian translation from Ukrainian.

## The sun has set (Seryozha)

The sun has set. The field grows dark. Dusk crawls from the ravine and spreads over the fields and meadows. It flows in all directions like a river. Then golden sparks flash on the tip of a poplar tree. That is the sun sending its last greeting. They flash and then die. Goodbye, sun!

## The bees drink water (Galya)

I saw how the bees drink water. Droplets of water flow down a slender reed onto a smooth willow stump. The tree stump is wet. The bees love the scent of the willow. They fly to the tree stump to drink water. They shake their golden wings. Have a little rest, bees. You have a long way to fly.

## The buckwheat is flowering (Varya)

The buckwheat has flowered. It is as if the field is covered in a white carpet. But this carpet is alive and smells so good. On each flower is a bee. The carpet is humming: that is the buzzing of the bees. A big furry bumblebee lands on a flower. The stem shakes and bends. The bumblebee cannot hold on, falls, and buzzes angrily.

## The combine operator (Yura)

My uncle is a combine operator. He drives a big machine. In front of him is the wheat. Sharp knives cut the stems and pass them to the threshing machine. The threshing machine threshes the wheat. The grain flows in a thin stream into the bunker. A truck drives up and takes the grain to the processing plant. There will be lots of white bread.

### Our threshing machine (Vanya)

Our school has a tiny, little threshing machine, about so big ... The students harvested the wheat on our school plot. They tied five sheaves. The little threshing machine started humming. It threshed the wheat. We sprinkled the wheat into a sack. And we will sow it.

### The apple trees are flowering (Pavlo)

Oh, how beautiful it is in the orchard, when the apple trees are flowering. The white flowers have opened their petals to the sun. The wind rocks the flowers, and they ring. Like silver bells. The whole orchard is ringing, smiling at the sun. And when the wind dies down, you can hear the buzzing of the bees. They are flying above the trees. They are looking for the bells that ring the loudest. And the orchard is singing, like a thousand strings. A bee sits on a bell, waves its paws and shakes its wings. Golden dust rises above the bell in a cloud.

### At Aunty Dasha's farm (Kolya)

We were at Aunty Dasha's farm. She milks thirty cows. Big, big churns of milk. They take the milk to the dairy. There they make butter out of it.

### In the evening the cranes call (Tina)

The sun has set behind the mountain. In the blue sky the cranes are flying. They call, 'Hello, green meadows; we have flown from the warm sea'. The branches shiver on the trees. The green grass rustles. The pond rings out, 'Hello, cranes; tell us what you have seen in the warm sea'.

## Gentle Grandpa Dusk (Sanya)

The stars come out in the sky. From out of the ravine comes gentle Grandpa Dusk. Old and shaggy—covered in hair. With a stick. He walks towards the village. He visits the huts. He takes the children in his warm, soft hands. And the children feel sleepy. They dream sweet dreams.
(Sanya thought up this story about dusk when she was attending the School of Joy, but it came back to her later when we were making up our stories at school.)

## Uncle Kuzma (Fedya)

We were at Uncle Kuzma's place. He is a builder. He lays the brick walls of homes. Now he is building a shop. Uncle Kuzma has already built fifty homes. Lots of people live in them. He says, 'My houses will live for two hundred years'. Many people will remember what a good builder Uncle Kuzma is!

## The snowdrop (Katya)

The sun woke up the forest. It melted the snow on the tips of the pine trees. A hot drop of water landed in the snow. It made a hole through the snowdrift and the dry leaves. Where it fell, a little green stalk appeared. And on it a light blue snowdrop flowered. It looked at the snow and marvelled. 'Have I woken up too early?' 'No, it's not too early; it's time, it's time', sang the birds. And spring began.

### *The sun and the storm cloud (Tolya)*

A golden field. The sun plays on each ear of grain. Field, field, how beautiful you are! But now a storm cloud comes floating above you. It has covered the sun. The golden sparks on the ears of grain go out. The field turns grey. As if someone has covered the earth with a grey blanket. Come out quickly, sun, from behind the storm cloud. The ears of grain are waiting. We are waiting for you too, sun!

### *Stars are falling from the sky (Lyuba)*

In August, stars fall from the sky. In the dark forest there is a big clearing. A star fell from the sky into the clearing. A purple flower bloomed there.

### *In our classroom it is warm (Sasha)*

In our classroom it is as warm as can be. There are hot radiators with water flowing through them. In the basement is a boiler. Coal burns in a big furnace. Miners dug it from under the ground. The sent it on the railway line and brought it to us. They unloaded it onto the ground. Then they loaded it onto a truck and brought it to our school. We are warm because the miners and railway workers work hard.

### *The starlings in winter (Misha)*

Last winter the starlings did not fly away to warmer lands. How did they know there would not be any heavy frosts? I saw how the birds gathered in the evening in a big flock, and flew from tree to tree. They were looking for the warmest place and chirping anxiously. During a blizzard the starlings flew into our barn.

They settled everywhere, even on the backs of the cows. And on sunny, frosty days, they bathed in the snow. A starling would drop like a stone into a soft snowdrift, and dig itself into the snow. Then it would climb out of the snow and chirp happily.

## The New Year fir tree (Danko)

Mum and I put a fir tree on the table. We decorated it with toys. Underneath we put Grandpa Frost. Night came. Outside, the moon was shining brightly. I wanted to see what Grandpa Frost was doing. He had lifted his stick and walked away from the fir tree across the table. He was walking and wheezing. On the branches, white snowflakes were whispering about something. A grey hare had found a place to hide on a twig. He was waiting to jump from the fir tree into Grandpa Frost's sack. Then there would be a present for New Year's Day.

## Grandpa Yukhim (Lyuda)

My Grandpa Yukhim is a forester. He has been working on the collective farm for twenty-five years. Near the village is an oak grove. Those are his oak trees; he planted them. Grandpa says that his oak trees will live for 300 years. I am also going to plant a little oak tree.

## The wicked spider (Kostya)

In a dark corner of the storeroom a spider spins its web. I watch to see what it will do. The spider hides against the wall and waves its legs, as if it is moving the web. A fly comes flying and buzzing. The spider turns and listens. The fly catches on the web and is stuck. Its buzzing becomes loud and anxious, and the spider is already hurrying towards the fly. No, I will not let you kill the fly, you wicked spider. I tear apart the web and free the fly. Fly away, and do not fall into the wicked spider's web.

## *Tomatoes (Slava)*

There are red tomatoes on green bushes. In the morning the tomatoes are covered in dew drops. The golden sun plays in each drop. A white butterfly settles on a red tomato. A bee is buzzing. The bee thinks that it is a big red flower. It circles the tomato and flies away.

Each one of these stories sparkles with living thought. Each word has been lived and felt. The children's compositions were the result of a great deal of work. We had to take children to the living source of thought and words, and make sure that the ideas and words associated with each object and phenomenon of the surrounding world had entered the hearts and souls of the children, and not only their minds. The emotional and aesthetic connotations of words, their subtle shades of meaning—these provided a life-giving stimulus for children's creativity. The words lived in each child's consciousness as vivid images, so when they wrote down their compositions in class, they supplemented their text with drawings.

It would be naïve to expect that children, influenced by the beauty of the surrounding world, will immediately create compositions. Creativity does not come to children instinctively. Creativity has to be taught. Children will only create compositions when they hear descriptions of nature from the teacher. The first composition that I narrated to the children was made up on the bank of a pond one quiet evening. I wanted the children to understand and to feel that it is possible to convey a visual image in words. At first the children copied my compositions; then, gradually, they progressed to independent descriptions of scenes from nature that excited them. Thus began the process of individual children's creativity. In this activity it is very important to feel the emotional and aesthetic nuances of words. Children will only learn to make up their own compositions when each word is seen clearly, like a brick prepared in advance to fit its predestined place. Then the children can choose the brick that fits a particular instance, and not just the first word they come across, so they can write with emotional and aesthetic sensitivity.

Writing compositions became one of my pupils' favourite activities. They tried to describe everything they saw and experienced. For children, words are a means of expressing their relationship to the beauty of the surrounding world. In grades two, three and four the children made up compositions about buds opening on an apple tree, a fading chamomile flower, the silver spider webs of an Indian summer, and the harvesting of apples in the collective farm orchard. Over a period of four years each student wrote forty or fifty miniature compositions. The following are examples of compositions written by the children in grades two, three and four.

### *The ice flowers on the window panes (Tanya, grade four)*

I asked Mum, 'Where do the ice flowers on the window panes come from?' Mum told me that they are drawn by the little grandson of Grandpa Frost. He walks with his grandfather at night, drawing on the windows ... I wanted to see how he does that. I went to bed, but I did not close my eyes. Everyone went to sleep. A tree creaked outside the window. A little boy came up to the window. He drew on the glass with a silver pencil and sang softly. I saw him draw a wonderful flower. Big, wide leaves and little petals. In the morning the sunlight sparkled and the flower seemed to be alive. I do not know if I dreamt it, or if I really saw it.

### *A world of flowers in the middle of winter (Galya, grade three)*

In autumn chrysanthemums bloomed near the greenhouse. They were not afraid of the cold mists. But then frost came from the north. Water froze in buckets. We needed to save the chrysanthemums from the cold. We transplanted them into pots and put them in the greenhouse. We pruned their stems. The chrysanthemums turned green again, and then flowered. In the morning I woke up and saw snow outside. Snow and sun. I quickly ran to the greenhouse. The chrysanthemums were flowering: white, dark blue and light blue. While on the other side of the glass snow was everywhere. The chrysanthemums smiled at the bright sun.

### *How we came back from the field (Pavlo, grade two)*

In summer I travelled with Mum to the field to get some hay. Mum loaded a big cart with hay. She tied the hay on with a rope. The horses plodded slowly. We sat high up on the hay. The sun set and the stars came out in the sky. I lay on the hay and looked up at the sky. Suddenly it seemed that our cart was not a cart, but a large boat. We were sailing over the sea. Above us were the stars. They were so close. If you lifted your hand you could pluck a star from the sky. Somewhere, far away, were green shores. There a quail was calling and grasshoppers were playing on violins. Our boat stopped and the stars flickered. Our boat had reached the shore. Mum got up, but I wanted to lie there a little longer.

### *An overcast autumn day (Shura, grade three)*

The days became shorter and the nights longer. In the mornings, clouds of mist floated over the river. Where was the sun? Why didn't it disperse the patches of mist? Little drops of autumn rain fell from the sky. The trees stood with drooping branches. Leaves fell. Large drops of water hung from the twigs. Somewhere in the mist a seagull gave a drawn-out cry. Perhaps it could not fly away to the south, and was complaining to people. In the forest it was as quiet as could be. A woodpecker knocked a few times and then fell silent. Golden acorns fell on to the leaves. The whole world was cloaked in white mist.

### *When autumn begins (Seryozha, grade four)*

In the morning the swallows were flying anxiously over the village. Then they gathered in a large flock. They settled in rows on the telephone wires and quietly chirped to each other about something. They were discussing when to fly to warmer lands. The next day there were no swallows left. When did they fly away? And how did they know that autumn is coming? The days are still warm. The sun gently warms us. I love the radiant autumn evenings. The crimson fire of the evening sunset blazes for a very long time. Even the leaves on the poplars seem crimson. That is the reflection of the sunset. The water in the sleeping pond is like the evening sunset. Only in the evenings it is noisy in the pond: birds flying south spend the night there. By morning the pond is covered in a veil of mist. There is dew on the grass. The dew is a greyish colour, not like in summer. Autumn is beginning.

## *What is the most important thing in life? (Varya, grade four)*

What is the most important thing in life? A miner will say the most important thing is coal. If there were no coal, the machines would stop, there would be no metal, and people would freeze …

A metallurgist will say the most important thing is metal. Without metal there would be no machines, no coal, no bread, and no clothes.

A grain grower will say the most important thing is bread. Without bread the miner and the metallurgist, the pilot and the border guard would not be able to work.

But which one of them is right? What is the most important thing in life? The most important thing is work. Without work there would be no coal, no metal and no bread.

## *A horse named Fire (Sanya, grade four)*

Mum told me this story. When the first collective farms were created in our village, the collective farm workers bought a horse. Its name was Fire. It would not submit to anyone. Even the bravest and most experienced people were afraid to approach Fire. It pawed at the earth with its hooves, bit with its teeth and snorted.

A young lad named Yurko managed to saddle the unruly horse. It reared, whinnied, jumped out on to the road and threw Yurko off. It ran several kilometres and stopped on the edge of the village. Two small children were playing in the middle of the road. They ran to the horse and hugged its front legs. Their mother's heart froze with fear. She thought it would kill or maim the children. But the horse stood quietly. It moved its leg and again stood quietly. It looked sideways at the children, as if it was afraid of hurting them. And the children kept playing. Then Fire walked away from the children and galloped through the village. They caught it and put it in the stables.

## *Hedgehogs (Fedya, grade four)*

Hedgehogs live under our porch. Each evening their whole family crawls out through a little opening and heads off for the pond. In front of them walks the old father hedgehog, then five little baby hedgehogs, and at the back, the mother hedgehog. What do they do there? I watched, and saw how they drink water and wash themselves. And then they dig in the soil with their little paws, and find some roots to eat. That's what the old father hedgehog and his wife do. And while they are doing that the little baby hedgehogs play and have fun. They have chosen a quiet little corner: nobody goes there.

One day, from out of nowhere, a dog appeared. It ran up to the old father hedgehog. The hedgehog rolled up in a ball and froze. All the other hedgehogs rolled up in balls too. The dog took the old hedgehog in its teeth and carried it to the pond. It dropped it in the water. The hedgehog swam to the shore. And the dog looked at it. Then it began to play with the hedgehog. I chased the dog away.

The next spring only the old hedgehog was left under our porch. What happened to all the others? They probably moved to another place. But the old hedgehog did not want to move. I put a saucer of milk near the porch. The hedgehog drank it. It stopped being afraid of me. I enticed it into my room. I turned on a lamp. The hedgehog stared at the lamp. I put some old newspapers on the floor. The hedgehog began to play with them, but at night time it went back to its home under the porch.

We also made up compositions collectively. One overcast autumn day the children were sitting in our Nook of Dreams by a blazing fire. I was telling them about distant tropical islands. For some reason the children recalled the hot summer, the river and our holiday at the melon plantation. From these recollections we put together a composition, which the children recorded in the album 'Our native language'.

### How we lived on the melon plantation

All over the hot earth were large watermelons. Blue, green and dove-grey. In the morning they were covered in dew. They were cold, oh, so cold. The grass was covered in dew, and our shelter was covered in dew. One day Danko got up early in the morning and brought a large watermelon to our shelter. He cut it up. As soon as anyone got up, he treated them to a cold slice of watermelon. 'Whoever gets up last', said Danko, 'will get the tasty core of the watermelon—the "grandpa"'. Everyone got up and only Sashko was asleep. We sat and waited—when would he wake up? We got sick of waiting and ate the 'grandpa' ourselves. We brought another watermelon and Sashko got the 'grandpa' from that one.

It was a quiet misty morning. Mist floated down from a gully and covered the whole plantation. The sun peeped out from behind a cloud and lit up the watermelons. They did not look so much like watermelons as like blue, green and grey glass spheres, floating on a white river.

During the afternoon a hot wind blew. Larks sang in the blue sky. Why do they never land in the plantation? Why do larks build their nests and raise their chicks only in wheat, barley and millet? And in buckwheat you find more larks' nests than anywhere else.

Next to the plantation, near a ravine, we found an ant-hill. Grandpa saw how ants were hurrying somewhere. He said, 'There must be a large ant-hill not far from here. The ants will tell us where it is.' He put several pieces of watermelon on the ant path. The sweet watermelon was immediately covered in ants. We saw how they took tiny pieces of sugar and carried them in one direction. We followed them and came to the ant-hill. The little grey hill under a bush seemed to be alive. The ants carried the sugar somewhere deep into their little tunnels, and then returned to the plantation. Grandpa explained to us how useful the ants are for the forest and for people. Each ant-hill protects several hectares of forest from pests. We began to protect ant-hills, and then Grandpa taught us how to create new ant-hills.

When we left for home Grandpa gave us each a big watermelon. The watermelons sat on our window sills at home for a long time. They reminded us of the hot winds, the wide steppe, the larks, Grandpa, and the resonant song of a cricket that made its home not far from our shelter. Where is that cricket now?

The beauty of language is embodied most clearly in poetry. When children find delight in a poem or song, it is as if they are listening to the music of words. In the best poems, words reveal the subtlest emotional nuances of our native language. It is because of this that children want to memorise a poem. Children derive real pleasure from repeating words that have touched their souls.

From the first days of the School of Joy, and during all the years of primary schooling, I tried to ensure that children felt and experienced the music of poetry. In the lap of nature, when children were enchanted by the beauty of the surrounding world, I recited poetry to them. One day we came upon an open field. In front of us stretched a beautiful view of a pond with a shimmering willow reflected in its mirror-like surface. I recited some lines from a poem by Shevchenko:

> *Quietly the wind blows,*
> *The steppe and fields dream;*
> *Between the gullies, above the ponds,*
> *The willows shine green …*

The children repeated the quatrain. They felt that the combination of words created a living image and gave rise to a musical form of speech, which not only lent the words new emotional nuances but revealed a new beauty in the surrounding world. Under the influence of some of the finest examples of world poetry, the children developed an urge to create musical language of their own. When taking delight in the beauty of a spring day, the children tried to describe that beauty in a way that used words melodically. The children's hearts were enthralled by poetic inspiration, and both boys and girls created poetry. On one occasion Larisa was looking at the fields stretching before her. Her eyes lit up, and she quietly uttered words while listening to their sound:

'Waves play in the yellow sea of wheat.'

'In the hot, mirage-like haze, a blue burial mound shimmers', continued Seryozha, picking up on her thought. Everyone was happily excited; everyone searched for their own poetic words. At such times, when a child's soul is gripped by poetic inspiration, words enter the spiritual life of a child: alive, full-blooded, displaying all the colours of the rainbow, giving off the sweet scent of fields and meadows. Children seek, and find in words, a means for expressing their feelings, thoughts and experiences. To awaken poetic inspiration in a child's heart is to unlock yet another life-giving source of thought. This source is particularly powerful because words convey not only the object or phenomenon that they denote in human speech, but also deeply personal perceptions, feelings and experiences.

We need to teach poetic creativity not in order to train the next generation of poets, but in order to ennoble every young heart. I took any opportunity to awaken poetic inspiration in children's hearts so that words might find a unique poetic articulation in the soul of every child.

A quiet winter morning. The trees are clothed in white hoar frost. The branches, covered in icicles as fine as needles, seem to be forged from silver. We walk through the school orchard trying not to touch the branches, so as not to break the spell of this unique beauty. We stop and I recite poetry by Alexander Pushkin and Heinrich Heine about the beauty of winter. Under the influence of poetry and natural beauty, the children find words to describe the trees covered in frost, and compose their own poem. They do this collectively, bit by bit, as we visit the frost-covered orchard several times. The poem brings to life fantastic images from stories created on previous occasions:

*A magic blacksmith came,*
*And brought his golden forge.*
*In it he melted silver,*
*And poured it over the orchard trees.*
*He forged all through the night,*
*Beating his golden hammer ...*
*Now our orchard is dressed in silver.*
*Should one needle catch another,*
*The orchard will ring and ring.*
*But where is our magic blacksmith?*
*On his golden wings*
*He has flown back to the sun.*
*He will gather more silver,*
*Put it in his satchel,*

*And return to us again.*
*Again he will melt the silver,*
*And again the orchard will sing ...*
*But the sun awaits the blacksmith ...*
*Where have you flown, my blacksmith?*
*Why are you spending so long in the orchard,*
*Melting my silver?*
*Have you forgotten, blacksmith,*
*That you need to forge my garland?*
*A purple ray of light comes peeping*
*Into our quiet silver orchard.*
*And the sun is amazed,*
*And cannot admire the beauty enough ...*

Every child is a poet. Of course it would be naïve to expect poetic inspiration to come to a child through some marvellous instinct. I am not one to get sentimental about natural talent and I do not believe that every child is a poet by nature. It is an appreciation of beauty that awakens the poet in the soul. Unless we educate that appreciation, a student will remain indifferent to the beauty of nature and of words, a creature for whom throwing a stone into a pond and throwing a stone at a nightingale are one and the same. To give children the joy of poetic inspiration, to awaken the wellspring of poetic creativity in their hearts—this is just as important as teaching children to read and solve problems. In some children this wellspring flows more abundantly, in others less. I saw that for some children poetic inspiration is not a short-lived flight of fancy or flash of light, but a constant spiritual imperative.

Poetic creativity is the highest stage of oral language development, while oral language development—the culture of speech—expresses the essence of human culture. Poetic creativity is accessible to everyone. It is not the privilege of the exceptionally gifted. Poetic creativity ennobles a person. It is very important that this most subtle sphere of creativity should be a deeply personal, heartfelt interest for every child.

In grade three, Larisa, Sanya, Seryozha, Katya, Varya, Kolya, Tanya and Lida began to secretly read me the poems they had composed in solitude. I knew that there were other children who wrote poetry but were too shy to speak of their interest. And that was very good.

I did not see anything exceptional in children writing poetry. This is a normal exercise of spiritual energy, a normal expression of that creative spark without which a rich childhood is unimaginable. But the fact that the children's spiritual life was so rich and flowed so abundantly gave me great joy.

I felt particular joy seeing how poetic inspiration ennobled Kolya. My friendship with him grew ever deeper. In the school garden was a corner where I liked to spend time by myself. I used to rest there, and in good weather I played my violin. Then one day Kolya 'discovered' my little corner. He was probably seeking solitude himself. Seeing me, the boy became embarrassed and wanted to leave, but I asked him to stay. I played on the violin, trying to express in sound my appreciation of the beauty of the summer evening. Kolya listened to the melody. I became so absorbed I did not notice that the boy had sat down next to me. I passed the violin to him. Kolya tried to repeat what I had played but it did not come out the way he wanted. The boy stopped playing. We sat silently watching the sun set and listening to the quiet of the evening. Probably because we had been brought closer by witnessing the beauty of the surrounding world, Kolya shared with me his poem about nature. Here it is:

> *Blue flowers among green foliage;*
> *A bee flies over the flowers.*
> *During the night a nightingale came,*
> *It sings in the lilac bushes.*

*In the morning a thunderstorm rumbled,*
*Rain washed the flowers.*
*A grey storm cloud floats over the garden,*
*But the lilac is as blue as the sky.*

That evening I sat with Kolya in the garden for a long time. The boy began to come to that spot regularly, and each time he recited a little poem to me. One of them made such an impression on me that I wrote it down a year after he recited it to me. Here it is:

*The red sun has set behind the mountain.*
*The crimson sky is ablaze:*
*Tomorrow will be a windy day.*
*A flock of ravens takes off anxiously into the sky,*
*Racing eastwards, towards the dark forest.*
*On a tall poplar the leaves are whispering.*
*All is still. Somewhere in the distance you can hear*
*A cart clattering along the ringing road.*
*The scarlet sky has darkened,*
*Its heat covered in grey ash.*
*A bright star twinkles in the sky,*
*Night is here.*

I knew that Kolya never wrote down his poems: he memorised them. Poems lived in his memory and in his heart. My pupils did not usually think up poems while sitting in front of an empty sheet of paper. Poems were not born to be written down. The children could not help composing poetry in the same way they could not refrain from drawing.

Shura also entrusted a secret poem to me in a private moment. One winter day we went into the forest to ski. A red sun was close to setting. The trunks of the pine trees seemed forged from iron. We stood on the edge of the forest admiring the beauty of nature. Shura began reciting his poem about the woodpecker:

> *Under its bark a pine tree has a thousand strings.*
> *The woodpecker sits on top of the pine tree.*
> *He knocks with his beak on the top string,*
> *The string rings barely audibly.*
> *Closer to the sun the strings are finer,*
> *But at ground level the string is not a string.*
> *At ground level a deep bell softly rings,*
> *A copper bell, under red bark.*
> *The woodpecker hops, and uncovers a string,*
> *Strikes with his beak, and the string rings out ...*
> *The forest sings, but the woodpecker is already looking for another string.*

Varya made up several dozen poems during childhood. This little girl had a sensitive, impressionable soul. I saw how once, spellbound by the beauty of a summer evening, Varya stood on the bank of a pond looking at the willows bending to the water, and at the reflection of the blue sky in the pond's mirror-like surface. A few days later, the girl recited her poem about that summer evening to me:

> *Blue sky, green willows, white huts—*
> *All reflected in the water.*
> *I stand in front of a blue mirror,*
> *Before me stretches a distant, endless world.*
> *I see a red sunset and a white cloud,*
> *A star twinkles, and above a distant road*
> *A bird takes off into the sky, saying goodbye to the sun.*
> *This wonderful world has its own music:*
> *Listen, someone has plucked*

*A thick string, and the blue heavens sing,*
*The willows sing, and the huts sing.*
*I hear this music only by the evening pond,*
*When the sun lights a fire beyond distant seas,*
*When white doves hurry to their night lodgings,*
*And a bat cleans its paws in a hollow tree,*
*When the wind, tired from the day, lies down to rest*
*In a dark ravine.*

Each year when autumn approached, the children wanted to say goodbye to summer. We went to our oak tree and made up poems about the past summer, about the cranes, and about the warm days of the Indian summer. Parting with summer for the fourth time, the children collectively composed a poem about the most dear and most cherished thing for us all: our homeland. I tried to translate the poem into Russian, like all the others, but in translation it lost the subtlety and the emotional and aesthetic nuances that only one's native language can convey. And so I am citing the poem in the original Ukrainian language:

*In the open sky a formation of cranes can be seen.*
*Cold winter, with its snow and frosts,*
*Approaches us from northern lands.*
*At dawn the cranes rose high into the sky,*
*They looked to the north*
*And saw white snows and blizzards.*
*The cranes called anxiously,*
*Said goodbye to the lake*
*And flew to warmer lands …*
*Beyond the forest, beyond the primordial forest,*
*Beyond high mountains and blue seas,*
*There is a warm lake, with green reeds.*

*Pure springs flow into that lake,*
*On its banks flowers bloom,*
*But the spring waters are not dear to the cranes,*
*Nor the sweet-scented flowers.*
*They do not build nests by that warm lake,*
*Nor do they raise their young there.*
*They wait impatiently*
*For the sun to melt the snows in our land,*
*For the spring waters to roar,*
*For a rainbow to shine in the sky,*
*For the sedge to grow green in the meadows.*
*The sun melted the cold snows,*
*The spring waters began to roar,*
*A rainbow shone in the sky,*
*And the sedge showed green in the meadows.*
*The cranes heard the spring coming to our land,*
*They rose into the sky,*
*Cried joyfully,*
*And flew to us ...*
*There are many warm lakes in the world,*
*Where winter never comes,*
*Where the grass is ever green and the flowers ever bloom.*
*But for us, our lakes are dearest,*
*Our grass and our flowers.*
*For this is our native land.*

In this poem there is a very subtle, rich emotional subtext expressing feelings of love for our natural heritage, sadness for the approaching farewell to summer, and anticipation of the joy of greeting a new spring with its flowering of new life.

The main feature deserving attention and praise is the way the children's imaginations have created such vivid images. I tried to make sure that the children, for whom poetic inspiration had become an integral part of their spiritual lives, read the best models of poetry. We created a little library of poetry. It was especially necessary for those students who did not yet feel a spiritual need for poetic creativity and who needed to develop sensitivity to poetic language. I repeat again that children's poetic creativity should not be seen as a sign of giftedness. It is just as normal a phenomenon as drawing, and everyone draws—all children go through that experience. But poetic creativity becomes a normal manifestation of children's spiritual lives only when the educator reveals to children the beauty of the surrounding world and the beauty of language. Just as one cannot educate a love of music without exposure to music, one cannot educate a love for poetic creativity without practising creativity.

People who love Pushkin and Heine, Shevchenko and Lesya Ukrainka, people who feel an urge to speak beautifully about the beauty that surrounds them, people for whom the search for the right word has become just as pressing as the need to contemplate beauty, people whose conception of human beauty is expressed in respect for human dignity and in affirmation of the most just, communist relations between each other—such people will never become coarse or cynical.

## Our Nook of Beauty

DURING THE SPRING THAT ARRIVED just before we completed grade one, we began to create our Nook of Beauty. The children had dreamed of this nook for a long time. We pictured it as a quiet, secluded spot, where nature's elemental beauty would be enhanced by beauty created by human hands. Our dream stretched into the future. We envisaged that with each year, there would be more and more plants in our little nook. Here we would rest and work, greet the spring and farewell the summer.

Between the school grounds and some thick undergrowth the children found a little clearing adjoining the grass-covered slope of a gully. A lot of moisture collected here when it rained. We weeded the clearing and began to transform it into a green glade.

'Our nook will be a realm of greenery', I told the children. 'The slope of the gully will be covered with a green wall of hops, and nightingales and orioles will settle in the thickets.'

This dream inspired the children. We worked hard to transform the clearing into a green glade. We had to bring slabs of turf from the field, lay them and water them. The children waited impatiently for rain to water the green grass. We found several young hop plants in the forest and transplanted them to the slope of the gully. Fortunately for us, the summer was a wet one and all the plants took well. In the forest we dug up several dozen lily of the valley rhizomes and planted them in one corner of our glade. We planted three dogrose bushes, on which we planned to graft roses. This was to be a kingdom of flowers. We planted forest nut trees all around the glade. The children wanted wildflowers to grow here as well. We found camomile and other plants. We transplanted several chrysanthemums from the greenhouse in the hope they would flower until deep into autumn.

Varya planted sunflowers. At the far end of the glade the children sowed a handful of buckwheat. Nina and Sasha's father gave us two dwarf apple trees to plant. Vitya told me that his grandmother grew tulips and we transplanted several clumps of tulip bulbs. One summer day the children saw a large flowering linden tree in the forest. In the branches of the tree thousands of bees were buzzing, and it seemed as if the whole forest was resounding like a harp. The children stood silent, enchanted by the beauty of nature. They were inspired to plant several linden trees next to their Nook of Beauty. In autumn we went into the forest, dug up some seedlings, and planted an alley. 'When the linden trees grow tall', the children dreamed, 'their thick crowns will merge, forming a shady corridor'.

It is difficult to find any other stimulus that awakens a desire to work as much as the urge to create beauty. This urge inspired the whole class. There was not one child who did not take part in looking after plants.

During the first and second summers nature rewarded us scantily for our work, but the children's dreams remained alive. When the second spring arrived, the glade became a continuous carpet of green and wildflowers bloomed. By the third spring, our nook was a kingdom of greenery and flowers. Hops covered the slope with luxuriant growth. When these vines were covered in golden cup-shaped flowers and the buckwheat was flowering, it seemed as if bees were flying there from all over the village, and bumblebees were coming from all the meadows and forests. On such days the children liked to sit under a green tent of hops and read or tell stories.

The greatest pleasure of all was to simply sit or lie on the grass. The hop flowers swayed above us and it turned out that the furry bumblebees liked hop nectar more than any other. Above our heads a wonderful harp resounded and vibrated, and it seemed that the music was coming to us from the sun. Like blue stars, lilies of the valley flowered in the midst of the emerald green glade. Several times during the day the colour of the green wall of hops changed, depending on the direction from which the sun's rays illuminated it. The children admired the beauty and I saw that every one of them wanted to spend time in that place, either on their own or with a friend. The beauty was particularly striking on summer mornings, when clear drops of dew sparkled on the grass. On such summer days poetic inspiration awoke in many a soul. The children wrote poems about the Nook of Beauty. These are the words that Galya used to express her admiration for the beauty there:

*Early in the morning I came to the Nook of Beauty.*
*The first rays of the sun fell on the hop vines,*
*And a thousand dewdrops sparkled,*
*A rainbow sprang to life in the green foliage.*
*Before me are not hop vines, but a waterfall:*
*Green waves plunge into the abyss,*
*The sun kindles sparks in a thousand drops of water,*
*And stars flash on the golden cups of the hop-flowers.*

In the summer when the children completed grade one, I grafted some roses to the dogrose stock. In late autumn of the same year we dug snowdrop bulbs from the forest floor. That was not easy but I did not want to deprive the children of the joy of welcoming in the spring. I will never forget how we came to the Nook of Beauty when the ground was still covered in snow, and saw the tender little blue bells of the snowdrops. Galya clapped her hands with joy. She was reminded of the fairytale about the melting snowflake: the drop of living water that brought a wonderful flower to life. Then the lilies of the valley flowered. This time the children did not pick the flowers, they admired them.

The hops spread, covering bushes with luxuriant foliage, and then a new joy came to us: we saw an oriole. On hot, sunny days, these beautiful birds sang. At such moments we were afraid of speaking loudly, for fear of startling the birds. Lida composed a poem about an oriole:

*A golden ball quivered in the bushes,*
*I hid and watched the wonderful bird.*
*Purple, dove-grey and orange feathers.*
*Give me, little bird, just one miraculous feather,*
*And on white silk I will embroider a rainbow.*

Every class began to create their own nook of beauty, trying to make it unlike any other. Then in the autumn of 1955 the school community began to create a common Nook of Beauty. Next to the school building we laid out a rose garden. We planted dozens of rose cuttings grafted onto dogrose stock. With each year this garden becomes more beautiful. In spring and summer it is a sea of flowers. Everyone comes here to admire nature and to labour to create beauty.

The rose garden is now adopted by the whole school community. When the roses begin to flower children, adolescents and young men and women come here and admire the beauty. The class that is judged to have made the greatest contribution in social work wins the right to care for the garden. More often than not, this is a junior or middle school class. They are allowed to cut several dozen roses each day. The roses are distributed to classes, and presented to teachers, mothers and the best workers in the village. On the day when we celebrate the first harvest, the children pick a large bouquet of roses and present it to the victors of the socialist labour competition.

Labour to create beauty ennobles young hearts and prevents indifference. In creating earthly beauty the children themselves become better, purer and more beautiful.

## *On the threshold of an ideal in life*

WHEN THE CHILDREN WERE PRESCHOOLERS and then became school students, I tried to imagine each of them as an adult human being. I could not stop asking myself: what sort of citizen, what sort of human being will you become, my little one? What will you bring to society, where will you find joy, what will you admire and what will you condemn, in what will you find happiness, and what trace will you leave upon the earth?

As a teacher and educator I aimed to instil in young hearts moral values created and fought for by humanity over many centuries: love for one's homeland and for freedom, steadfast resistance to oppression or enslavement of one human being by another, a preparedness to devote one's life and energy to high ideals such as happiness and freedom. It is very important that in the minds of our pupils noble words about the homeland and lofty ideals should not turn into loud but empty phrases; that the meaning of such words should not fade and become worn out from frequent use. It is better if children do not talk too much about the highest ideals, but that those ideals should live in their passionate young hearts, in feelings and actions, in love and hatred, in devotion and steadfastness.

There is among the 'divine commandments' a very interesting one: You shall not take the name of the Lord your God in vain. The composers of the commandments were clearly good psychologists. We are atheists but we also have sacred truths, sacred principles and sacred names. We should not take them in vain. We should not turn them into empty chatter. That which is dear to people should live in their hearts. It is especially dangerous to put words into the mouths of children that they do not understand. Otherwise that which is sacred to a nation could, in the child's mind, turn into an empty sound.

Just as a careful gardener nurtures the roots of a young tree knowing that the life of the plant will depend on the strength of the roots for several decades, so a teacher must take care to instil in children feelings of boundless love for the homeland, devotion to working people, loyalty to the ideals of communism. The education of these qualities begins from the time when a child begins to see, know and evaluate the surrounding world.

It is very important that children should hold dear everything created by previous generations, everything won and achieved in the difficult battle for freedom and independence. For a child the homeland begins with a piece of bread and a field of wheat, with a little pond by the edge of a forest under a blue sky, with a mother's bedside songs and fairytales. During the golden age of childhood—when a child is particularly sensitive to language, images and another person's inner world—we must reach children's hearts with everything the older generations are proud of, and explain at what cost the happiness of free labour has been won. I tried not to allow children to enjoy life's pleasures without a care in the world. A child's knowledge of the surrounding world and of themselves should not be one-sided. As they get to know the world and themselves, children should gradually become aware of their responsibility for the material and spiritual wealth created by previous generations.

Journeys into the past of our native region: that is what we called our excursions and hikes to fields, forests, the river bank and neighbouring villages. I tried to show the children what connects the past and present in the spiritual life of our people. I told the little ones:

'In front of you stretches a fertile field with ripening ears of wheat. In this field, by the edge of the forest, soldiers of the White Guard shot a red partisan during the civil war. And during the difficult summer of the first year of the Great Patriotic War [1941–1945], a battle raged here between a handful of our fighters and a company of fascists. Here our heroes died. Look at the wide field children. Those little mounds are nameless graves. The earth preserves the memory of their heroism. Thousands of mounds represent thousands of nameless graves. The earth preserves the noble blood of heroes, and the people's hearts preserve the eternal memory of their deeds. If they had not given their lives for the homeland you would not have been able to enjoy the beauty of your native land. The fascists would have made you slaves.'

Let little children ponder the fate of their native land. Let them feel care and concern for its future. May the events of the distant past rise up before them as precursors of the present.

During childhood—that age which we consider an age of carefree joy, play and fairytales—we are on the threshold of an ideal in life.

It is at this time that the roots of our civic mindedness are established. What sort of citizens your pupils become will depend on what they discover in the surrounding world during childhood, what inspires amazement and admiration, what inspires indignation and makes them cry—not from personal hurt, but from taking to heart the lives of other people. Before each child's gaze a complex world is revealed, with contradictions and complications. In it children see beauty and ugliness, happiness and grief. Everything that happens in the surrounding world, everything that concerned people in the past and concerns them in the present, children classify as good or evil. In order to lay a foundation for humaneness and civic mindedness in childhood, it is necessary to give children a just vision of good and evil.

What I mean by these words is that everything children become aware of in the surrounding world—all social intercourse, all people's actions in the past and the present—should arouse deep moral feelings in their young hearts. By 'a just vision of good and evil', I mean that children take to heart everything they come to know. Goodness arouses feelings of joyful excitement, admiration, an aspiration to follow in the footsteps of moral beauty. Evil arouses feelings of indignation, steadfast resistance, and a surge of spiritual energy to battle for truth and justice. A child's soul should not be a cold receptacle for truths. Indifference and a lack of feeling are a major vice that I tried to prevent. Little people with icicles in their hearts may become future philistines. It is necessary in childhood to kindle in every heart the spark of civic mindedness and steadfast opposition to anything that is evil or panders to evil.

It is not difficult to convince children that it is a great evil for one person to oppress another. Children will respond correctly if asked to explain what is evil about it. But if children have not been shocked by vivid images of such oppression, if they have not felt hatred for those who commit this evil, they will not become true citizens and people with high ideals.

Human indifference is dangerous and sickening. Childish indifference is frightening. I wanted each of my pupils to experience in childhood the noble feeling of deep personal concern for the lives of other people, however distant, perhaps living on the other side of the world, perhaps living one hundred years ago. Such feelings are a reliable antidote to indifference and a treatment for any icicle in the heart or dangerous seed of philistinism.

I read my pupils books and told them life stories that challenged them to fight for human dignity, and clearly expressed the idea that oppression of one human being by another is totally unacceptable. The children listened many times to Henryk Sienkiewicz's moving story *Janko the musician*. The first reading stunned the children. They called the landowner who destroyed the life of a defenceless child a bloodthirsty monster. The children clenched their fists and their eyes blazed with rage. Janko the musician would remain part of the children's spiritual lives forever. We read the story many more times, and some children even memorised it word for word. Why did the children want to hear about Janko the musician again and again? I think it is because the moral outrage gave rise to a surge of spiritual energy. In feeling that they were steadfast opponents of evil, the children became stronger. They wanted to experience the full extent of their moral force and convince themselves yet again that they were prepared to fight for justice. A heart in which this feeling is developed becomes sensitive to good and evil in the surrounding world.

In grades three and four we twice read Harriet Beecher Stowe's novel *Uncle Tom's Cabin*. The children were deeply moved by the fate of the slaves. It was hard for them to imagine that people were bought and sold like animals. Travelling mentally around the world, the children then learnt that there are still some corners of the globe where slavery has survived. The little ones could not bear the thought that they were unable to help children their own age who were sold in slave markets. Gradually the children developed a picture of the battle between good and evil in our time: millions of people are working not for themselves, but for landowners and capitalists. The children do not know what it means to have a childhood. The best young sons and daughters—fighters in the battle for freedom and independence—are shot, hanged or sent to work in forced labour camps.

The children will remember for the rest if their lives the tragic fate of Greek hero Nikos Beloyannis. During the fascist occupation of Greece, Beloyannis fought against the invaders, but when his country was liberated from the Nazis a bourgeois court condemned the patriot to death, accusing him of betraying his country. Beloyannis met his death with a red carnation in his hand and on the same day his wife, also condemned to death, gave birth to a son.

Shaken by the fate of the boy who lived in prison, the children asked how they could help Nikos Beloyannis junior. Noble feelings demand actions. The children wrote to the mother of Nikos Beloyannis junior via the International Red Cross and sent a present they had made: a red carnation embroidered on white silk. Then every year the students sent a letter to the hero's wife and a present for the boy on his birthday: a flower embroidered on white silk—a rose, a poppy, or a lilac. These actions, which may appear at first glance to be insignificant, left a deep impression on the children's hearts because they embodied a condemnation of evil and duel with injustice.

Leading the children into the world of social activity, I persuaded them that even during the darkest periods of human history, when the forces of evil oppressed millions of people, there were always those who stood up against injustice. The names of those people, their lives and accomplishments, are bright, guiding stars for the next generation. As an affirmation of human dignity I tried to ensure that my pupils were inspired by the endurance, courage, heroism and conviction of the finest sons of humanity, of those who fought and gave their lives for the freedom and independence of their homeland, for liberation from exploitation.

I strove to ensure that the moral values created and fought for by humanity in the past, and now finding full expression in socialist society, became the spiritual inheritance of every child, exciting their hearts and motivating them to act to promote the victory of truth throughout the world. Antonio Gramsci said that the truth is always revolutionary. I tried to reveal moral truths in all their beauty, without empty talk about beauty. The beauty of humanity's moral inheritance will only become part of a child's spiritual wealth when its revolutionary significance is demonstrated through vivid examples that move the heart. A Latin proverb says that words teach, but examples inspire. The example of a shining life, of heroic deeds in the name of humanity's happiness—these provide a light that illuminates a child's life. But even examples will only teach one how to live when they are a living embodiment of humane, progressive, revolutionary ideas. The German poet Goethe wrote that in the final analysis, anyone who distances themselves from ideas is left only with feelings.

During the childhood years I exposed the children to vivid descriptions of people who have been our guiding stars for many generations. Of course you cannot explain everything to a small child. We should not overburden little ones with an avalanche of images and pictures, endlessly agitating their hearts and souls. Let children learn a little for now, but enough to discover the beauty of moral values. Let children reflect on those things that have moved and shocked them, allowing a blend of thought and feeling to take shape in each child's heart. Over a period of four years I told my pupils about the heroic achievements of people who had fought for lofty human ideals: Spartacus, Campanella, Ivan Susanin, Stepan Khalturin, Sofia Perovskaya, Nikolai Kibalchich, Taras Shevchenko, Thomas Müntzer, Hristo Botev and Janusz Korczak. I told them about the life and struggles of Vladimir Lenin, about the communist heroes Julius Fučík, Ernst Thälmann, Nikos Beloyannis and Kamo (Ter-Petrossian), about the war heroes Nikolai Gastello and Aleksander Matrosov, about the courageous defender of scientific truth Giordano Bruno, and about the humanist scientist Miklouho-Maclay.

Such striking examples have great power to influence the spiritual world of a child. An idea is embodied in living human passions, actions and achievements. It is not necessary to explain to children the essence of any particular act. When an idea is expressed through a shining example, children understand the idea perfectly well. The heroes whom I described to my pupils shared one important characteristic representing the essence of moral beauty: a preparedness to give all their energy, and even their life, for the happiness of others. It is this characteristic that arouses admiration and makes children think about the lives of other people. People who have found happiness in serving humanity come to exemplify a moral ideal.

It is hard to imagine a complete education that does not at some stage involve children sitting up until midnight reading a book about moral greatness, while their heartbeat quickens from a feeling of inspiration. A moral ideal is born in the heart when people examine themselves and compare themselves with someone whom they conceive to be a model of moral beauty, of loyalty to convictions, of courage, perseverance and steadfastness in the face of difficulties.

\* \* \*

My stories about Janusz Korczak, a national hero of the Polish people, made a deep impression on the children's hearts. The boys and girls were stunned by the fact that this human being faced death with the children he loved. Janusz Korczak could have saved his own life, but considered it to be dishonourable when thousands of innocent children were dying at the hands of fascist executioners. Janusz Korczak became a symbol of true humanity for the children.

\* \* \*

## *Not a day without concern for others*

LIFE TEACHES US THAT IF children only 'consume' joys without earning them through work and spiritual effort, their hearts may become cold, unfeeling and indifferent.

Showing kindness to others is a great moral force that ennobles children. One of my educational objectives was to ensure that children felt in their hearts that there were people around them who needed help, care, affection, warmth and sympathy. It was most important that children's consciences would not allow them to ignore these other people, and that children showed kindness to others—not in order to draw attention to themselves, but from altruistic motives.

The source of a child's conscience, of a readiness to show kindness to others, is in empathy for the feelings of people who experience grief and misfortune. Sensitivity to the spiritual world of another person, a capacity to respond to another's misfortune—in these are the origins of the highest human joy, without which there can be no moral beauty. Even in the School of Joy my pupils had taken their first steps on the path that leads to the pinnacle of moral beauty: they had grasped the rudiments of the great science of humanity. They had learnt to recognise grief, sadness, sorrow and anxiety in the eyes of those with whom they came in contact in everyday life. This ability can only become part of one's moral character in adulthood and a permanent feature of one's spiritual life, if not a day goes by in childhood without heartfelt concern for others.

I always taught my pupils to empathise with the feelings of others. I tried to ensure that each child put themselves in the shoes of those who needed sympathy, help and heartfelt concern, and that they experienced the feelings of others as their own. The misfortune of another person must become the child's own misfortune, and force them to think about how to help those in need. A vital role is played by personal relationships in the education of humaneness. It is easier to feel love for humanity than to help one's neighbour. One cannot know people in general without knowing concrete human personalities. Human suffering will not reach children's hearts if they cannot read sorrow in the sad, pleading, suffering eyes of their friends. A child who has not seen both sides of human life—happiness and grief—will never become sensitive and responsive.

There was no small amount of grief in our class. You did not have to go far to find it. Joyful laughter rang out in our group and a spirit of cheerfulness reigned, but some children's eyes were sad. Three years after Valya started school her father's health took a sharp turn for the worse. The girl became silent and thoughtful. Nina and Shura's mother was seriously ill, and the girls often stayed home to help their father with domestic work. Sashko's grandmother fell ill. She was in and out of hospital, sometimes for a week, sometimes for a month. This brought the boy much grief. During his grandmother's illness he was cared for by an aunt, a very good woman who cared for him well, but separation from his grandmother caused the boy suffering. One cold autumn day Sashko decided to visit his grandmother. Without saying a word to his aunt he walked to the hospital. On the way he was soaked by rain, caught cold, and fell ill. A few days later he was admitted to the same hospital as his grandmother.

Misfortune visited Volodya's family. His mother worked as a plasterer and every day she travelled to work by bus. When the roads were made slippery by spring ice, the bus collided with a truck and Volodya's mother was seriously injured. Doctors said she would be disabled for the rest of her life. At the same time Volodya's grandfather, who had done a lot to keep Volodya on the right track, fell ill and died.

Vanya also experienced a great misfortune: his older brother was one of the first young people from our area to travel east to open up virgin farmland. He perished in a snowstorm. While his mother and father were in Kazakhstan to bury their son, another misfortune struck the family. Vanya's sister's husband received a severe electric shock and barely escaped with his life.

A misfortune of another kind visited Kolya's family. His father was arrested and sentenced to two years in prison for handling stolen goods. The moral atmosphere in the family improved but the boy could not help being shaken by what had happened.

Each day when I met the children, I looked into their faces. A child's sad eyes—what could be more difficult in the complex process of education? When children have grief in their hearts they are present in body only. They are like a tightly stretched string: if you touch it carelessly you will cause pain. Each child experiences grief in their own way: if you show affection to some they will feel better, whereas a kind word will cause others new pain. Pedagogical skill in such situations consists of human wisdom: find a way to spare an aching heart; do not cause your pupils more suffering; do not rub salt in their wounds. Of course pupils who are dazed, confused and shaken by grief cannot study as they did before. Grief affects the way they think. The most important thing for a teacher is to see a child's grief, sadness and suffering, to see and feel a child's soul. How teachers relate to a child's grief and the extent to which they are capable of understanding and feeling a child's soul—this is the basis of their pedagogical skill.

We should not expect a student who is experiencing grief to answer questions in front of the class. We should not demand diligence and hard work. We should not ask what has happened—it is not easy for a child to talk about it. If children trust their teacher, if the teacher is their friend, they will tell what it is possible to tell. If they remain silent, do not probe the child's aching heart … The most difficult thing in education is to teach how to feel for others. And the older the child the more difficult it is for a teacher, figuratively speaking, to touch those subtle strings of the human heart that resonate with noble feelings.

In order to teach children to read the eyes of those close to them and to feel for them, an educator must know how to spare children's feelings, and most importantly feelings of sadness. There is nothing more grotesque in the emotional and moral relationship between an adult and a child than an older person's attempts to dispel feelings of grief with frivolous assertions of the sort: 'You're just a child. You're exaggerating your grief ...'

First of all we need to understand the movements of a child's heart. You cannot learn this with the aid of any special methods. This is only arrived at through a high level of emotional and moral development on the part of the teacher. Whatever the origins of a child's grief, it always finds expression in sad, melancholy eyes, which strike you with their unchildlike thoughtfulness, lack of engagement, anguish and loneliness. Children experiencing misfortune do not notice their friends' games and amusements. Nothing can distract them from their melancholy thoughts. The most sensitive and kindly way to help such little people is to share their grief without probing that which is deeply personal and private. Insensitive interference may provoke bitter animosity. And if there is no genuine human feeling behind it, advising not to give in, not to despair, or to be firm with oneself, is seen by children as irrelevant hot air.

To teach children how to feel for others means first and foremost to pass on to them our own emotional and moral culture. The cultivation of feeling is impossible without a deep understanding of people's inner states. Such understanding comes to children when they mentally put themselves in the shoes of someone who is experiencing sadness or anxiety.

When Sashko's grandmother fell ill, the boy became sad, thoughtful and at the same time wary. You would say something to him and he would wince as if you had touched a sore spot. One day I noticed that his big, dark eyes were full of tears. The children told me, 'Sashko is crying'. It would be naïve to expect a child to be overcome with sympathy for a friend or an adult just because he is a child. Empathy needs to be taught just as thoughtfully and carefully as we teach children to take their first independent steps. Empathy is one of the most subtle areas of cognition, involving both mind and heart. For an experienced teacher one of the most powerful means for educating empathy is language.

I chose a moment when Sashko was out of the classroom and said to the children, 'If someone is experiencing grief we should not express surprise. And Sashko is going through a really hard time. The only close relative he has is his grandma. He does not remember his mother. And now his grandma is ill. Perhaps they will put her in hospital and then who will the boy live with? Put yourself in his place and then you will understand what grief is. Do you remember the old man we met by the roadside? Do you remember what sad eyes he had? You felt then that the old man was grieving. Why don't you notice the sadness in your friend's eyes? You have seen that Sashko has been quiet and thoughtful for some days now. He is sitting in class but all his thoughts are at his grandma's bedside. If the boy stays home for a few days, do not rush to ask him why he was not at school. It is not easy for someone to talk about their misfortune. And in general, if you see that someone is grieving and suffering do not be too inquisitive, but help them. Don't rub salt in the wounds of their heart. If you know that someone in our class is going through a hard time, do everything you can to make sure that not a single word or action of yours should cause more suffering. And also think about what you can do to help Sashko and his grandmother. But your help should not be boastful: look how good we are, we are helping our friend. To make a show of your kindness will not help anyone. If your heart does not tell you that you need to help your friend, no amount of outward kindness will make you kind.'

Sashko came back to the classroom and I did not say another word about him. The children understood why I immediately began to talk about something else. During the break they began to discuss how to help the boy and his grandmother. The children brought their friend apples and fish, and all this was done with the purest of motives. When Sashko's grandmother was admitted to hospital and he began to live with his aunt, the children often visited him. When they learnt that the boy had got soaked in the rain, fallen ill and was in hospital with his grandmother, they took his misfortune to heart. On our day off, we all set off for the hospital. The children took apples and pastries for their friend. Shura brought a slab of chocolate that his father had brought for him. We waited half a day while all the children had a turn in Sashko's ward.

This both delighted and troubled me. This was the result of a collective impulse. Some of the children wanted to show kindness to their friend mainly so others would see their noble act. Volodya told me that he would bring a present to the hospital for Sashko: some new skates that his father had recently bought him.

'Will your father let you?' I asked.

'Yes, Dad says it's OK.'

'Then there is no point bringing them to the hospital. Sashko cannot skate at the moment. When Sashko is well you can take the skates to his home.'

Volodya did not give the skates to his friend. It turned out that his generous impulse was short-lived … This incident forced me to think more deeply about the education of kindness, warmth and empathy. These are very subtle, complex things. How do we teach a little person to do something good without looking for praise or reward, but from a subjective impulse to do good deeds? What does it consist of, this impulse to do good things, and where does it come from? When educating empathy collective impulses are important, but at the same time compassion must involve deeply personal spheres of each child's spiritual life.

I tried to ensure that all my pupils did good deeds—helping their friends or other people—from an intrinsic motivation, and that they experienced a feeling of deep satisfaction. This is probably one of the most difficult tasks in moral education: to teach a person to do good things without direct advice to follow a specific course of action. How is one to do this in practice? It seems that the most important thing is to develop children's inner capabilities so they cannot help doing good deeds, in other words to teach them to empathise. But how do you do that? How do you teach children witnessing another person's grief to mentally put themselves in that person's shoes, so they clearly intuit the other person's feelings? It is very important that the personality of the little child should identify with the personality of the person who is experiencing suffering in their life, so that the child can see and feel themselves in the grieving person.

The more the children gave of their spiritual reserves to a friend experiencing grief, the more sensitive their hearts became. One cold winter's day in February (at that time the children were in grade three), Misha, Katya and Larisa came running to my home. They were upset about something.

'Vanya's brother Lenya has died', said Katya. 'His father got a telegram. He is going to Kazakhstan tomorrow. What should we do now?'

The children's eyes implored me: teach us how to help our friend.

That day we learnt how the tragedy had occurred. Lenya, an eighteen-year-old tractor driver, had been carting hay to an animal breeding farm. On the way a blizzard struck. The young man could have left his tractor and walked to a village not far from the road; but he did not do that, hoping the blizzard would end and he would be able to deliver the hay to the farm on time. But the blizzard strengthened, the temperature plunged, and Lenya froze in the tractor cabin … For several days Vanya did not come to school. The children were sad and their chatter fell silent. Everyone was asking how to help their friend. Someone suggested going to visit Vanya at home. I advised against that. 'The boy, his mother, father, brothers and sisters are going through a terrible time. If we arrive at their home, the mother will see us and remember how Lenya went to school and it will become even more difficult for her. We'll visit Vanya later, when his mother's heart has had some time to heal. And when the boy comes to school, do not ask how his brother died. It is very hard to think and speak about that. Be attentive and very careful with Vanya; do not cause his heart pain in any way."

When Vanya's father came back from Kazakhstan he told me that a street in the state farm village had been named after his eldest son. I repeated what he had told me to the children. At that time the students in our class were preparing to join the Pioneers. The children were thinking about whose names their troop and each of the three patrols should bear. And then they themselves said what I was expecting to hear from them: that Vanya's patrol should bear the name of his brother Leonid, who had died following the call of duty. The boy took that news home to his mother. I advised the children: let's get an album and each of us can draw something about school in it. Of course the children wanted to draw something connected with Leonid and his school years. The senior students showed us an apple tree planted by Leonid when he was in grade three. In the physics laboratory we found a model of a crane made by Leonid and his friends. Leonid loved birds and some people in the school still remembered how he had made a dovecote with other members of his Pioneer patrol. The children described all these things in their album. I drew a portrait of Leonid. They presented the album to Leonid's mother. For her this was a priceless gift. She was glad that the school community preserved the memory of her son. We made a similar album for the Pioneer patrol that would bear Leonid's name.

It is very important not to turn good feelings and good deeds into activities put on for show. It is better to talk as little as possible about what has been done and not to praise children for kindness. These are guidelines one should adhere to in educational work. The greatest danger is that children will mentally want to take credit for simple human acts of kindness and consider them almost as acts of valour. Usually the school is guilty when this happens. A student finds a coin that someone has lost and hands it in, and soon the whole school knows about it. I remember one interesting case that happened in a neighbouring school. A girl brought a five kopeck coin that she had found to her class teacher and the teacher praised her lavishly ... The following break three girls and one boy came running to the teacher. All had found one or two kopeck coins lost by their friends. The children expected to be praised. The teacher sensed something was not right and expressed her indignation ... In this way children learn to dispense 'portions of goodness', and if they are not praised for their good deeds they feel dissatisfied.

Kindness has to become just as normal a human state as thought. It has to become habitual. Our school staff tried to ensure that sincere, heartfelt acts of kindness left feelings of deep satisfaction in the children's hearts. Heartfelt sensitivity to the spiritual world of another human being develops in childhood under the influence both of a teacher's words and the psychological climate in the group. It is very important to awaken heartfelt impulses of sympathy, of a readiness to act with kindness, in all the children. But this impulse only ennobles the heart when it is expressed in individual activity.

My pupils did not forget their old friend Grandpa Andrei. During the winter months the old man lived in a little hut not far from the winter quarters of the apiary. The children visited him, bringing apples and drawings. The old man appreciated every kind word. The children sensed that loneliness was a difficult burden to bear and tried to show kindness to the man.

One warm spring day in March the children were in a hurry to get to Grandpa Andrei's house. They were going to help him put out the hives. This was a special day for everyone. The children were overjoyed to observe how the golden-winged messengers of spring completed their cleansing flight after the winter. On the way to the bees' winter quarters we called in on an old lady to get a drink of water. She treated us to some home baking and suggested we visit her more often.

During the war years Olga Fedorovna experienced great loss. Her two sons, her husband and her brother died at the front, and her daughter died from hard labour in a coal mine in Nazi Germany. I told the children about her difficult life and the children felt an urge to befriend Grandma Olga. The little ones visited her frequently. Olga Fedorovna showed us the medals and decorations earned by her husband and sons. The children wanted with all their hearts to bring some joy to Grandma Olga. As soon as the time arrived to plant fruit trees, we planted five apple trees in her yard and the same number of pear trees, cherry trees and grape vines—in memory of her sons, daughter, husband and brother. We also planted trees for the old lady herself. It is hard to convey in words the feelings of gratitude that Olga Fedorovna experienced. On hot summer days we came to water the plants, though Olga Fedorovna did that without our help. During the summer the children spent whole days with her.

Grandma Olga became the children's friend. The children would not spend a special day without her. We tried not to miss the times when the cherries, apples, pears and grapes ripened. We came to the old lady's orchard, picked the first ripened fruit, and presented them to her. When the children were studying in grade seven the old lady fell seriously ill. She died a week after the school year ended. This was a great loss for the children. Sometime later, we learnt that Olga Fedorovna had left her hut and orchard to the children. This bequest presented a problem to the collective farm management. In what sense could the students be considered owners of the hut and orchard? The collective farm workers helped them to make sense of something that did not fit into any legal framework. They said, 'Let the children do their good deeds on this little property'. We invited Grandpa Andrei to live in the hut, and he was very happy to move there. It was close to the apiary. When Varya and Zina were studying in grade four they had made friends with some Little Octobrists[29] and helped them prepare to join the Pioneers. These little ones spent whole days in the orchard.

Great is the grief of a mother whose son has died fighting for the freedom and independence of his homeland. Let our children feel, experience and share this grief. May the thousands upon thousands of mothers, whose sons lie in unmarked graves from the Volga to the Elba, from the Arctic Ocean to the warm waters of the Mediterranean Sea, become friends with our school students. It is impossible to ennoble children's hearts if they have not felt and experienced the greatest loss of our homeland: the loss of 22 million lives; the grief of terrible torture, fires and destruction; everything that we can never forget nor forgive the Nazis.

The more deeply children comprehend and experience a mother's grief, the more sensitive their hearts will be, the firmer their civic convictions will be, and the stronger young people's sense of responsibility for the future of their homeland will be. For this reason we need great tact when approaching such an important event as inviting a mother, whose son has died heroically on the battlefield during the Great Patriotic War, to a Pioneer gathering (or in general to the school). Meeting a person whose personal grief expresses the nation's grief should leave a deep impression on young hearts.

Educating a citizen is one of the most complex questions, not only for educational theory but for the practical process of education. In this area, it is very important that knowledge should pass through the heart and be reflected in one's personal, spiritual world. Knowledge

---

29 Translator's note: The Little Octobrists was a communist youth organisation for children aged seven to nine. Children typically joined this organisation at school in grade one, and continued in it until grade three when they joined the Pioneers.

about the homeland, about that which is dear and sacred to the Soviet people, is not simply information that one can use in everyday life once it is memorised. These are sacred truths that must touch the personal lives of pupils. They will only become sacred for a child if the greatness of the homeland is perceived through the greatness of human beings.

## Work inspired by noble feelings

WORK BECOMES A GREAT MOULDER of character when it enters the spiritual life of our pupils, giving them the joy of friendship and comradeship, developing curiosity and a thirst for knowledge. It allows them to experience the joy of overcoming difficulties, revealing more and more beauty in the surrounding world, and awakening the first stirrings of civic pride—the pride that comes from creating those material benefits without which human life is impossible.

The joy of work is a powerful educational force. During their childhood years every child should have a deep experience of this noble feeling.

It was the first autumn of our school life. The senior students had set aside several dozen square metres of soil for us in the school plot. We hoed the soil: rural children are accustomed to such work. I told the little ones, 'Here we will sow winter wheat, harvest the grain, and mill it. From it we will bake our first bread.' The children knew very well what bread was, and strove to work like their mothers and fathers. At the same time there was something romantic about what we had undertaken, incorporating elements of a game.

Dreaming of our first bread inspired us and helped us to overcome difficulties. And the difficulties were not insignificant: the children carried small baskets of humus, mixed it with the soil, dug furrows for the rows of wheat, and sowed one grain at a time. The sowing turned into a real celebration. All the children were inspired by the work. The plot was sown but no-one went home. We felt like dreaming and sat under a tree where I told the tale of the golden grain of wheat. I thought about the tale, and about how to ensure that in childhood, my pupils would find not only a child's joy in their work but also their first experience of civic joy.

While waiting for the first shoots to appear, the children were excited: would our plot soon turn green? And when the first shoots appeared the boys and girls came running every morning to see how quickly the little green stalks would grow. In winter we sprinkled the plot with snow to keep the wheat warm. In spring the children experienced the joyful excitement of seeing how the shoots carpeted the earth with green, how the wheat grew tall stalks and formed ears of grain. The little ones took a keen interest in the fate of each ear.

The harvest was an even more joyful celebration than the sowing. The children came to school in their finest costumes. Each child carefully cut the wheat and bound it in a little sheaf. We celebrated again with the milling. We gathered every last grain and sprinkled it into a sack. Grandpa Andrei milled the wheat and brought us some white flour. We asked Tina's mother to bake us some bread. The children helped her: the boys brought water and the girls supplied the wood. And there they were: four big, white loaves of bread, the fruits of our work, care and concern. A feeling of pride filled the children's hearts.

At last the long-awaited day arrived: the celebration of the first bread. The children invited Grandpa Andrei and all the parents to their celebration. They spread white, embroidered table cloths. The girls laid out the fragrant slices of bread and Grandpa Andrei put out plates with honey. The parents ate the bread, praised the children and thanked them for their work.

That day remained in the children's memories for life. At the celebration no-one said any lofty words about labour and human dignity.

The thing that so moved the children on that day was a feeling of pride: they had grown the grain and they had brought joy to their parents. And human pride in one's work is a major source of moral purity and nobility.

Our celebration of the first bread attracted the attention of other classes. Every class wanted to grow its own grain. The children gave their teachers no rest: why did other classes have a celebration of the first bread and not theirs?

This event provoked a lot of reflection amongst our staff. Everyone could see that the simplest matter—working the soil and fertilising it—could be just as desirable an activity as a walk in the forest or reading an interesting book. Teachers told of instances where the laziest children, who seemed not to be interested in anything, became unrecognisable in this work. 'What is going on?' we wondered. And we all came to the conclusion that the main thing was the feelings experienced by the children, the fact that they were inspired by a noble goal. A love of work is connected above all to the children's emotional lives. The children wanted to work when that work brought them joy. The deeper the joy they found in their work, the more the children valued their honour, and the more they saw themselves in their activity—their effort, their name. The joy of work is a powerful educational force that helps children become aware of themselves as members of a group. This does not mean that work becomes merely an amusement. It demands effort and persistence. But we must not forget that we are dealing with children who are just discovering the world.

The children decided to make our celebration of the first bread an annual event. The following autumn they took on a new plot, and when they had produced a new crop of winter wheat they invited their parents and little preschool friends to the celebration. Even when my pupils became senior students they were still very excited to harvest the wheat from their little school plot, to mill the grain and bake the bread. In all of this there were elements of romanticism and play.

The joy of work cannot be compared with any other joy. It is unthinkable without a sense of beauty, but in this case the beauty lies not in what the children receive but in what they create. To find joy in work is to find beauty in being alive. Knowing this beauty, children experience a feeling of self-worth and pride, conscious of the fact that they have overcome difficulties.

This feeling of joy is only accessible to those who know how to make real efforts, who know perspiration and tiredness. Childhood should not be one long holiday. If there is no hard work, at an age-appropriate level, children will never know the happiness that comes from work. In work education, the pinnacle of educational wisdom is to establish in children's hearts a traditional folk attitude to work. For society as a whole, work is not only a necessity of life without which human existence is unthinkable, but also a sphere for expressing many aspects of spiritual life, the spiritual richness of the human personality. The richness of human relations is expressed in work. To educate a love of work is impossible if a child has no sense of the beauty of these relations. The people who make up a nation see work as a major avenue for self-expression, for the affirmation of their personalities. A folk saying suggests that without work, a person becomes an empty shell. One of our major educational objectives is to ensure that each pupil's feelings of personal worth and pride are based on success in work.

During the first spring of their school lives the children planted the 'Mothers' Orchard': thirty-one apple trees and the same number of grape vines. 'Children', I told my pupils, 'this will be an orchard for our mothers. Our mother is the dearest, closest human being. In three years' time these apple trees and grape vines will bear their first fruit. The first apple, the first bunch of grapes, will be our present for our mothers. Let us bring them joy. Remember that our mothers do a lot for us. Let us show our appreciation for their care and concern by giving them joy.'

Work in the Mothers' Orchard was inspired by the dream of bringing joy to our elders, to our parents. Some of the children did not yet know the full depth of that noble human feeling: love for one's mother. I tried to awaken that feeling in each child. Galya planted a tree for her stepmother, Sashko for his grandmother, Vitya for his aunt. No-one remained indifferent to the work. In spring and summer the children watered the plants and eradicated any pests. The apple trees and grape vines turned green. During the third year the first flowers appeared and the first fruit set. Each one wanted their fruit to ripen as quickly as possible.

I found great happiness in seeing how delighted Tolya, Tina and Kolya were. Juicy apples were ripening on their trees and amber coloured grapes swelled on the grape vines. The children picked the ripe fruit and carried it to their mothers. Those were unforgettable days in the lives of the children. I remember the tenderness that shone in Kolya's eyes when he picked an apple to take to his mother.

During the second year of their school lives the children's work was inspired by noble feelings. Each child planted fruit trees in their parents' home plots, for their mother, their father, their grandfather and their grandmother. 'This is the apple tree for my mother, father, grandfather or grandmother', the children would say with pride. Sashko planted trees in memory of his father and mother. Galya and Kostya planted fruit trees in memory of their mothers, and did not forget their stepmothers, for each of whom they also planted a tree.

There was no other work for which the children showed the same touching level of care as when they looked after these trees. All waited impatiently for the apple trees to flower. To watch for the first fruit from these apple trees, to pick them and carry them to their mothers—these were not simple work processes that the children carried out one after another. These were steps in their moral development, during which the children experienced the beauty of what they were doing.

The most sacred and beautiful thing in a person's life is their mother. It was very important that the children felt the moral beauty of work that brings joy to one's mother. Gradually a wonderful tradition took shape and established itself among our class members. In autumn, when earth and toil bestow abundant gifts, we began to observe the Autumn Mother's Day. On this day each student brought their mother the fruit of their own labour, something they had dreamt of all summer and sometimes for several years: apples, flowers, ears of wheat grown on a tiny plot of land (each child had a corner for their favourite work in their parents' yard). 'Take care of your mothers.' This was the thought we impressed upon the boys and girls as we prepared them for the Autumn Mother's Day. The more spiritual energy the children invested in work to bring their mothers joy, the more humanity there was in their hearts.

We also initiated a Spring Mother's Day. We found a remote clearing in the forest the children named the 'wild strawberry clearing', where many berries grew in summer. In spring the clearing turned light blue as snowdrops flowered. The children experienced great joy when they visited this wonderful place. They wanted to share this joy with their mothers. And then the children came up with an idea: the first flower to grace the earth would be for their mother. That was how the Spring Mother's Day began. On that day the children presented their mothers not only with the tender little bells-shaped snowdrops, but also with flowers grown in the glasshouse. When conducting celebrations dedicated to mothers, we should avoid fuss and formality. We tried to ensure that honouring our mothers was an intimate, family affair. The important thing here is not grand words, but deep feelings.

To love humanity is easier than to show kindness to your own mother, according to an old Ukrainian saying attributed to our popular eighteenth century philosopher Grigory Skovoroda. This saying contains deep wisdom from our folk pedagogy. It is impossible to educate the quality of humaneness if attachment to a close, dear person has not already taken root in the heart. Words about love for others do not constitute love. The true school for educating heartfelt warmth, soulfulness and empathy, is the family. Our relationships with our mother, father, grandfather, grandmother, brothers and sisters are a test of our humanity.

The work children do should create beauty. This is what is required if we are to combine aesthetic and moral education. In the first autumn of our school lives we collected dogrose seeds and planted them in a little garden bed set aside for us in a secluded corner of the school grounds. Onto the dogwood bushes we grafted buds from white, red, purple and yellow roses. We created our own 'Rose Garden'. It is difficult to convey in words the joy the children experienced when the first flowers appeared. The boys and girls were afraid to touch the bushes in case they harmed them. The children were in raptures when I said that roses would flower here all summer, if the flowers were cut correctly. Each one wanted to take a flower for their mother. They were delighted to think that they would be able to present their mothers with a little bouquet of roses, together with their apples, on Autumn Mother's Day.

During the first spring of our school studies we sowed many flowers. The plants needed constant attention. Watering was especially difficult. At that time the senior students constructed a small water-tower with a pump. The water was fed to the flower-bed, which lightened the children's work, and it became attractive to all of them. Even the tiniest, Danko, could now water all the flowers in half an hour.

But I was not satisfied by collective work. I wanted the cultivation of flowers to become every child's personal hobby. There is probably no work that ennobles the heart, and that combines beauty, creativity and humanity more than the cultivation of roses. I managed to kindle in each child's heart the desire to grow flowers at home. In grades three and four my pupils were already able to admire the roses they had grown in their yards at home.

Life convinced me that if a child has grown roses in order to admire their beauty, if the sole reward for their labour was to take pleasure in beauty, and to create beauty for the happiness and joy of another human being, that person would be incapable of evil, meanness, cynicism or heartlessness. This is one of the most complex issues in moral education. Beauty in itself does not contain any magic power capable of educating spiritual nobility in people. Beauty educates moral purity and humanity only when the labour required to create beauty is humanised by a higher moral motivation characterised by respect for others. The deeper this humanisation of work is, creating beauty for others, the more people respect themselves, and the more intolerable it is for them to stray from the norms of morality.

The role of beauty in the education of morality was taken up for discussion by our staff. While giving great significance to beauty as a means of influencing the spiritual world of a student, particularly their emotions, we were wary of overvaluing the role of its influence. Under what conditions did beauty become an educational influence? This was a question we addressed at a psychological seminar. The answer was arrived at through a general analysis of the laws of the education process. Sharing our experience, analysing the methods and techniques that teachers used to influence the spiritual world of students in the junior, middle and upper school, we became more and more convinced that there is not, and cannot be, any single, all-powerful method that guarantees the success of education and at the same time compensates for any deficiencies and weak areas in other spheres of educational influence.

Aesthetic education may be conducted wonderfully well, but if other components and elements of our education process have serious weaknesses, then the educational influence of beauty is weakened and may be reduced to nought. Each influence on the spiritual world of a child acquires educational force only when it is accompanied by other influences that are just as important. In some circumstances a person may carefully cultivate flowers and take delight in their beauty, while at the same time remaining an indifferent, heartless cynic. It all depends what other means of influencing the spiritual world of the personality accompany the particular influence upon which we, as educators, are placing our hopes.

Our staff became convinced of these truths. Discussion of the lives of particular children led us to the issue of the harmony of pedagogical influences. In my view this is one of the fundamental laws of education. I do not think for a moment that this issue has been completely resolved in the educational practice of our school, but we have done a lot to investigate and address this issue. The essence of this concept, which encapsulates one of the most important laws of education, is as follows. The educational effect of each means of influencing the personality depends on how well thought through, how well directed, and how effective all the other means of influence are. The strength of beauty as an educational influence depends on how skilfully work has been developed as an educational influence, and on how deeply and thoughtfully the education of reason and feeling have been developed. A teacher's words acquire educational impact only when the personal example of elders is functioning, and when all the other educational influences are characterised by moral purity and refinement.

Between educational influences there are tens, hundreds, thousands of interrelationships and interdependencies. In the final analysis, the effectiveness of education depends on how these interrelationships and interdependencies are taken into consideration, or more precisely, how they work out in practice. In my view, the tiresome accusations that educational science has not kept up with life are due to our having ignored the fact that any means of influencing the personality loses its strength in the absence of hundreds of other influences. Any rule will be no more than an empty sound if hundreds of other rules are not followed. Educational science falls behind to the extent that it does not investigate the multitude of interconnections and interdependencies between various means of influencing the personality. It will only become a precise science, a true science, when it researches and explains the most subtle and complex interdependencies of educational phenomena.

We began to hold special days to celebrate flowers. There were several of them. The spring flower day was to celebrate the appearance of lilies of the valley, tulips and lilacs. On this day we visited the forest and the lilac bed planted during the first autumn of our school life. Each pupil gathered a small bouquet, trying to find a unique combination of colours. We assembled on the lawn and admired each other's bouquets. We took them to our mothers and to our friends, Grandpa Andrei and Grandma Olga. We invited the little preschoolers to our celebration and gathered bouquets for them as well.

The second celebration was rose day. We picked bouquets in the school rose garden and from the home gardens. By the second year of studies nearly every child had rose bushes at home. We took the most beautiful bouquets to Grandpa Andrei and Grandma Olga.

The third celebration was wildflower day. This brought the children the greatest joy of all. We went into the fields in the morning, when the flowers are especially beautiful. Picking a beautiful bouquet of wildflowers requires real creativity. We brought the bouquets to school, rested, and dreamt of a time when wildflowers would bloom at school. We recalled where the most beautiful flowers grew, gathered seed in autumn and dug up rhizomes, and in time, cornflowers and camomile flowers bloomed in the school grounds.

Autumn flower day, or chrysanthemum day, was when we said a sad farewell to summer. We worked hard to mark this day as late as possible. We defended the chrysanthemums from cold winds and frosts by covering them overnight with paper hoods. After autumn flower day we transplanted the flowers to the glasshouse.

During their third year, the children celebrated snowdrop day for the first time. The forest was still carpeted with snow but the earth had already woken from its winter slumber. The first lilac-blue and white bells appeared in clearings. The children took little bouquets to their mothers on this day.

I do not want to give readers the impression that my pupils' childhood was one continuous celebration. Here I am describing in a few pages the children's experiences over a period of four years, and each celebration was the result of work.

My aim was that the children would see work as a source of spiritual joy. People should work not only for bread, clothing and to build a house, but also so that flowers will always bloom next to their homes, giving joy to themselves and others. Even during the childhood years, people should work for joy.

Little nooks of beauty appeared in the gardens surrounding our children's homes a year after the children started studying at school. Nearly all the children cultivated roses. Apart from that each child had their favourite flowers. Varya, Lida, Pavlo, Seryozha, Katya, Larisa and Kostya loved chrysanthemums. Sanya, Zina, Lyuba, Lyuda and Saskho cultivated carnations and tulips. Vanya, Vitya and Petrik planted several lilac shrubs. I showed the children how to care for the flowers, how to cultivate seedlings and how to select the best locations for the plants.

Kolya's love of flowers led to conflict with his mother. The boy loved to work in the glasshouse. I gave him three chrysanthemum plants and showed him how to plant them. At that time we also distributed some excellent tomato seedlings to the children. Kolya took home ten tomato seedlings with his chrysanthemums. The mother planted the tomatoes and Kolya planted the chrysanthemums. Two weeks later the mother saw the chrysanthemums, which were already well established, and pulled them out. The boy found the discarded plants by the fence, burst into tears and ran to his mother. The woman laughed at him: 'What a fuss to make over some flowers! What do we need them for? We've managed very well without flowers up till now.' The boy took the flowers and planted them in a corner behind the barn.

After some time had passed the boy brought his mother some light blue flowers and said, 'Look, Mum, how beautiful they are.' The boy experienced complex emotions as he said these words. He probably wanted to say, 'Mum, I want our family life to be as beautiful as these flowers'.

The children worked with a lot of compassion in the bird clinic.

After storms we would go into the forest and we always found young chicks that had fallen from nests. Then the bird clinic would ring with the sound of children's voices. And during bitter frosts in winter, the children set up feeders with pumpkin seeds by the windows of the clinic. Many tomtits came to feed there and cheeped demandingly when the food ran out. The children sprinkled grain on a table and the tomtits flew into the room to peck at the food. Gradually the birds became accustomed to the children and spent more and more time in the room. On frosty nights they stayed inside. They cheeped happily, and landed on the children's shoulders, hands and heads. On sunny days the birds came for feed and flew away at once. The children did not want to part with their feathered friends. The birds seemed to sense this. In their cheeping the children thought they detected a plea. 'Please excuse us', the birds seemed to say. 'We cannot stay for long.'

Kolya, Yura, Sashko, Kostya and Pavlo spent hours at a time in the bird clinic. I advised the children to build little feeders at home. Little shelves with pumpkin seeds appeared near their ventilation windows and Pavlo made a little house.

At first glance this may seem to be of little substance and unrelated to education. But in reality caring for another living creature is an education in heartfelt sensitivity and warmth, in empathy.

In grade three the children began celebrating the Day of the Lark, described earlier, which became a unique celebration of work and artistic creativity. The girls baked little larks from wheaten dough. Each one tried to capture the bird's precipitous ascent in their simple creations. This was a unique form of artistic creativity. The girls showed each other their larks and found in them not only movement, but song. 'Your lark is silent, but mine is singing', you might hear during those days.

When the children grow up they will go to work in agricultural brigades and animal breeding farms; they will become tillers of the soil and milkers, agronomists and horticulturalists. It is essential that the little ones should feel the beauty of simple work on the land and on farms from an early age. It is very important that simple agricultural work should give children joy. And this is impossible without play, without collective enthusiasm for the work activity, friendship and mutual help. My pupils always took the common task to heart and thought about its results. The class was always a collective working group.

In early spring we visited Tanya's father at the animal breeding farm. They set aside a warm corner in a barn for us and put four little lambs there—Tanya's father chose the very weakest. 'Children, we will care for these warm little bundles of life. We will visit them every day and feed them a warm mix of milk and hay until they are strong and healthy', I told the children.

You often hear people say, 'There are some lazy creatures who cannot be interested in doing anything. There are some hearts that are so hardened, that you just can't get through to them.' It is not true. Inspire little ones (and I mean little ones and not adolescents—at eleven or twelve years of age it is already too late) with work such as looking after little lambs on an animal breeding farm. Work with the children for a month or two and you will see how the icicles melt in even the most indifferent heart. To collectively inspire children with the beauty of work is a powerful way to foster a love of work. In our class we had not a single indifferent student, not a single lazy child, and that was the result of inspiring children with simple work.

We found some nutritious hay, prepared some meal from it, and boiled a 'lamb soup'. We fed the lambs milk. When they began to eat green grass the children brought them shoots of barley and oats from the glasshouse. As soon as grass started to grow outside whole armfuls of juicy feed started to appear in the lambs' enclosure. Tanya's father fenced a small area near the barn for the lambs and we used to let them roam there all day. It was our little 'sheep farm'.

In their third year of school the children acquired new, more serious responsibilities. The boys and girls wanted to look after calves and an area was set aside for us at the dairy farm. The children spent all winter growing green barley and oats in the glasshouse. In summer we dried hay for the calves. Many of the boys and girls visited the dairy farm nearly every day.

When spring came and the sheep and lambs were transferred to the field camp, the children missed them. They wanted to live for at least one day out in the fields, in natural surroundings. On Sunday we walked to the field. We grazed the sheep and lambs and collected hay cut by the shepherds. The first spring grass provides a medicinal feed for young lambs in winter. And in summer, when our lessons had finished for the year, the children came to the field camp nearly every day. Experience has convinced me that people will never fall in love with simple agricultural work if they have not appreciated the beauty of everyday work in childhood.

The children's work on the school's experimental plot was illuminated by the fire of romanticism. Even in grade one we were allocated 0.1 hectare [1000 square metres] of land, and together with the senior students, built a little house there—brick walls, a tiled roof, a wooden floor, a little stove, water pipes, electricity—everything you would find in a real house, only smaller. The 'green house', as the children named this structure, became one more cosy nook where the little ones could read and listen to stories about nature. When the children were studying in grade three we conducted experiments there, trialling seeds.

The construction of that little house was both work and play. When the work was completed, the children took great care of what they had created with their own hands. They understood very well that the little house was the result of their work. No explanations can take the place of such life experience.

In order for children to appreciate and take care of the fruits of society's labour, they must first have some personal experience of social construction, however insignificant. The essence of public property is only understood when people hold dear what society has created. This understanding must be acquired in childhood. Teachers often complain that some adolescents squander public resources and wonder why they are so insensitive. If you want teenagers to look after pubic property and be self-disciplined, for their concern to be sincere and not just for show, for them to be genuinely concerned about property that does not belong to them, then make sure that something public becomes dear to them in childhood, and is inseparable from their personal happiness.

Next to the green house was our plot of land, where we grew wheat, barley, millet, buckwheat, corn and sunflowers. In the house we selected seed, stored our harvests and prepared fertiliser. The children's work was inspired by the romanticism of discovery. The children thought while they worked, and worked while they thought. They were discovering the secret laws of nature. I tried to ensure that in childhood my pupils were convinced by their own experience that knowledge helps people to harness the forces of nature, and that such knowledge is only acquired through work. I told the children about a grain of wheat and how work shapes its life story. The children discovered the wonderful world of soil biology. We introduced organic matter into our plot and the soil became fertile. The children each planted one hundred grains of wheat and observed with great interest how the plants developed. The children were inspired by the goal of 'feeding' the soil so well that large, heavy grains would form in the ears of wheat. Each one wanted to feed their plants as well as possible with liquid fertiliser. This was a truly creative endeavour, inspiring the children and motivating them to carry out the simplest of work operations. Carefully cutting the ears, the children counted out a thousand grains and weighed them. Whoever harvested the biggest crop was filled with pride. The other children strove to improve.

I was delighted to see that Shura, Misha, Pavlo, Sashko, Yura, Larisa, Tina, Vanya, Nina, Zina and Kolya were falling in love with plants and sensed the life in the soil. In grades three and four they grew grains of wheat twice the size of those normally grown in the field.

In the green house and in the glasshouse we grew cucumbers and tomatoes hydroponically. During the winter the children prepared a fertile mixture of humus and black soil. In spring they transferred the mixture to our outdoor plot, and in autumn they harvested a large crop of potatoes and tomatoes.

Some children worked in the 'green laboratory', a little house built for children in the middle school years. Here, under the supervision of older students, my pupils conducted interesting horticultural experiments. It was also here that I showed the children how to graft different varieties of fruit trees to wild rootstock. In grade two all the children learnt this delicate skill, experiencing the power of knowledge over nature and the bringing together of theory and practice.

The boys and girls could not wait for spring so they could see the results of their grafting. When the first leaves appeared on the grafted buds there was no end to the children's joy. We planted a collective nursery. We decided to raise our own trees for planting every year. This nursery became yet another favourite place of work. Vanya, Lyusya, Kolya, Volodya, Lyuba, Lida, Zina, Fedya, Katya,

Varya, Larisa, Seryozha, Tina and Galya especially liked to work there. In the summer after completing grade three, we found a wild plum growing in a remote thicket and each of us grafted onto it a different variety of fruit tree: plums, apricots and peaches. All the grafts took. The children observed with amazement how the different varieties of fruit tree developed on one crown. After two years the first fruit appeared.

It has already been noted that nature provides a rich stimulus for thought, helping to develop creative and inquisitive minds. As children understand nature's laws they gradually become more human, because they gradually become conscious of themselves as the highest step on nature's long developmental ladder. But nature is not of itself capable of creating miracles, of developing children's natural powers, educating their intellects and enriching their thought. Without conscious efforts, without work, it is impossible to discover and learn her secrets. Only when human beings take the first conscious steps to harness the forces of nature does she reward them, at first sparingly, then more and more generously as people make fresh efforts, simultaneously discovering and creating. The more children work, the more the secrets of nature reveal themselves to their minds, and the more new mysteries they become aware of. And the more mysteries there are the more active their thinking becomes. Perplexity is the surest way to prime thought. From the moment when a grain of wheat is planted in the tilled soil, to the harvest of the crop, more than two hundred questions arose among the children. How? Why? It is hard to think of any other interaction with nature that would provoke thought and reflection as much as work on the land: growing trees, grain and industrial crops.

I tried to ensure that the children's work was varied and facilitated the discovery of their talents and interests. Next to the school workshop we set up a room for the little ones. Here we put worktables with vices. I managed to realise a long-held dream. The senior students made two miniature lathes and one drilling machine. In a cupboard and on shelves, there were little planes and saws. In the metalwork drawers were collections of tools for metal working and also metal plates and wire. All of these things are necessary for construction and modelling. Many boys and girls were interested in working in this work room. Gradually a club for young tradespeople was formed. Seryozha, Slava, Yura, Tolya, Galya, Misha, Vitya, Lyuda, Tanya, Sanya, Vanya and Pavlo showed particular interest in construction, modelling and fretsaw work.

Gathering after dinner in the work room, we worked on several interesting models at once: a wind-powered generator, a grain-cleaning machine, a winnowing machine, a model house, a desk, and a cupboard for our tiny metal working tools. The children worked collectively, preparing both wooden and metal parts. The smaller and more delicate the model, the harder it was to make it like a real 'grown-up' one (to use the children's words), and the more interesting they found the work.

My main aim in getting the children involved in this work was to awaken their talents and interests, to develop skills and habits that would be essential in the future. I tried to engage the children through my own example. I showed them how to work with wood and metal, how to use the tools. The skill of the person who is instructing acts as a spark to kindle the fire of interest and awaken inspiration. Our activities in the work room began when, before their eyes, I made a doll's bed from wood. The more that little bed became like a real bed, the brighter their eyes shone. The little ones wanted to join in the work. Many of them began to help me on the spot: planing and sanding parts for the bed. By the time we started making a wind-powered generator, I already had not only reliable helpers but real workmates. Yura, Vitya and Misha quickly learnt how to use the tools. Everyone wanted to work at once, so we began to make several models at the same time.

Here I would like to make a little digression. The source of children's abilities and gifts is in their fingertips. Figuratively speaking, there are little channels that flow from the fingers to the centres of creative thought. The more confidence and inventiveness there is in the movements of children's hands, the more delicate the interaction between the hands and the tools of trade. And the more precise, subtle and complex the movements required for this interaction, the more brightly the creative element in children's minds shines. The more deeply this interaction of the hands with nature and with socially useful work has entered the spiritual life of the child, the keener their observational skills, inquisitiveness, perceptiveness, attentiveness and capacity to conduct research.

In other words, the more masterful children's hands are, the more intelligent they are. But such mastery is not achieved through some sort of intuition. It depends on the mental and physical strength of the child. Strength of mind grows with the development of manual skill, but this skill in turn draws on the powers of the mind. I tried to ensure that the discovery of the surrounding world was accomplished through an interaction between the children's hands and the surrounding environment so that children would observe not only with their eyes but with their hands, and they would manifest and develop their curiosity not only through questions but through work.

From the first days of the School of Joy my pupils gathered herbariums, seed collections, and samples of timber from different species. They studied the properties of materials, not only through the process of observation but also thanks to the interaction of their hands with various materials, armed with simple tools like knives, scissors, hammers and chisels. In grades one and two the children learnt to work with small knives. The children cut thin layers of timber from various species—willow, ash, poplar, oak, pine, pear, cherry—sanded them and pasted or sewed them to paper to compare their hardness and other properties. From knotty excrescences on the trunk of an ash tree (a particularly supple material) they made letters and the figures of animals and birds. All the boys and girls carved a 'wooden alphabet', as they called these letters carved from ash tree excrescences. Not far from our village there is a granite cave. We often walked there to collect mineral samples. With interest the children used little hammers to chip off small pieces of mica, gathered collections of stones of various colours, formed toy bricks out of clay, dried them in the sun and then built little houses. During the harvest in summer, we cut even stems from wheat and rye, plaited them into straw bands and sewed hats.

All of this was not just a preparation for technical creativity. In developing manual skills, I was developing the intellect. When we were constructing the model wind-powered generator, the children suggested replacing the metal blades of the windmill with wooden ones. 'There is a very strong and light timber', said Seryozha. 'From it you could make blades that would turn in the slightest breeze …'

During their four years of study in the primary school the children made more than thirty working models, which were comparable to the model wind-powered generator in the complexity of their construction. With each year the individual interests of the children became clearer. Shura, Vitya, Misha, Seryozha and Yura loved metal and mechanisms. They could work for several hours at a time at their vices, and the time flew by for them unnoticed. Sometimes it took a great effort to make them go home. Observing the boys at work at their vices or their miniature lathe, where they fashioned simple parts out of wood or soft metal, I remembered how in the School of Joy and in grade one, the children had learnt to carve their wooden letters. It would be naïve to see in this boyish enthusiasm a prediction of their future trades or professions. Life experience shows that a person's vocational development goes through many transformations. It is very rare for people to become what they dream of becoming in childhood.

Physical work is closely connected with intellectual development. Manual skills are the physical manifestation of an inquisitive mind, quick wittedness and a creative imagination. It is very important that during childhood all children should use their hands to bring their ideas to life.

In grade four the children made their own tools: little rough and smooth planes. The boys did not forget the simplest of tools either: they used a knife to carve amusing figures of wild and domestic animals, a fairytale witch and a wizard for our puppet theatres. Seryozha and Misha made two aquariums, one for our classroom and one for our Story Room.

The children derived great joy from another interesting project: we constructed a small generator driven by a little internal combustion engine. The generator produced a low-voltage current, safe for children.

In grades three and four the children had two hours of their favourite work every week. Some children went to the green house, some to the work room, some to the glasshouse, and some to the experimental plot or the orchard. Those who had fallen in love with work on the animal farm went to look after the lambs and calves. Each student chose work after their own heart. Sometimes I accompanied the children to one work area, sometimes to another. In each group there were children who showed a clear aptitude for a particular type of work. They became the organisers of these little work groups, enthusing their friends through their example. In the work room the group leader was Yura. Among the horticulturalists it was Vanya, among the orchardists it was Varya, and in the animal husbandry group it was Sasha. I was very pleased to see that these children had many skills and knew significantly more than their classmates. The other children tried to catch up with them, and the work activities took on the character of a competition to demonstrate their work skills.

Work entered the spiritual lives of my pupils as a joyful play of physical and intellectual abilities, as an affirmation of self-worth. It is very important that all children should achieve significant success in their favourite work, should see with their own eyes a manifestation of their creative ability, and should achieve mastery in their favourite pursuit—to the degree that this is possible for a child, of course. During the school years they should learn to do something very well and beautifully. The feeling of pride that comes with success in a favourite pursuit marks the beginning of self-awareness, the first spark igniting the fire of creative inspiration in a child's soul. And without inspiration, without an uplifting emotion of joy and a sense of being at the height of one's powers, there is no human being; there is no deep conviction that a person will occupy a worthy position in life. I tried to ensure that there was not a single child in the school who had not discovered a unique individual talent for work.

When I look back on each of my pupil's childhood years, I see eyes shining with joy and burning with pride in their work success. I see Seryozha with his little radio. He made it in grade four—three months of persistent work rewarded with great joy. I see Fedya standing next to a flowering peach tree. He had grafted a peach bud to wild plum rootstock, and waited for it to flower and bear fruit. I remember Valya at that joyful moment when she carried a young lamb from a shed on the animal breeding farm. The little girl had raised it in spite of its weakness and sickliness. Tina has a broad smile as she looks up at the sun and the clear blue sky and gazes at some purple roses. She had grafted three rose buds to a dogrose bush, and created a shrub of exquisite beauty. When I hear Sashko's name, I see a dark-eyed boy with a little sheaf of wheat. When we weighed the grain he had grown on three square metres of land, we calculated that such heavy grains would have yielded a crop of eight tonnes per hectare ... Not far from the school well grows a spreading apple tree. Each year when it flowers I admire the unique shades of pink, and I cannot help thinking that at any moment a little girl with blonde pigtails will come running up to the tree and say, 'This is my apple tree'. That is what Katya said when the apple tree first flowered. I remember Kostya with a sad face: he is hugging a little calf, but the calf does not respond to his affection—it has fallen ill.

This is how I remember all the children. I see them in love with their work. However, I do not think that this love necessarily predicts the future life path of each child. Just because children have fallen in love with the natural world and find joy in working in the orchard or the fields, does not mean that they will definitely become orchardists or agronomists. Talents, abilities and interests are like the branches of a flowering rose bush: some flowers die off and others open their petals. Each child had several interests and it is impossible to imagine children having a rich spiritual life any other way. But each child shone most brightly in some particular pursuit. Until children achieved significant success in some particular form of work, they did not stand out as individuals. As soon as work began to give deep personal joy, the human individuality shone through.

Work in which a person achieves mastery gives affirmation to the personality and is a mighty stimulus for the education of character. Feeling oneself to be a creator, a person strives to improve. It is difficult to exaggerate the significance of children discovering their creative powers and abilities in childhood, on the threshold of adolescence.

## *You are future custodians of our homeland*

IN GRADE ONE MY FIRST assistant appeared: a twelve-year-old Pioneer from grade six named Olya. She asked the council of the Pioneer group to entrust her with the preparation of the Little Octobrists to join the Pioneers. Olya loved children and that was the main requirement. (At our school the leaders of the Octobrist groups and Pioneer troops are not appointed. The ones who are most strongly motivated and who love children are the ones who take on the role of working with little ones.) Olya helped me in many ways: playing with the children, taking them on walks in the forest and the fields, telling them about Pioneer heroes and about the heroism of Soviet people during the Great Patriotic War.

For Olya regular contact with the children was a spiritual imperative rather than an obligation. To feel such an imperative is a remarkable talent in my view, a talent for being human. Those who are blessed with this talent become wonderful teachers and find great happiness in their work. Observe the children in a school community closely and you will find some that cannot live without doing something for their little friends. Among boys this often expresses itself in mischief, pranks and cunning tricks. The boy wants to be a leader and to take his friends with him, but does not know how to direct his energies. I feel like advising teachers not to supress this bubbling energy. These boys, these jokers and tricksters, are your potential helpers. Find a way to get closer to them and channel their energy in the necessary direction.

I tried to ensure that the preparations to join the Pioneers, and indeed the whole life of our Pioneer troop, educated in the children a deep feeling of love for our sacred land, so plentifully drenched with the blood of those who fought for its freedom and independence. Love for our homeland begins with admiration for the beauty that children see before them, in which they invest a part of their souls. Olya and I opened the children's eyes to the beauty of our countryside, and to the beauty of what has been created by Soviet people.

We walked into the steppe, sat on the summit of an ancient burial mound, and gazed at the wide fields sown with wheat. We admired the flowering orchards and tall, slender poplars, the deep blue sky and the song of the lark. Admiration for the beauty of the land where our grandfathers and great-grandfathers have lived, where we too are destined to live out our lives, repeat ourselves in our children, grow old and depart into the earth that has given birth to us—this is a major source of love for our homeland. There are countries in the world where nature is more striking than our fields and meadows, but the beauty of our native land must become the dearest of all to our children. It is important that children do not see this beauty with their eyes only. When they see how the trees are covered in a veil of white during the spring, how the bees hover above the golden bells of the hops, and how the apples and tomatoes swell and turn red, they must experience these things as part of the joy and plenitude of their spiritual lives. Let their childhood be remembered in bright and sun-drenched images: an orchard clothed in white flowers, the unforgettable droning of the bees above a field of buckwheat, the deep cold autumn sky, a formation of cranes passing on the horizon, the dark blue burial mounds seen though a shimmering haze, the crimson sunset, a willow leaning over the mirror surface of a pond, tall slender poplars by the roadside—may all of these leave an indelible impression in their hearts, epitomising the beauty of life during childhood and enshrining memories of all that is dearest to them.

But let the appreciation of this beauty also be accompanied by the thought that there would be no flowering orchard, no bees droning over the buckwheat, no tender mother's song, no sweet dreams at dawn when your mother carefully adjusts your blanket over your feet, none of these things would exist if on one cold winter morning nineteen-year-old Aleksandr Matrosov had not fallen to an enemy bullet while defending his battle comrades from bullets with his own chest; if Nikolai Gastello had not directed his blazing plane at enemy tanks; if thousands upon thousands of heroes had not shed their blood from the Volga to the Elba. It is this thought that we bring to the children's minds when they are experiencing the joy of existence. I tell my pupils how soviet soldiers fought for the freedom and independence of our homeland here in our village, in these fields, under these trees.

The joy of existence is not only the most striking expression of an individual's self-awareness, but also an evaluation of the surrounding world, expressing children's active relationship to what they see around them. The logic of life in a socialist society is such that the beauty of the surrounding world is naturally one of the contributing factors to the joy of childhood, the joy of existence. But is the surrounding world dear to children only because it is beautiful? The joy of existence is after all only a combination of pleasures that the child receives from the older generations. The surrounding world will become even dearer to little people when they see and feel the blood, sweat and tears that their grandfathers and great-grandfathers shed in the name of the freedom and independence of our homeland. This merging of the joy of existence with civic feelings is expressed very well by the Lithuanian poet Justinas Marcinkevičius in his poem 'Blood and ash':

> *Instil, mothers, in your children*
> *Love for our homeland, so that your children's*
> *Hearts from these lofty feelings*
> *May become more courageous and more sanctified.*
> *Inspire them with the thought that our sky,*
> *In the midnight glimmer of its guiding stars,*
> *May not be higher or more beautiful,*
> *But is not the same as everyone's.*
> *And let those be close to children,*
> *Who are united with them by the same feeling.*

Our native land becomes boundlessly dear to us when the joy of existence merges with a feeling of indebtedness to those people who have defended its beauty. In this mingling of feelings, the moral and aesthetic education of the younger generation is combined. The joy of existence should not be carefree. Educators are greatly mistaken if they think the joys of childhood should not be darkened by tales of grief, suffering and sacrifice undertaken in the name of our happiness.

The sunny days of early autumn arrive. Apple-laden branches hang low, grapes ripen, huge piles of yellow wheat appear on the threshing-floors of the collective farm, and silver cobwebs float in the transparent air. Olya and I take the children to the edge of the village. Here an ancient burial mound dominates the landscape. From it we have a view of a valley covered in grey watermelons; beyond it an orchard; beyond the orchard, tall, slender poplars; beyond them the steppe, with green fields of winter wheat; and on the horizon, distant burial mounds in a blue haze. The boys and girls are experiencing an unforgettable moment. In the beauty that they see before them, they feel their happy childhood. From those distant fields their mothers and fathers return in the evening, bringing some of that sunlight in their tender eyes. We sit down on the burial mound. I tell a tale of good and evil, and the children rejoice in the victory of the good.

A week later we return to the burial mound and the children discover something new in that beautiful landscape. The first autumn colours have appeared, covering the apple trees and poplars with gold, and the emerald fields of winter crops have turned an even deeper shade of green. The sky seems deeper. Every week at the same time we come to this place, admire the beauty, experience the battle between good and evil in our wonderful folk tales, listen to the music of the autumn steppe, breathe the clear air, and dream of how we will come here in spring to greet the lark. This little corner of the steppe enters the spiritual life of the children and becomes dear to them. It is the first striking image of their homeland, forever imprinted on the children's hearts.

It is impossible to awaken feelings for our homeland without perceiving and feeling the beauty of the surrounding world. Before explaining at what dear cost the older generations won the joys of childhood, we must open the children's eyes to the beauty of their native land. May memories of a little corner of their distant childhood remain in the children's hearts for the rest of their lives, and may the idea of their great homeland be connected with that little corner.

On a quiet autumn day I show the children a barely perceptible pit on the summit of the burial mound and say:

'Look at this hole in the ground. Time has weathered it and it is overgrown with grass. On a sunny autumn day, just like today, our troops were retreating along this road to beyond the Dnieper. A young machine-gunner came here, to the top of this burial mound. He set up his machine-gun here to hold up the enemy and prevent them from getting to the Dnieper. Enemy troops on motorcycles appeared on the road. He killed them. The fascists began to bombard the burial mound with mortars and cannons. You can see how on the south side it looks as if it has been dug up. The earth here is sown with deadly metal. The explosions fell silent and motorcyclists again appeared on the road. The burial mound came to life again, and again the enemy fell from the soviet soldier's bullets. The fascists sent a tank to the burial mound. It came up to those trees and opened fire with its gun. The shots fell silent and again the motorcyclists appeared on the road, and again the burial mound came to life. The warrior was seriously wounded in his arm, his head and his chest, but he kept on fighting. His eyes filled with blood, and he knew he was seeing the blue sky of his native land for the last time. Only when a shell exploded next to the machine-gun did the young man's heart stop beating. In the evening collective farm workers came here, dug a hole and buried his bloodied body. The soldier's remains lay here until the village was liberated from the enemy by the Soviet Army. The soldier's army friends came to the top of this burial mound, dug up his remains, and transferred them to the village where he was buried with honour in a communal grave. We do not know the name of that hero, and his mother does not know where her son is buried.'

The children's hearts ache. The beauty of life, the beauty of this little corner of their native land, is even dearer to the children. The children see the world through the eyes of a hero. That young man gave his life so that they could live happy and peaceful lives, so that they could see the stars twinkle in the sky, smell the scent of the grasses and the apple trees, and listen to the song of the grasshoppers in the steppe; so that on New Year's Eve their mothers could place a present from Grandpa Frost under their pillow ... The children fell silent, looking at the earth on which so much blood has been shed. They felt like caressing each clump of soil, each stem of wormwood and thyme.

Probably many of my pupils had trouble getting to sleep that night. In their mind's eye they could still see their native steppe, sometimes bathed in bright sunlight, at other times shrouded with the smoke of battle. Their hearts ached: never again would that hero see the beauty that they saw today, that they would see again tomorrow and in a year's time. From that thought tears appeared in their eyes and in their dreams they sensed the warm, tender hand of their mother.

The next morning before our lessons begin, Varya comes to me. She reads a poem she has composed the day before:

*By the steppe road stands a tall burial mound.*
*Over it for many years the wind has whispered,*
*The bright sun has shone,*
*And autumn mists have drifted.*
*A cruel enemy came to our land.*
*A young hero climbed the tall burial mound.*
*He barred the enemy's way.*
*Here, on the ancient burial mound, the young warrior fell,*
*A shell tore apart his chest,*
*His bloodied heart quivered on the earth,*
*The blue sky became dark,*
*The sun hid behind a black cloud ...*

*We will never forget you,*
*You died, so we could live.*
*There, where your heart fell to the ground,*
*We have planted an oak.*

A week later we again walk to the burial mound. The children want to know who that hero was. Where was he born? Where did he study? Is his mother alive? Everything that the children can hear and see they now see through the eyes of the hero who gave his life for his homeland. The children want to do something to express their feelings. When the leaves have fallen from the trees we bring a little oak to the summit of the burial mound. Words are unnecessary when children's hearts are moved by kindly feelings. The children are deeply moved by what they are doing. We are not planting a tree just to decorate the summit of the burial mound with greenery. We are establishing a living monument to a hero.

It will be difficult to grow an oak tree on top of a burial mound—the children know that—but they are not discouraged by any difficulties. In winter we protect the oak from winter winds by covering it with snow. In spring when the burial mound is covered with fresh grass, the children run every day to see if any buds have opened on the oak. This is not just caring for a tree; this is an encounter with a hero. The little oak turns green and in every leaf the children feel the breath of that bleak day. The old men who buried the soldier help us to establish the day of his heroic act. We mark it every year as a day of glory, remembrance and sorrow. The children come to school early in the morning, each with flowers to make a living wreath, and place it where, according to the old men, the hero fell.

For the children, that little patch of earth on the summit of the burial mound has become a symbol of the heroism of older generations who have defended the freedom and independence of our homeland. 'You are guardians of this land, where the blood of previous generations was shed.' This is the thought I impress upon the children. 'You must work to ensure that our homeland remains rich and powerful.'

One warm day, Olya and I took the children to the 'Garden of Heroes'. This is a war memorial created by the student community of our school on the spot where, during the fascist occupation in the late autumn of 1941, a tragedy played out, full of heroism and self-sacrifice. Cutting down the collective farm orchard, the fascists set up a prisoner-of-war camp here. Behind its barbed wire under the open sky, six thousand wounded, starving, unclothed soldiers and officers of the Soviet Army were condemned to die. Those people were deprived of water, and on cold autumn nights they gathered frost from the frozen earth and ate grass. Dozens of prisoners died every day. With animal cruelty the fascists waited for all the prisoners to die so they could explode a bomb depot next to the camp and blame the soviet troops, accusing them of bombing their own people.

Soviet patriots in the camp created a secret organisation and prepared a mass escape. One cold night when thousands of people were shivering in the wind and the rain, in twenty different locations, soldiers and officers crept up to the barbed wire. They went to their deaths, lying over the barbed wire, while most of the prisoners climbed over their bodies and fled into the steppe. More than four thousand people found shelter that night with the collective farm workers. Neither the Gestapo nor the treacherous police could find them. Four hundred heroes gave their lives so that 4000 of those condemned to die could again take up arms and join the ranks of those fighting for the freedom of their homeland.

After the liberation of the village from the fascists, the school students decided that this sacred place should become a lush, living memorial, dedicated to the heroes. They cleared the area, filled in the trenches, and planted 400 oak trees: 400 living monuments to those who had given their lives to save their comrades. The little oak trees grew, and from generation to generation the true legend of those heroic deeds was handed down. A few years after the establishment of the oak grove, on the occasion of their entry into the Pioneers, a new generation of students planted their own oak trees next to the first plantation. They wanted trees with great longevity to grow in that place where the blood of heroes had baked on the barbed wire, and where the ashes of their hearts were mixed with the soil. Each pioneer planted their own little tree. This became a tradition: when they joined the Pioneers, each student planted an oak tree in the Garden of Heroes.

We went there with the children. Olya told them of the heroes' deeds and showed them her oak tree. The children were impatient to join the Pioneers themselves.

Spring came and only a few weeks remained until the anniversary of Lenin's birthday, when each year we conduct a celebratory gathering of the Pioneer group in order to receive a new intake of Lenin's young successors. Once again we gathered at the Garden of Heroes and each child brought a young oak tree, a spade, and a basket of humus. The children planted the trees and watered them. Here on 22 April, on that sacred site commemorating heroic events, the children were presented with their Pioneer scarves by their older comrades. Here Lenin's young successors solemnly swore to be faithful patriots of their socialist homeland.

We went to the Garden of Heroes several times a year. In early spring we cleaned the trees of dead branches and leaves, and planted new trees in place of any that had been damaged by frost. In late autumn, on the day when the heroes had performed their courageous deeds, we held a gathering of our Pioneer troop. In place of the barbed wire fence a line of shapely oak trees now grew. In solemn silence the children walked past, each placing flowers at the foot on an oak tree. Asters and chrysanthemums blazed where on that fateful night the earth had turned red from blood.

We also went to the Garden of Heroes on our happiest days, on the eve of the summer holidays or before a distant excursion. In this sacred place silence always reigned. Even now there is no running, playing or shouting there. This is a place for admiring the beauty of nature, resting and reading. Boys and girls whose fathers gave their lives during the Great Patriotic War come to this place. Here a son bows his head and thinks of his father's grave in some distant place on the shores of the Arctic Ocean or in the Carpathian Mountains. From generation to generation the tale is passed down of those heroes who through their sacrifice made it possible for Soviet people to enjoy the sunshine, the flowers and free labour.

The oak on the burial mound grows ever taller. When my students, who are now young adults, see that tree proudly raising its branches to the blue sky their hearts beat more rapidly in their breasts and their homeland becomes even more close and dear to them.

Decades will pass, the participants in those unprecedented historic battles will pass away and ever newer generations will remember, with astonishment and gratitude, those who saved humanity from the threat of fascist domination.

We should never forget the countless calamities and horrors of war, the glow of the fires, the groans of those dying from bomb explosions, the cries of those driven to camps in fascist Germany, the strong embraces of fathers leaving for the front, the weeping of mothers receiving news of the heroic deaths of their husbands and fathers ... The younger generation must lay a foundation for an eternal monument to the fallen heroes. Here in the school where we now study, a transit prison was set up for young soviet men and women sent to forced labour camps during the fascist occupation. Our children should never forget that.

I told the children, 'Before the war there were 5100 inhabitants in our village. During the Great Patriotic War 837 of our villagers—785 men and 52 women—died heroic deaths at the front. Apart from the

837 who did not return from the front, 69 inhabitants of our village died in fascist death camps overcome by starvation and inhuman torture. They were tormented, killed, and then burnt in crematoriums. The fascist murderers traded with their ashes. The ashes of your brothers and sisters, of your mothers and fathers, were used to fertilise the soil in the area around Weimar not far from the fascist camp at Buchenwald. May the ashes of your brothers and sisters, fathers and grandfathers live on in your memories. Never forget that 276 young people were taken from our village to fascist camps in Germany and that 194 of them were killed in death camps, dying from hunger and overwork, some burnt alive in crematoriums. Pavlo's brother, who was taken to the city of Bochum, had his eyes burnt out with a red hot poker by fascist criminals and was nailed alive to a tree for sabotage. The Nazis buried Tanya's sister alive for communist propaganda. Kostya's uncle was thrown naked into an iron cage, where he suffered several days of torment before he died in agony. Yura's cousin was thrown to a pack of Alsatians and torn to pieces for trying to escape. A fascist officer took a baby from Valya's cousin and before the mother's eyes smashed its head against a stone. Lyusya's aunt, a twenty-six-year-old woman, was sent to the fascist camp at Auschwitz with her two children, a four-year-old daughter and a three-year-old son. At the camp the mother was separated from her children. The woman said to a fascist officer, "They are sick. I beg you, let them stay with me." The fascist shouted, "If they are sick, we will cure them ..." and before the eyes of the grief-crazed mother he threw the naked children on the stone floor and trampled their bodies with his steel-capped boots.'

'We should not only never forget these things ourselves, but like a baton we should pass on these memories of the human conscience to all future generations', I told the children. Together we decided to create a village pantheon, a gallery of portraits of the heroes who fell fighting for the freedom and independence of our Soviet homeland.

At the end of grade three and at the beginning of grade four the children visited every family in our village.

The mothers gave us photographs of the heroes who had fallen in battle and of the victims of the fascist death camps. Portraits drawn from these little photographs were placed in our 'Room of Remembrance and Sorrow'. This would be the beginning of a pantheon whose final shape would be gradually formulated by later generations of school students: such was the aim we set ourselves. This was our duty, which must be carried out so that war would never again visit the earth, so that nations would live as brothers and sisters, so that children would be born for peace and happiness and not for death and destruction. This was our duty to the nations of the whole world. We should never forget or forgive so that the horrors of fascism would never be repeated.

During one of our hiking trips we camped for the night on a high bank of the Dnieper. Several times the children clambered down to a spring in a gulley in order to fetch water, and each time they had to take a circular route to get round a large stone boulder that lay in their path.

'Why is that stone lying there?' wondered the children. 'Why do people keep going around it instead of pushing it aside into the bushes?' With the best intentions they rolled the stone aside and freed up the path. But in the morning an old fisherman approached us and asked where the stone was. The children thought he would praise their efforts but the old man shook his head and said, 'That stone has lain here for many years, and this is where it belongs ...' And he told them about the heroic deeds of three soviet reconnaissance officers. Crossing the river during the great battle for the Dnieper, they sheltered behind this stone with their machine guns and for a whole day engaged the enemy in an uneven battle. The fascists employed cannons and mortars, and shells exploded for several hours, but the stone remained an impregnable fortress. During the night our troops crossed the river and rescued the scouts. The soldiers lay behind the rock bloodied and wounded by bullets and shrapnel, but unbroken. The scouts were sent to a military hospital on the other side of the Dnieper and no-one knows their names. Only this granite boulder remains as a memorial to the heroes' deeds. The children went over to the stone and stood before it for a long time. They rolled it out of the bushes and put it back where it had lain. Only now did they notice that the granite stone was pitted with holes from bullets and shrapnel. On the ground we found many fragments of stone and each child took a small piece for remembrance.

From that time on our hiking routes always took in that special stone. Like the oak on top of the burial mound, that grey granite boulder became a symbol of the beauty of heroism for the children, stirring lofty patriotic feelings in their young hearts.

A person's moral character, how they relate to social issues and to work done for the sake of our homeland, depends on their attitude in childhood to the heroic deeds of their fathers and grandfathers. I tried to ensure that children's hearts beat more rapidly with the thought that on the little hill where we were working that day, a hero had shed his blood. Such feelings strengthen the conviction that to work on your native land for the benefit of your homeland is a great privilege for which people went into mortal combat. In the secret recesses of a child's heart the voice of conscience awakens: you are walking in the bright sunlight and admiring the blue sky because under these poplars and birch trees, under these oaks and apple trees lie those who gave you a life in the sunshine.

This voice reminds Lenin's young successors that they are the future custodians of their native land. A feeling of being responsible for the material and spiritual wealth created by older generations is the root of civic maturity. Olya and I thought about how to inspire the children to work from a sense of duty towards those who had defended their current life under a bright sun and a blue sky. One day the children came to their field. They had to carry several hundred kilograms of humus to a small plot of infertile land so that wheat could grow where nothing had grown before. The work was hard and monotonous. Before beginning the work, Olya told the children about the heroic deeds of a young Ukrainian member of the Communist Youth League, Mikhail Panikako, during the dark days of the great battle on the Volga.[30]

The nineteen-year-old youth stood in a trench barring the way to fascist tanks. An enemy tank was advancing towards the trench. The soldier drew back his arm to throw a bottle containing flammable liquid at the tank. At that moment a bullet smashed the raised bottle. The liquid caught fire and flames spread over the young man's clothes towards his face. A living torch leaving a trail of fire and smoke behind, he rose from the trench and approached the tank. In his other hand he held his last bottle. Now he had clambered on to the tank's armour-plating. He smashed the bottle over the tank's turret and it went up in flames, spinning around. Just before the tank exploded, and covered in flames, Mikhail stood tall, raised his arm and shouted. The other soldiers responded to his battle cry, poured out of their trench, swept the enemy before them, and took the street.

This story stunned the children. It was as if the hero was standing in front of them, eternally alive and saying to them, 'I gave my life for just such a little patch of our sacred land as this. Is it possible not to care what grows on it, weeds or wheat?' At that moment in each and every heart the voice of conscience spoke up: I must not be indifferent.

I do not mean to suggest that before every work activity you need to tell children about deeds of heroism. You should not encourage children to think that if they have been a bit lazy and not done something properly that they are not carrying out their duty to our homeland. A sense of duty is a sacred feeling, and children must treasure

---

30 Translator's note: The reference here is to the Battle of Stalingrad.

it in their hearts. At the same time it is important that heroic deeds teach us how to live, and give rise in children's minds to their first civic convictions. I advised Olya to speak only of Mikhail Panikako's deeds, without any moralising, so that the children could see that little patch of land with the eyes of a citizen.

## The children join the Pioneer Organisation

IN THE SPRING OF 1955, shortly before they completed grade three, the children joined the Pioneer Organisation that bears Lenin's name. The Communist Youth League committee appointed Olya as their leader. She was studying in grade eight.

A ceremonial gathering of our Pioneer group, which bore the name of Zoya Kosmodemianskaya, was traditionally held on the anniversary of Lenin's birth on 22 April. Long before that day, Olya and her friends began preparing the children to join the Pioneer Organisation. The grade eight students told the children about the heroic past of Lenin's party, the Communist Youth League and the Pioneer Organisation.

'Your Pioneer troop should bear the name of that person who inspires you most', Olya told the children, and they unanimously decided to adopt the name of Mikhail Panikako, the hero of the Battle of Stalingrad. Our troop's motto was 'To fight and overcome, like Lenin'; our symbol was oak leaves and acorns to signify our campaign to enrich our natural environment.

The Pioneer gathering was attended not only by students but by parents, participants in the October socialist revolution, veterans of the partisan movement and the civil war, and founding members of the Communist Youth League who had set up the organisation in our village in 1919.

The gathering took place on a large green lawn. The grade eight Pioneers lined up opposite the grade three students who were about to enter the ranks of Lenin's successors. The leader of the grade eight troop council announced that their troop was standing down and handing over its baton to the grade three students.

The solemn moment when the red scarves were to be handed over arrived. We have a school tradition that the Pioneer troop that has come to the end of its activity hands over its red scarves to the Young Octobrists who are joining the Pioneers. The boys and girls took off their Pioneer scarves and tied them round the necks of their young friends. Each student passed his scarf on to a little one he or she had made friends with. Among the grade eight and grade three students there were brothers and sisters, and the older children passed their scarves on to their younger siblings as a treasured family heirloom.

Having accepted their scarves, the children pronounced their solemn oaths as young successors of Lenin. They swore to be strong and courageous patriots like Mikhail Panikako, and to follow the motto 'To fight and to overcome, like Lenin'.

To commemorate their induction into the Pioneers, each child received a present: a book about the life and struggles of a famous person.

That gathering remained forever in my pupils' memories. In the sacred rite of induction into the Pioneers, the most important thing is that the red scarf should be passed on from generation to generation of young followers of Lenin. The red scarf, a symbol of our revolutionary struggle, is not bought and sold in shops; it is entrusted into a child's hands and carefully looked after. It is not worn every day, but only on special days, at ceremonies, and at Pioneer gatherings. This is the tradition we follow in our school Pioneer group.

# To fight and overcome, like Lenin

VLADIMIR LENIN TAUGHT US THAT the fight for communism is carried out in mundane things, in our ordinary, everyday work. Olya and I thought about how to ensure that the children took to heart everything that happened around them, that each child was concerned about what happened to the material wealth that belonged to the people. Olya organised a group of young nature conservationists within our troop. The children began to monitor a green belt of forest adjoining fields not far from the school. They walked right through the green belt and saw that someone had ring-barked several trees. Clearly someone wanted the trees to die so that they would have a justification for cutting them down. If the trees are dead, why leave them standing? The children were outraged. How could this happen? We plant the trees and care for them, and someone else is destroying them? They needed to find out who it was.

From that day the young nature conservationists began to carry out Pioneer raids. They set off for the green belt in the evening and waited for uninvited guests. A few days later the offenders were caught red-handed: two collective farm workers came with saws to cut down trees. The children informed the farm management about the people who were destroying the trees. The offenders were required to plant ten trees for each one they had destroyed. The children were delighted: justice had prevailed. This is an essential precondition for complete moral development. Children need to see the triumph of justice over injustice. Its victory inspires them, giving them the strength to overcome new difficulties.

The young nature conservationists became enthusiastically involved in a new game. During one of their Pioneer raids they noticed that the yards of some collective farm workers were overgrown with weeds.

The children brought these collective farm workers young apple trees, and suggested they pull out their weeds and plant fruit trees instead. There were three negligent workers who were too lazy to do this. The Pioneers wrote them 'Warning notices from the young nature conservationists', containing the following words: 'It is very difficult for us, the young nature conservationists, to see how your yards have become nurseries for weeds. Soon you will have wolves breeding amongst your forests of thistles. How can you live in such a 'forest'? We request that you destroy your weeds, plant apple trees and grapes, and grow some flowers. We have left five apple trees and three grape vines in some soil near your house. They need to be planted tomorrow. Please plant them and water them well. If you are too lazy to do this we will come and dig holes, pull out all the weeds and plant the trees ourselves. Then there will be a garden, but it will not be your garden, it will be our Pioneer garden.'

The 'warning notices' were delivered in an original way: lowered through open ventilation windows and left on the table. And in the evening, when no-one was looking, they left the trees and vines. In all of this there was an element of play, which took the children's fancy. They waited impatiently for the following day. What would those lazy people do? They walked along the street after school and could not recognise the vacant lots. Where weeds had been growing, now trees had been planted ... News of the young nature conservationists' group quickly spread through the school. Our troop began to organise nature conservation groups for Pioneer troops throughout the school. The collective farm management asked our senior Pioneers to defend their mulberry plantation: some collective farm workers were indiscriminately breaking branches off. The Pioneers conducted several raids and the destruction stopped.

In summer our troop took on the responsibility for preparing twenty kilograms of high grade wheat seed for an experimental plant breeding plot. The children chose the very best heads of wheat, found a dry place in one of the school rooms to store it over the winter, threshed the grain in spring and passed it on to the agronomist. So much care and concern went into this work that when the wheat planting began, the children (who were by then in grade four) went into the field to see the seed planted with their own eyes. When the shoots appeared the children again just had to go and have a look. During the harvest the Pioneers decided to assist the senior students. I was delighted to see that having devoted some of their energy to helping others, the children became more receptive to everything that was going on in the surrounding world. When we went to the field, the children were excited to see that their seeds had taken well. When we went past the collective farm orchard and saw caterpillars on a small apple tree, the children were alarmed. At such moments the Pioneers did not think about their duty to society. They were simply unable to pass by indifferently when another living creature was threatened. The children went into the orchard, killed the caterpillars, saved the apple tree, and examined the neighbouring trees to see if they had any pests on them.

The feeling of being custodians of our native land is an important patriotic feeling that we need to foster in young hearts. The ones who will become real patriots are those who in childhood, adolescence and early youth, care about what happens to every head of grain in the collective farm field, every tree in the communal orchard, every handful of grain on the collective farm's threshing floor; for whom these things are as dear as the things that bring them deep personal joy: a toy given to them by their mother or father, a favourite picture book, their skates or skis ... Communal property will become valued as something deeply personal only when children invest part of their souls in work that creates something for others, when the material results of their work bring them deep personal joy, when the path that leads to this joy involves care, concern and failures. I was always concerned about what stirred children up or upset them. What did children take to heart: only those things that related to their own well-being, or also things that affected the welfare of others? The answer to this question was always an indicator of children's moral development. I was delighted to see that Kolya and Valya were upset when heavy rain bent the stems of wheat on our experimental plot. Until children have experienced such misfortune and have worried and suffered, educators cannot rest because their pupils may embark on life as indifferent observers.

Egoists and selfish people grow from those who live through childhood without worrying about others, who are just consumers of pleasurable things. I was alarmed to see that this danger threatened two of my pupils: Volodya and Slava. In their families people went out of their way to make sure these children were fed a surfeit of pleasurable things. The only thing that upset these children was when their parents did not buy them some nice new thing. These egoistic concerns needed to be balanced by concerns of another sort: concern for the material and spiritual needs of others. One hot summer I noticed that a lime tree we had planted during the School of Joy had begun to dry out. 'Our friend does not have enough moisture', I told Volodya and Slava. I took the boys into the orchard promising to show them something interesting, and directed their attention to the little tree drying out in the heat. 'The lime tree needs our help and we can help her if we want to', I told the children. 'Trees of this species, especially young ones, like moist air, dampness and cool shade. Let's help our friend, children. We can lay a thin pipe from the water main to this spot (it is not far), direct it at the lime tree and create some rain. The tree will feel constant coolness.' At first the boys were indifferent to my words, but when I told them about artificial rain their eyes shone with curiosity. The work now seemed like an interesting game and what child does not like to play? And the boys began to play. We laid a pipe to the tree, attached a fine sprinkler, and a barely perceptible cloud of fine water droplets appeared above the lime tree. In the midday heat the boys turned on the 'rain' and in the evening they turned it off. Gradually the boys developed feelings of concern for the little tree. How did it feel under the rain? The children were delighted to see how the lime tree's branches straightened up, and how tender new leaves appeared on them. In this way the boys acquired an interest that was not connected to their own personal well-being.

But that was only the beginning. Just as a jeweller cuts a diamond, examining each facet, wondering where next to make contact with the precious stone in order to produce a jewel, so an educator has to ponder how to approach the secret recesses of a child's heart. Several times I went into the forest with Volodya to locate and collect the largest fruits of the dogrose bush, then sowed their seeds and watered the green shoots. When it was possible to graft onto their stems, we found some white rose buds and grafted these to the dogrose stock. This was not merely work but an attempt to reach out to a child's heart. Gradually the boy's joys and disappointments became linked to the surrounding world, and not just to his own personal well-being.

I had to devote a lot of attention to Slava as well. Together with Olya he raised a sick lamb on the animal breeding farm. At first this concern for another living creature resembled a game. Then it developed into an enthusiasm for work, and gradually Slava became an industrious young animal breeder. I will never forget how one cold winter's day he came to me with tears in his eyes. The boy complained to me that his favourite calf loved green oats and we were only growing barley in the glasshouse. How could he go to the farm without oats? We began to grow oats as well.

Concern for things that are not connected directly with one's own needs is a wonderful antidote to childish egoism. If children develop personal interests that find expression in concern for the common good, their hearts will never become seed beds of self-pity. That egoistic feeling takes over the souls of children whose joys and sorrows are concerned only with themselves.

# The Brave and Fearless Patrol

A TIME CAME IN MY pupils' physical and spiritual development when their uncontrolled childish energy found expression in strange, seemingly inexplicable behaviour. Before my eyes a sudden change took place: shy children became reckless and timid ones became bold and decisive.

One day we went into the fields to watch the collective farm workers and senior students construct a haystack. The boys and girls were interested in how the tractor driver was able to lift a large mass of hay to the very top of a high stack by attaching a thick cable to his vehicle. The cable stretched taut, lifting its burden to a height of about fifteen metres. From the haystack we walked to the combine harvester. And then I saw from a distance how one of the boys, grabbing hold of the cable, was rising higher and higher into the air. I looked around and Shura was missing. That was him dangling fifteen metres in the air. The other children saw Shura and ran to the haystack shrieking with joy. No doubt all of them wanted to experience the joy of rising to such a dizzying height. I was beside myself until Shura came sliding down the haystack as if he was on a sled. I did not know whether to rejoice at the happy completion of an unusual journey, or get the children away from there as quickly as possible.

I had difficulty calming the children and restraining them from undertaking the same journey. I could see that were very displeased with my caution. My feelings told me that I had to find a way of making the journey safe and not just forbid it. We put a pile of hay underneath the cable and then one after another they made the journey, first the boys and then the girls.

In those days we did not yet have a constant supply of electricity, and in order to charge our batteries the senior students constructed a wind-powered generator. The windmill was mounted on top of a twelve metre tower. At the top of the tower was a flat wooden platform with a little trapdoor through which an electrician could climb, when necessary, to reach the generator. One day when there were strong winds, the children were flying kites. Each child was trying to fly their kite as high as possible. Vanya said, 'My kite will fly higher than anyone's'. The boy climbed up the tower, leant against a wooden rail that ran around the platform, and began to let out his kite string. With horror I saw that the trapdoor, pushed aside by Vanya, had slid to the side of the platform and fallen to the ground. The boy was running around the opening not noticing the gaping hole at his feet. His eyes were fixed on the kite. It was only good fortune that prevented an accident.

Children are irresistibly attracted to heights. The sweet sensation of being up high gives children great joy, whereas for educators like us these childish impulses provoke only anxiety. Nearly everything the children did that caused me great agitation was connected with the attraction of heights ...

Not far from the school stood an old church. The twenty metre bell tower was crowned with a steep, round dome. Looking up at the dome one sunny spring day, I saw the figures of three children next to the cross. I recognised Seryozha, Kolya and Shura. My heart froze. The children saw me and began to hide, running from one side of the dome to the other. There was no sense in calling out to the children. That would have only made things worse. I went into the school and asked the teachers to quietly remove all the children. Some could be taken for a walk in the forest, some to the fields, and senior students could be sent home. To put it simply, I wanted to make sure that no-one paid any attention to the children and that no-one raised the alarm. I myself went to the workshop, from where there was a good view of the church, and sat by the window with my head in my hands. Perhaps I had kindled the children's desire to experience the pleasure of heights by allowing the game in the hay stack. Then I saw how the boys climbed down from the church dome via rusty old pipes that in places were barely holding on to the wall.

After a summer downpour a waterfall appeared under a bridge over the pond. An old lady from the collective farm came to me and told me to come and have a look at what the children were doing. I went to the pond. I could not see anyone on the dam, but from under the bridge I could hear children's squeals. Tolya and Vitya had tied long ropes to the rails of the bridge and made a swing. Swinging back and forth above the raging waterfall, they were squealing with joy.

From somewhere or other, Petrik, Vitya and Kolya dragged a wooden barrel with one end knocked out to the top of a high bank overlooking the pond. Each of the boys in strict order, for none of them wanted to give up his turn to the others, crawled into the barrel and the others gave it a gentle shove down the slope. The barrel rolled down the slope, stopping a few metres from the water. To this day I cannot understand how this game could have ended without misfortune. In such cases a fortunate outcome is probably only possible for children.

During one of our walks in the forest we observed some timber cutters preparing lumber for the collective farm. The children could not tear their eyes away from the spectacle of a sawn tree crashing to the ground. On the way home the children did not notice that Shura and Danko had remained behind. We were resting in a clearing when an old timber cutter came up to us and brought the boys with him. The old man told us that Shura and Danko had tried to climb up a tree so they could fly down in its branches when it was felled.

All of these incidents occurred during a six month period in grades three and four. I felt that to restrain the children from such behaviour and worry about preventing an accident was not the solution. The children's irrepressible energy required more than just a high level of activity. The children wanted to affirm their courage in the face of danger. Their thirst for brave deeds showed that the children wanted to experience the romanticism of valour. I needed to channel their energy in a positive direction.

The reader will have noticed that these acts, which seem so irrational at first glance, were mainly carried out by boys. There was not a single boy who did not give me pause for thought. Even Danko, who I considered to be timid and indecisive, astonished me in the autumn of 1955. He crossed the pond over very thin ice. To reduce the risk of falling through the ice he put his schoolbag full of books on the ice and pushed it in front of him. The ice cracked and bent, and over the deepest place it was covered with water, but by some miracle it did not break and the boy reached school safely. Two grade three children tried to cross the ice after him and the ice gave way beneath them, fortunately right next to the bank.

Do we need to protect children from accidents? Of course that is very important, but it is not the only thing that matters. It is also necessary for children to face danger and to overcome it.

And that is how we came to form the 'Brave and Fearless' patrol. All the boys joined it and after a little while some of the girls did too. I thought up games and activities that required strength of will, boldness and fearlessness. On the bank of the pond we found a high cliff. We investigated the bottom and it turned out to be safe. One hot day in July the boys came here to swim. I showed them how to jump from the cliff and how to direct their flight. Immediately after me Shura, Seryozha, Kolya, Vitya and Fedya jumped. The next day Yura, Kostya and Petrik summoned up the courage to jump. On the third day Tolya, Misha, Sashko and Vanya jumped. There were only four reluctant boys remaining: Pavlo, Volodya, Danko and Slava.

Their friends teased them. There were some girls swimming below and they also started to egg the boys on. Tina joined us on top of the cliff. She also wanted to jump. She leapt gracefully into the water.

Larisa and Valya followed her example. In the end Pavlo, Danko and Slava overcame their fear.

Only Volodya could not bring himself to jump. I could see that the boy was ashamed of his fear, but at the same time could not bring himself to cross that threshold beyond which a person discovers the pride of a courageous act. We had to find a lower cliff for Volodya to jump from. He jumped there, together with the girls, but still could not find the courage to jump from the higher cliff. I had to spend a lot of time working with him, motivating him to carry out courageous acts. When the children were hanging out birdhouses for the starlings in spring, I managed to convince Volodya to climb a tall tree. This was the boy's first victory over his fear. The children told me in secret that Volodya had gone to the cliff by himself, undressed, and sat for a long time. He had run at the cliff several times but each time had been afraid to jump.

After the three bravest girls, the next to jump was Valya. Nobody had expected it of her. Valya's act was a shock to Volodya. The boy screwed up his eyes and jumped into the water. After Valya had jumped, Nina, Galya, Lyusya, Zina, Katya and Sasha also ventured to jump. After them, all the girls began to jump. I became convinced that the girls had significantly more will power than the boys. They were able to overcome their fear with greater courage and did not celebrate as loudly as the boys when they succeeded in forcing themselves to carry out a courageous act.

When we were holidaying in the lap of nature after completing grade three, the children invented a polar explorers' game. According to the game, on an island overgrown with shrubs—an iceberg surrounded by water—there were some shipwrecked polar explorers. We were on the mainland. We had to float supplies (bread and potatoes) over to the survivors. Between the 'iceberg' and the 'mainland' was a small lake. According to the rules of the game, the supplies had to be floated over during a bleak polar night.

And now it was necessary to find some volunteers from the Brave and Fearless patrol. The children were a bit frightened. It was said that someone had seen a wolf's lair on the island, but Shura and Seryozha were ready to undertake the night crossing. We tied a bundle with bread, potatoes, matches and lard to a thick pine plank. We lowered two inflated rubber inner-tubes into the water: these were our 'launches'. The sun set, mist descended over the lake and the island, and the stars came out. The boys undressed, tied their clothes to the plank, and quietly swam away. A minute later they were no longer visible: we could hear a quiet splashing for a few minutes and then all was silent. The whole Brave and Fearless patrol sat on the bank of the lake, together with a little dog named Travka ... An hour passed and the night became impenetrably dark. We could not see the island or the lake. Suddenly in the darkness a weak light flared up. The young polar explorers had reached the 'survivors' and were sending us a signal to send over the next two launches.

Again we tied bread, potatoes, lard and onions to a plank and lowered the 'motorboats' into the water. Vitya and Yura undressed. One of the girls told us that in the old days large pikes lived in this lake and they might still be here ... The tale was obviously intended to frighten Vitya and Yura. Of course the boys were afraid to lower themselves into the dark water, but now they would not refuse to cross for anything in the world. When Yura and Vitya stepped into the water a splash was heard up ahead. Of course it was a fish, but the boys had not forgotten the tale of the pikes. Another hour passed, a second light appeared on the island, and immediately both lights went out: a sign that the two parties of polar explorers had joined forces. We lay down for the night but no-one could fall asleep.

A campfire flared up on the island: the boys would keep watch all night. They would not close their eyes until dawn. Huddled together, they would look with impatience towards the east, waiting for the first light. The next day, as soon as the tops of the trees were lit up with the first golden rays of the sun, the boys would swim back. Those who were yet to experience the joy of overcoming their fear would envy them. And having overcome their fear, they would reply calmly, as becomes men, 'It's not scary at all'.

We prepared all the boys in turn for these secret night crossings, and Volodya went too. At the height of the game the girls also wanted to join in. Why could the boys go and not them? I was expecting this request. Tina crossed the lake with Kolya, and Varya with Tolya. The boys found some dry hay on the island and made up a bed for the girls.

The night, the quietness, the isolation: all of these things attracted the children. In all of these things they felt the romanticism of overcoming difficulties. The children invented another interesting game, pretending to be geologists. During the day in the depths of the forest, about five kilometres from its edge in an impenetrable grove, the girls constructed a shelter from branches and set up camp. This was the main base of a geological party. The game was for a group of geologists—the boys—to make their way through the taiga to the main base in the dead of the night … In the geologists' backpacks were mineral samples. The boys left the school as darkness descended, and within an hour had reached the edge of the forest. They had to accurately determine their direction, and apart from that they had to pretend they were crossing a raging taiga river and a mountain range. The girls were forbidden to give signals of any kind. It took two hours to cross the forest. The boys reached the main base after midnight, tired, but happy and excited.

During a heavy downpour in August, fourteen calves became separated from the collective farm herd. The animals had run away into the flood-meadows. Adults conducted a prolonged search for the calves but could not find them. 'Why don't we look for them?' Shura and Vitya suggested to me. And so it was that nine members of the Brave and Fearless patrol—six boys and three girls—set off with me in a search party. We took food supplies, a tent, a compass, and two motor boats for crossing the lake. The children were elated. We searched the flood-meadows section by section. In some places we had to divide into groups of two or three. After four days we found eleven calves grazing in a forest glade. The remaining calves had probably drowned, caught in the torrent that was created during the downpour. The days of that search remained in the children's memories forever. They were especially memorable for Galya, Lyusya and Sanya, as the girls were afraid of the darkness, frogs and grass-snakes. On this trip we even encountered a fox and an eagle owl.

In the summer that followed grade four, we played at mountain climbing. We lowered a rope ladder from a clifftop into a deep ravine, making sure it was securely fastened. Below was our base camp and we were mountain climbers. Our assignment was to clamber up the rope ladder to the top of a sheer cliff, to climb onto the cliff top and then to clamber back down into the ravine. Many of the boys were no longer afraid of heights, but even they were a bit scared at first. Vitya was the first to climb to the top and back, followed by Shura and Seryozha. Yura came back after climbing half way up. We had to find a cliff that was not as high and we played there for several days. The girls competed with the boys. The bravest and most fearless were Tina, Larisa and Kostya. They teased Volodya and Slava who began to get dizzy at a height of three metres.

In the end all the boys and girls conquered the cliff. When children show bravery and fearlessness they experience a deep feeling of joy. Bravery and courage are manifestations of one's moral character and willpower, and are necessary for every person, not only in exceptional circumstances, but in everyday life and work.

The closer we approached to the end of primary school, the more I was bothered by the thought that the children would soon be adolescents. They were already agitated by thoughts about themselves, wondering 'What sort of person am I? What is good or bad about me? What do my friends think of me?'

The age of adolescence was approaching: the time for self-education. Thinking about the future, when the most important educational force would become the children's own will and persistence, I strove even now, in childhood, to awaken an interest in self-education. Each student had a routine for work and rest. The children rose at six in the morning, did their morning exercises, washed themselves with cold water, had breakfast and did their homework. Each one studied for at least an hour before leaving for school. I tried to ensure that regular adherence to routines became a matter of self-education. It was difficult to persuade Volodya and Slava to get up early independently. The parents were reluctant to wake them up and could not make them go to bed early. I talked not only with the boys but with their parents. I managed to inspire Slava with the prospect of self-education. The boy learnt self-control. But for the time being I was not able to inspire Volodya in the same way. His family encouraged him to be soft.

## *We say farewell to summer*

AFTER COMPLETING GRADE FOUR, ALL the children—sixteen boys and fifteen girls—progressed to grade five. Twelve students received excellent grades in all subjects and the staff council awarded them with certificates. Thirteen students had a mixture of good and excellent grades. Six children had a mixture of satisfactory, good and excellent grades.

In my view, the greatest success of my educational work was that the children had passed through a school of humanity; had learnt to sense the feelings of those around them, to take to heart their joys and sorrows, to live with others, to love their homeland and to hate its enemies. The children had a wonderful command of their native language and had learnt five things: to observe, to think, to read, to write, and to convey their thoughts in words. I had become convinced that it was possible to teach children to read by the age of seven; that is, essentially before they commenced studies in grade one. If that goal is achieved the spiritual powers of the child are freed for thought and creativity.

No less important was the fact that the children were morally and spiritually prepared for the difficult years of adolescence. During the primary school years I had planned for the time when the children would reach that invisible boundary that separates childhood from adolescence. Some had already crossed that boundary. The difficulties of adolescence had in essence already begun in grade four.

One quiet August evening we visited our Nook of Beauty to say farewell to summer.

The last rays of the sun were playing on the tops of the trees. Apples were ripening on the tree that we had planted four years ago. A bumblebee was hovering over bunches of grapes and the rumble of a tractor carried to us from a distant field. The girls had brought a sheaf of wheat and had plaited bunches of guilder rose berries between the ears of grain. We sang a song about the quiet summer evening. The sound of the song died away and the children gazed at the evening sky. The music of nature, memories of the summer that we were farewelling today, all of this found a response in the children's hearts. The surrounding world—the evening sky, the scarlet sunset, the amber-coloured apples, the bunches of grapes, the green wall of hops, the white chrysanthemums, the buzzing of the bumblebee—the whole world presented itself to them as a wonderful harp. The children touched its strings and magical music issued forth, the music of words. This was the music of joy and sorrow. I also experienced joy and sorrow. All my life I will remember the poem that the children composed that evening as they parted with summer:

*Summer of beauty, we part with you today.*
*Golden sun, you wear a garland of wheat,*
*With guilder rose berries among its ears,*
*A white rose, apples and bunches of grapes.*
*Summer of beauty, you have given us so much joy:*
*A green forest glade on a hot day,*
*Warm rain with peals of thunder,*
*A fragrant haystack and a night by the campfire.*
*We lay on the hay; stars twinkled in the sky,*
*The fragrant haystack sailed like a ship,*
*Over the green sea of grass, while the stars twinkled,*
*And a grasshopper sang in the green grass.*
*You gave us the scarlet morning dawn,*
*Golden sparks kindled in the drops of dew,*
*The ears of wheat and the red tomatoes ripened.*
*Above a white carpet of buckwheat the bees hummed,*
*Amber honey dripped from the yellow honeycomb,*
*We ate fresh bread with fragrant honey,*
*While around us the wasps droned ...*
*We swam in the warm river,*
*In the blue sky light clouds floated.*
*Summer of beauty, we farewell you today,*
*But you will visit us again.*

You will soon become adolescents, children. What will those years bring you? I will not leave you for a single day. I will lead you on to youth and maturity. For five years I have led you by the hand and given you my heart. There were moments when it tired; and when its strength was fading I hurried to you, children. Your happy chatter poured new strength into my heart. Your smiles gave birth to new energy. Your searching eyes, scanning the surrounding world, stimulated my thought … I give you all the strength of my heart, children, because with you I feel the joy of living.

The evening sunset's embers die down, the stars twinkle, and a wave of cool air floats to us from the river. We walk to the river. The children do not want to part with nature. They have fallen in love with it. For them nature has become a source of spiritual wealth, beautiful thoughts, wisdom and moral beauty.

When the children become adults, when I see them off on their life's journey, I will remember this evening. I will remember how I wanted to speak of my work in the words of Walt Whitman:

> *Now I see the secret of the making of the best persons,*
> *It is to grow in the open air and to eat and sleep with the earth.*[31]

In a few days' time I will climb another rung of the ladder with you, children. You will become grade five students. This is the age of adolescence, the threshold of young adulthood. I will tell about those years, full of troubles and joys, in another book.

---

31 Translator's note: These lines are from Walt Whitman's 'Song of the open road'.

# Other Publications

http://www.ejr.com.au/publications

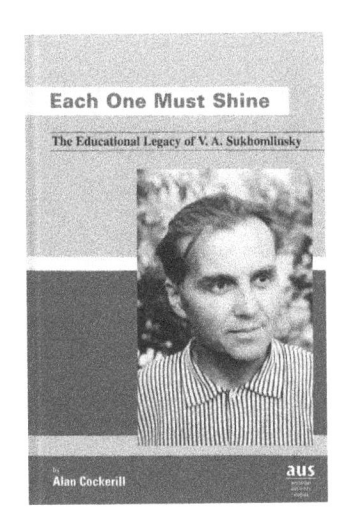

### Each One Must Shine

The definitive English language study of the educational legacy of Vasily Sukhomlinsky.

*'My utmost favourite book on what education can be.'* Mother and educator from Washington State.

Hardcover: AU$35.00

Pdf: AU$9.99

### Tales from Pavlysh: A World of Beauty

A selection of Sukhomlinsky's short stories for children, beautifully illustrated by students from Ukraine and Belarus.

Softcover: AU$14.95

Pdf: AU$9.99

Note: This title is also available as a pdf in Russian, Ukrainian, Chinese and Japanese editions.

More information about Sukhomlinsky may be found at:
http://theholisticeducator.com/